A GUIDE TO 1 CO

TEF Study Guides

This SPCK series was originally sponsored and subsidized by the Theological Education Fund of the WCC in response to requests from Africa, Asia, the Caribbean, and the Pacific. The books are prepared by and in consultation with theological teachers in those areas. Special attention is given to problems of interpretation and application arising there as well as in the West, and to the particular needs of students using English as a second language. More advanced titles in the list are marked (A).

General Editors: Daphne Terry and Nicholas Beddow

1. A Guide to the Parables
2. A Guide to St Mark's Gospel
3. A Guide to Genesis
4. A Guide to Amos
5. Church History 1: The First Advance AD 29–500
6. A Guide to Psalms
7. Old Testament Introduction 1: History of Israel
8. Church History 2: Setback and Recovery AD 500–1500
9. Applied Theology 1: 'Go . . . and make disciples;
10. Old Testament Introduction 2: The Books of the Old Testament
11. A Guide to Romans
12. A Guide to Religions
13. A Guide to Exodus
14. Church History 3: New Movements AD 1500–1800
15. Old Testament Theology 3: Theology of the Old Testament
16. A Guide to Isaiah 40–66
17. A Guide to 1 Corinthians
18. A Guide to Philippians
19. Applied Theology 2: 'Tend my sheep'
20. A Guide to the Revelation
21. A Guide to Isaiah 1–39
22. Church History 4: Christianity Worldwide AD 1800 Onwards
23. A Reader in African Christian Theology (A)
24. New Testament Introduction 1: Jesus Christ: His Life and His Church
25. A New Teaching, A New Learning: A Guide to Teaching Theology (A)
26. New Testament Introduction 2: The Formation of the Christian Scriptures
27. A Guide to Acts
28. A Guide to Galatians

IN PREPARATION

A Guide to Deuteronomy
A Guide to Jeremiah
A Guide to Hosea
The Inter-Testamental Period
Readings in Indian Christian Theology (A)

TEF Study Guide 17

A GUIDE TO
1 CORINTHIANS

John Hargreaves

First published in Great Britain 1978
SPCK
Holy Trinity Church
Marylebone Road,
London, NW1 4DU

Fourth impression, with amendments 1991

The photographs in this book are reproduced by courtesy of
Mark Shearman (p.119), the Royal National
Lifeboat Institution (p.172) and Camera Press Ltd.

ISBN 0 281 03617 9 (net edition)
ISBN 0 281 03618 7 (non-net edition for Africa,
Asia, S. Pacific, and Caribbean)

Printed in Great Britain by
Dotesios Printers Ltd, Trowbridge, Wiltshire

Contents

Preface

I should like to express grateful acknowledgements to:

St Luke's congregation, Sevenoaks, England, who allowed me to take time off away from the parish in order to write this between 1972 and 1977;

David Anderson, previously Principal of Immanuel College, Ibadan, to whose unpublished work on 1 Corinthians I was privileged to have access;

Yoramu Bamunoba, Bishop of West Buganda, and Enos Bagona, Chaplain of Ntare School, Uganda, with whom I discussed 1 Corinthians as they prepared for the East African Diploma of Theology many years ago;

John Dobson, then on the staff of Bishop Tucker College, Mukono, who generously commented on my theological statements in an early draft of this book;

Alan Chilver, of the Theological College of Northern Nigeria, who was kind enough to give a long list of my questions to his students and pass on their comments to me; and

Harold Taylor who did the same with students at Rarongo Theological College in Papua New Guinea;

John and Helena Parry and John and Dorothy Lowe, of the CMS Fellowship House, Foxbury, who enabled me to discuss 1 Corinthians with visitors from many parts of the world and gave me ideal conditions for writing;

Stephen Ridout, who at my request filled three large exercise books with suggested amendments;

Jim Bergquist, Associate Director TEF and more recently teaching at the Lutheran Theological Seminary, Columbus, Ohio, who gave valuable advice at several stages in the development of the manuscript, and, with Dr Merle Hoops, also of LTS, vetted the final draft.

Daphne Terry, who as editor continues to combine in a unique way stimulation and efficiency with encouragement and kindness.

Sevenoaks 1977   JOHN HARGREAVES

Using this Guide

In the Introduction (p. 1) we explain why it is important for Christians to study Paul's letters to the congregation at Corinth. But before beginning their study, readers may find it helpful to consider how they can make the best use of this book to guide them.

Each section of the Guide consists of:

1. An *Outline* in which the Bible passage is re-told very briefly so as to make quite clear what chief subjects Paul was dealing with, and the most important message he was sending to the Corinthians about them. Of course, reading this Outline is not meant to take the place of reading the actual passage in the Bible. We need to read carefully the words of the Bible itself at each stage of our study.
2. An *Interpretation* of the passage, in which we discuss what it meant to the Corinthians of Paul's time, and how we should understand and apply it to our own lives as Christians today.
3. *Notes* on particular words or verses which seem to need further explanation or discussion; and
4. *Suggestions* for revision and further study.

SPECIAL NOTES

These four notes are separate from the sections dealing directly with the Bible text, partly because of their length, and partly because each relates to more than one section. If any reader finds that these Special Notes raise questions which he is not himself asking, he is free not to study them further. But those on Paul and Corinth contain background information relating to the letter as a whole, and some people may prefer to read them immediately after the Introduction, before going on to the detailed work on the text of the letter.

STUDY SUGGESTIONS

These suggestions for further study appear at the end of each section and each Special Note. They are intended to help readers who are working alone to study more thoroughly and understand Paul's teaching more clearly, and to check their own progress. They can also be used in the classroom or at seminars, and provide topics for group research and discussion. They are of four kinds:

1. *Words:* These are to help readers check and deepen their understanding of some important words and phrases.

2. _Content:_ These are intended to help readers check the work they have done and make sure they have fully grasped the ideas and points of teaching given.

3. _Bible:_ These relate the ideas and teaching in Paul's letter with ideas and teaching found in other parts of the Bible.

4. _Discussion and research:_ These are intended to help readers think out the practical applications of Paul's teaching to their own lives and to the mission of the Church in the world. They are especially suitable for use by a group.

The best way to use these study suggestions is: first, re-read the Bible passage itself; secondly, read the appropriate section of the Guide carefully once or twice; and lastly, do the work suggested, in writing or group discussion, without looking at the Guide again except where there is an instruction to do so.

The _Key_ at the end of the book (p. 229) will enable readers to check their work on those questions which can be checked in this way. In most cases the Key does not give the answer to a question: it shows where an answer is to be found, either in the Guide or in the Bible.

All these study suggestions are only _suggestions._ But in some cases they provide further interpretation of Paul's letter. Some teachers will want to select only those which are relevant to a particular situation, or may prefer to substitute questions of their own.

INDEX

The Index (p. 241) includes only the more important proper names of people and places and the main subjects which occur in the first Letter to the Corinthians, or which are discussed in the Guide.

BIBLE VERSION

The English translation of the Bible used in the Guide is the _Revised Standard Version Common Bible (Ecumenical Edition)_ (RSV). The _New English Bible_ (NEB) and _Good News Bible_ (GNB) are used in a few cases where they shew the meaning more clearly. Other translations mentioned are the _Authorized_ (or 'King James') _Version_ (AV) and the _Revised Version_ (RV).

FURTHER READING

The Bibliography on p. ix lists some books which readers may find useful for further study of 1 Corinthians.

Bibliography

INTRODUCTORY BOOKS

William Barclay *The Letters to the Corinthians* (Daily Study Bible) St Andrew's Press

F. F. Bruce *I and II Corinthians* (New Century Bible) Nelson

W. B. Harris *The First Epistle of St Paul to the Corinthians* (Christian Students' Library) CLS Madras

Leon Morris *The First Epistle of Paul to the Corinthians* IVF and Tyndale Press

E. H. Robinson *Corinthians 1 and 2* (Fontana) Collins

W. G. H. Simon *The First Epistle to the Corinthians* (Torch) SCM Press

Margaret E. Thrall *The First and Second Letters of Paul to the Corinthians* (Cambridge NEB Commentaries) Cambridge University Press

MORE ADVANCED BOOKS

C. K. Barrett *A Commentary on the First Epistle of Paul to the Corinthians* A. and C. Black

J. Ruef *Paul's First Letter to Corinthians* Penguin

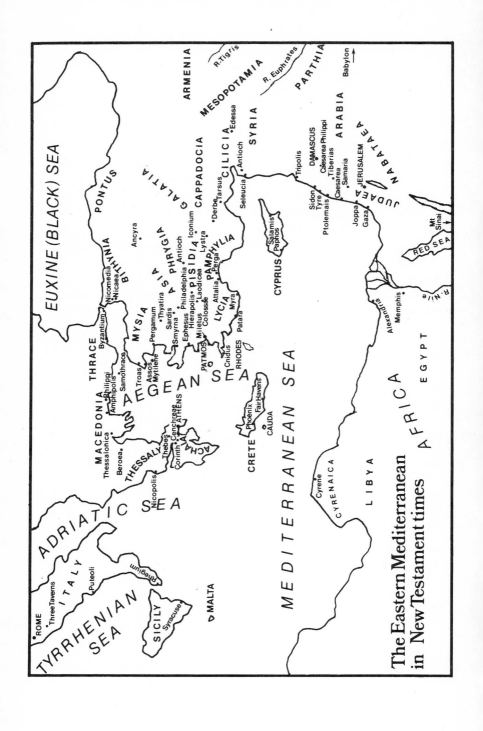

The Eastern Mediterranean in New Testament times

Introduction
Why do we read 1 Corinthians?

Some people read 1 Corinthians chiefly because of beautifully-written passages which it contains, e.g. Chapter 13. Certainly there is great value in studying a passage such as this, perhaps learning it by heart and using it for the rest of our lives. But this is not the main reason why 1 Corinthians is important.

Other readers may above all want to find in this letter answers to their questions. It is true that there are some questions to which we can find clear answers in 1 Corinthians. For example, if someone asks, 'Why do Christians use bread and wine in Holy Communion?' he will find the answer in chapter 11: 'Because this is what Jesus used at the Last Supper.' But Paul did not write this letter in order to answer questions which we ask nearly 2,000 years later. Therefore, although we do find some of our questions answered in this letter, we shall be disappointed if we regard the letter chiefly as a book of answers or rules.

1. The chief reason why this letter is important to us is because in it Paul showed that the Gospel is true for all people of all times and for all races and under all conditions.

Jesus lived and taught in Palestine. Very few of His hearers and followers had received advanced education. Most of them lived in villages or small towns. Most of them were Jews. We today know that what Jesus said and did was true for the whole world and for all ages. But no one could know that at the time. It was necessary for someone to show that it was as true for Jews living in Egypt, Greece, and Italy as it was for the Jews of Palestine whom Jesus Himself had taught. And (what is even more important) someone had to show that it was as true for non-Jews as it was for Jews. If no-one had done that, the Christian Church would be no more than a Jewish sect. It was Paul who first did it. This is the main reason why we read 1 Corinthians today.

Paul's task was two-fold:

(a) He had to show that the Gospel was as true for those who were highly educated in Asia Minor and Europe as it had been for the less well-educated people of Palestine. There were plenty of people to say that Jesus had good news for simple peasants but that His teaching was of no value to university people. This is why Paul wrote so much about the true meaning of 'knowledge' and 'wisdom' in 1 Corinthians chapters 1 and 8 (see pp. 11 and 101).

1

(b) He also had to show that the Gospel was good news for non-Jews. This is what his letter to the Galatians is mainly about. He showed that it is not necessary to be a Jew in order to be a Christian (see Gal. 3.25).

Having shown that the Gospel was true for non-Jews, Paul had also to show that it was possible to live it in a non-Jewish society, in spite of the difficulties. This is what 1 Corinthians is about. Paul was saying: 'The Gospel is true for the people of Corinth, and it is possible to live the Gospel in Corinth,' e.g. where people frequently take each other to court (chapter 6), where the Greeks hold different ideas about marriage from Jewish ideas (chapter 7), where some of the food has been offered to idols (chapter 8).

But Paul's task was very difficult. He had to show that the Gospel was true for all sorts of people without changing the Gospel. This is why he repeatedly referred to Jesus, e.g. 'I decided to know nothing among you except Jesus Christ and him crucified' (2.2). See also note on 15.3a. This is a difficulty for us today also. It is fairly easy, for example, to show that the Gospel is true in a Hindu (or Muslim) country if we first change the Gospel and make it as much like Hinduism (or Islam) as possible.

At the same time, Paul had to interpret the Gospel, just as we have to today. It would have been fairly easy to keep the Gospel unchanged if he had made no effort to interpret it, i.e. to show how it can be lived in one particular country at one particular time.

2. The second important reason why we read 1 Corinthians is because as we read it we see that Christians have to continue the work which Paul began. He led the way, but he taught the Christians at Corinth that his work was their work too: '*we* preach' (1.23). In addition, he told them that they could not preach effectively, i.e. they could not show that the Gospel was true for the people of Corinth, unless they showed it by the way in which they lived as a fellowship. A chaplain in Hong Kong wrote recently: 'Nearly all the workers in our big dye factories who became Christians did so because they saw that the Gospel was being lived by a group of worker Christians from these factories whose members loved each other.' This is the reason why Paul wrote so much about 'unity', e.g. in chapter 1.10–17 and chapters 12, 13, and 14.

What was true for the Christians in Corinth is, of course, true for present-day Christians. Paul, as we saw, led the way, but not even he can do for modern Christians what they themselves have to do, i.e. show that the Gospel is true for this generation and can be lived in present-day circumstances. This is the reason why it is a mistake for readers to use this letter as if it was a book of rules or answers to their questions. But this does not mean that they are without help. They can, as they read Paul's letter, open themselves to the same Holy Spirit who guided him, and in this way carry on the work which he began.

1.1–9 Greetings

I greet you and thank God for you

OUTLINE

1.1–3: I, Paul, greet you Christians of Corinth.
(Verse 1 is about Paul himself, v. 2 about the Corinthians, and v. 3, the greeting itself, is about God.)
1.4–7: I thank God that He has given you:
    (a) Knowledge and the ability to express it (v. 5);
    (b) All the gifts which you need (v. 7a);
    (c) A willingness to await the coming of Jesus (v. 7b).
1.8,9: I praise God because:
    (a) He never ceases to look after His people (v. 8);
    (b) He keeps His promises (v. 9).

INTERPRETATION

1. As Paul began his letter to the Christians at Corinth, he had a difficult task. He had to answer the questions which they had sent to him. He had to build them up as a strong congregation. And he had to point out the ways in which they had gone wrong.

But if he wrote too severely they might feel that he had ceased to love them, and might not take his letter seriously. So for the first nine verses he wrote about matters on which he and they could agree.

They could agree about the things that God had done. For example, God had 'called' both Paul (v. 1) and the Corinthians (v. 2). Jesus Christ was his Lord and their Lord. See 'ours' in v. 2c. The Corinthians agreed about this, even though many of their members sometimes forgot that they owed their belief to God's calling, and spoke as if they had created it themselves (see 1.29).

Then Paul thanked God that He had given His grace to the congregation of Corinth (even though many of them had not made use of it).

2. The other great truths which Paul expressed in these greetings are the following:
    (a) The Church is the new chosen people of God,
    (b) Jesus Christ is 'Lord' and 'Son of God',
    (c) Jesus will come again.

3. However, this was a letter, not a sermon. So Paul began it according to the custom of those who wrote letters in Greek at that time. Every

3

country has its own 'letter-writing' customs. In Iran you begin by saying that you are not worthy to write at all. Arabic letters begin with a string of greetings. An English letter-writer begins with the person's name to whom he is writing, and calls him 'dear'. Paul, following the custom of his time, put his own name first (together with the name of his friend Sosthenes), then the name of the congregation to whom he was writing, and lastly the greeting itself.

Note: We have said that Paul 'wrote a letter'. But it is not likely that he sat down and wrote it all at once. It is much more likely that while he was living in Ephesus he wrote down messages from time to time (with the help of his secretary) for the Christians in Corinth. Finally, perhaps after some months or a whole year, he put these messages together and sent off the package by Timothy (see 4.17).

During this time (AD 54) he received information from Corinth: from Chloe's household (1.11), and in letters (7.1), and through Stephanas and others (see 16.17). He may also have travelled in the neighbourhood of Ephesus and heard more news of Corinth. Because he was receiving information from time to time, it is likely that he added to or emphasized what he had written earlier.

We cannot prove that this is how Paul wrote 1 Corinthians, but it is a probable suggestion. And it explains some statements in the letter which would otherwise puzzle us. For example he said in 4.19 that he was coming to the Corinthians very soon, but later (16.8) that he was delaying his coming. So it seems that he wrote 16.8 some time later than he wrote 4.19 and after things had happened which made him change his mind. See also note below on chapter 10 (p. 134).

NOTES

1.1a. Called by the will of God: In this verse it is Paul himself whom, he said, God had called. In v. 2, it is the members of the Church at Corinth. What does 'being called' mean?

1. God calls people as part of His continuing creation. He has a 'will' or purpose for the world, and calls human beings to join in completing it.

2. When God calls people, He is inviting them to dedicate their lives to live as followers of Jesus Christ. See note on 7.17 (p. 90).

3. Sometimes people believe that God is also calling them to do special work or accept special responsibility or live in a special place. Paul believed that God had called him to the special work of being an apostle. He believed this because of his experience on the road to Damascus (Acts 9.15,16). Students are in theological schools because they believe that God has 'called' them to special work.

4. But it is not easy to find out if God has really called us to special work. We may say 'God has called me to this' for wrong reasons. The staff

of a theological school was interviewing candidates, and asked each of them, 'What makes you think that God has called you to be a Church Leader?' One replied, 'My people have sent me.' A second, 'I cannot get further education in any other way.' A third, 'I had a dream.' A fourth, 'My mother promised God that if He gave her a child she would give him to the Church.' A fifth, 'I have known that this was God's will since I was very young.'

How can we find out if God has really called us or others to do a special job or work in a special place? There is no one method. But we are more likely to avoid mistakes if:

(a) We keep in touch with God day by day, e.g. through prayer and Bible study.

(b) We consult other Christians, remembering that God has given His Spirit to them as well as to ourselves.

(c) We understand that the most important call is to follow Christ – i.e. that what matters most is the sort of people we are. What sort of work we do and where we do it are far less important to God.

1.1b. To be an apostle of Christ Jesus:

1. **Apostle:** The Greek word *apostolos* means 'someone who has been sent as a representative'. Paul used this word nine times in this letter to refer to himself and others whom God had sent out into the world with special authority. For a fuller note see p. 109.

2. **Of Christ Jesus:** Why did Paul not say 'apostle of God'? Because it was through Jesus Christ that Paul had come to live a new sort of life. When he was converted, as he told his listeners, he experienced God in the form of Jesus Christ (see Acts 22.8). And since Paul's time this is what Christians have experienced. They can communicate with God most personally, and commit themselves to serve Him most definitely, when they see 'the glory of God in the face of Christ' (2 Cor. 4.6).

So it is not surprising that Paul used Jesus's name nine times in the first few verses of this letter.

In v. 1, he referred to three truths about Him:

1. Jesus is the Messiah for whom the Jewish people have been waiting. 'Christ' means the 'anointed one', the special one whom God has chosen to bring peace to His people.

2. Jesus was truly human during His time on earth. 'Jesus' (the same name as 'Joshua') was a name which Jewish parents often gave (and still give) to their sons.

3. It is through Jesus that Christians communicate with God. When Paul said he was the 'apostle of Christ' he meant that he was a messenger who received his messages from God through Christ.

1.2a. To the church of God which is at Corinth: As Paul used the word 'church' twenty-two times in this letter, we shall study its meaning again later (see p. 151).

5

The word 'church' is a translation of the Greek word *ecclesia*, which means 'those whom God has called out'. When the Hebrew Scriptures were translated into Greek, the translators used this word for those Israelites whom God called out to worship Him in the assembly of His Chosen People. When Jesus came, His followers used this word for the Church because the Church had now taken the place of the Israelite People. Now it was the Christian Church whom God had called out to be His special people, to do His work in the world.

In vv. 1–9 Paul had the following thoughts about the Church in his mind:

(a) It is people, not a building. There were no special church buildings until about 100 years after Paul wrote. Christians met in one another's homes. See note on 1 Cor. 16.19 (p. 224).

(b) It is 'all those who . . . call on the name of our Lord' (v. 2b), i.e. those who have accepted Jesus as their Lord, and who have shown this by being baptized. It is the 'fellowship of his Son' (v. 9).

(c) 'The church . . . at Corinth' means 'that part of the whole great Church which is visible in Corinth'.

(d) It is 'of God', i.e. it belongs to Him. His members are answerable to Him for the way in which they treat it. It does not belong to them.

Paul would have been distressed at the way in which Christians today sometimes use the word 'Church', e.g. 'my Church', and 'the Church of England', 'the Lutheran Church', 'stone church'.

1.2b. To those sanctified . . . , called to be saints. The words which are translated 'sanctified' and 'saints' in this verse, and 'holy' in 3.17, are all connected with the one Greek word *hagios*.

1. The meaning is 'dedicated'. When Paul said that his readers had been 'sanctified', he was reminding them of what had happened some years earlier when they listened to his preaching and were baptized. At that time God had dedicated them, i.e. marked them out for the special purpose of doing His work in association with Christ (see also 6.11). When Paul said that they were 'saints', he was reminding them of what they were now. They were members of the Church. Therefore they belonged to Christ. Therefore they were saints.

2. These 'saints' or 'holy' people are those who have a special purpose in living. But the word 'saints' does not mean good or faultless or perfect people. From Paul's letters to the Corinthians we see that the members of that Church were in many ways not good. They quarrelled among themselves. Many of them paid more attention to the teaching of non-Christians than to the Gospel. In spite of this, Paul called them 'saints' and 'holy'. 'Saints', then, are people who sin but who can receive forgiveness from God through Jesus Christ.

3. The word 'saints' does not mean people who have withdrawn from the life which other people live. The people to whom Paul was writing were

'at Corinth' (v. 2), i.e. they were in the middle of the life of that city. They were 'called' or 'marked out' by God to serve Him, but they had to serve Him *in* the city. They were like the lambs or bullocks which the Jews used to mark and set aside for sacrifice. These animals were marked out, but they lived with the rest of the herd.

So modern saints are members of groups of people such as town-councils, school staffs, factories, or firms, or trade unions. One result of this is that sometimes they face situations where whatever they do seems to be wrong. A Christian who is an employment officer said recently, 'The manager of my firm has told me to dismiss a number of workmen. If I do, I know that some of them will not get other work. What ought I to do? It is hardly possible for me to do what is right.' Saints often face difficulties like that.

4. In the years after the New Testament was written, people began to use the word 'saint' to refer to a very good person (like St Francis) or to a leader of the Church in the early days (like St Paul). But no writer in the New Testament used the word in that way.

1.2b. In Christ Jesus: In the note on v. 1b we saw three truths about Jesus which Paul expressed in v. 1. We note here further truths to which he referred in the rest of this section:

1. Jesus is the head of God's Church and the Church is His Body. That is what Paul meant when he wrote that Christians are 'sanctified *in* Christ'. See also vv. 4 and 5. Christians belong to each other because they are 'in' Christ, in His Body the Church. See chapter 12.

2. Jesus is 'Lord' (vv. 2, 3, 7, 8, 9). When the Hebrew scriptures were translated into Greek, the word used to translate 'Yahweh' (the name of God) was *kyrios*. This is the word which Paul used when speaking of Jesus, which is here translated 'Lord' (see note on p. 163).

3. Jesus will one day show Himself again (see note below on v. 7).

4. Jesus is God's 'Son' (v. 9). What did Paul mean when he used this word 'Son'? It is picture-language which he and other Christians used in order to say that Jesus had a special relationship with God. But at this time Paul had not had to answer the questions which people soon asked, e.g.: 'Was Jesus really God? If He was God, how could He also be truly man?' Later, other Christians did their best to answer those questions. See note on pp. 104, 145.

1.3. Grace to you and peace: Greek-speaking people often used these words 'grace' and 'peace' in their greetings. But Paul used them in a new way, because of his experience of God through Jesus Christ.

'Grace to you' means, 'May you appreciate God's grace more fully than in the past'. 'May you be more and more grateful to God because He came to us in the person of Jesus, although we did not deserve it.' See also v. 4, 'the grace of God which was given you in Christ Jesus'.

'Peace to you' means, 'May you enjoy God's peace, i.e. the effect of His grace on your whole lives. Let God restore the fellowship between Himself and yourselves, for that fellowship is true peace.'

1.5. In every way you were enriched: Some people have thought that in this verse (and in v. 7a) Paul was not being sincere, and that he was flattering his readers so that they would take seriously what he was about to say. But this is unlikely for two reasons:

1. 'You were enriched' means 'God did not miss you out when He was distributing His gifts'. See also v. 7. Later (in v. 11) Paul showed that many of the Corinthians did not make use of these gifts. But they had received them.

2. 'You' means the congregation as a whole, to whom God gave His gifts.

1.7. You wait for the revealing of our Lord Jesus: See also the phrases: 'Will sustain you to the end' and 'in the day of our Lord' (v. 8). So Christians not only look back to what God has done in Christ, they also look forward to what He will do to complete His work. They can trust Him totally concerning the past, present, and future.

The Jews before Christ believed that God would one day put right what is wrong in the world. A 'day' would come when He would 'come' to the world as judge. Paul, because of his experience of Christ, said more about that 'day':

1. It is Jesus whom God has appointed to be the judge.

2. At the present time Jesus is an unseen Lord, but at that day He will be 'revealed' to all people as their Lord.

3. The Christian's part is:

(a) To wait for that day, and to trust in God who is faithful (v. 9), i.e. He does not change His character.

(b) To accept the grace and forgiveness of God now. Although Christians are sinful, He loves them as much as if they were guiltless (v. 8).

Paul refers to the 'end' or 'the day' or 'coming' also in such passages as 1 Cor. 3.13; 10.11; 11.26; and (especially) in chapter 15. See notes on pp. 37, 129, 156, 201ff.

STUDY SUGGESTIONS

WORDS

1. 'Paul would have been distressed at the ways in which Christians today sometimes use the word "Church"' (p. 6).

(a) What is the meaning of the word in each of the following sentences?

(b) In which *three* of them does the word mean what it meant to Paul?

(i) The church was very hot this morning.

(ii) I believe in the Holy Catholic and Apostolic Church.

(iii) The head of the Roman Catholic Church is the Pope.

(iv) The Church at Bida welcomes visitors.

(v) The Church's one foundation is Jesus Christ the Lord.

2. 'Called to be saints' (1 Cor. 1.2).

(a) What word is used for 'saints' in that verse:

(i) In another English version?

(ii) In another language you know?

(b) What do the words which you have quoted in your reply to (a) mean when they are used in ordinary conversation?

(c) How, if at all, does that meaning differ from the meaning it had for Paul?

3. What does the word 'grace' mean? (vv. 3 and 4).

CONTENT

4. Why did Paul begin this letter by thanking God for the gifts which God had given to the Christians at Corinth?

5. What did Paul mean by saying that those Christians were '*in* Christ'?

6. (a) How many times did Paul use the name of Jesus Christ in 1 Cor. 1.1–9?

(b) What did Paul say about Jesus in each of the following verses? 1 Cor. 1.1; 1.2c; 1.7; 1.9.

(c) Why did Paul call himself 'an apostle of Christ' and not an 'apostle of God' in v. 1?

(d) What are people missing who worship God but who do not worship Him 'through Jesus'?

BIBLE

7. In the following passages the word 'holy' (or 'saints' or 'sacred') occurs. What or whom did the writer refer to in each case?

(a) Mark 6.20　(b) Acts 4.27　(c) Rom. 15.26　(d) 1 Cor. 1.2
(e) 1 Cor. 6.1　(f) 1 Cor. 7.14　(g) Phil. 1.1　(h) 2 Tim. 3.15.

8. 'I give thanks to God' (1 Cor. 1.4). For what did Paul thank God in each case, according to the following passages:

(a) 1 Cor. 1.4–7　(b) Phil. 1.3–6　(c) Col. 1.3–5　(d) 2 Thess. 1.3,4.

9. What single truth was Paul referring to in the following passages? 1 Cor. 1.7,8; 3.13; 5.5; 11.26; 15.24.

DISCUSSION AND RESEARCH

10. On p. 5 we read about the staff of a theological school asking candidates why they thought that God had called them to be ordained leaders. If you were interviewing them:

(a) What further question would you put to each of them?

(b) How, if at all, would you decide if God was really 'calling' that candidate to that work?

11. (a) 'The word "saints" does not mean people who have withdrawn from the life which other people live . . . they are members of groups such as town-councils, school staffs . . .' (pp. 6, 7). To what groups (other than Church groups) do you and your Christian friends belong?

(b) We read on p. 7 of an employment officer who felt that whatever he did, he could not do right.

(i) What is your opinion of his remarks?

(ii) Do you think that you can be a 'saint' if you do work like his?

Give reasons for your opinion in each case.

12. Christians look forward to what God will do to complete His work, i.e. at the 'revealing' of Jesus (p. 8). What difference, if any, would it make to your own behaviour if you thought that there would be no completion of His work by God, and no 'revealing' of Jesus?

1.10–31 Unity in the Church

You will not be united unless you follow the crucified Jesus

OUTLINE

1.10–13a: I beg you to unite and to stop quarrelling. For I hear that you are divided into rival parties, each party saying that it follows a different apostle.

1.13b–17: Thank God I did nothing to create a party of my own. I did not even baptize more than a few people.

1.18–25: You are divided because you have followed teaching which the world calls 'wisdom', and because you have despised Jesus who was killed on a cross. But in truth, God's plan which most people call 'foolish' is wiser than what such people call 'wisdom'.

1.26–31: You can see what I mean if you look at the sort of people whom God has called into His Church. The world does not regard them as 'wise' or 'great'. So if you want to boast about anyone, do not boast about them. Boast about God and what He has done for us all.

INTERPRETATION

Verse 10 is the beginning of a long section of this letter which continues to the end of chapter 4. In this section Paul wrote about: (a) the need for

10

unity, (b) the message which Christians preach, (c) the work of those who lead and preach and listen in the Church.

In this section (1.10–31) Paul was encouraging the congregation at Corinth to be a united body. He had heard of their divisions. We notice among others three important words: 'dissensions', 'cross', 'wisdom'.

(a) **'Dissensions'** (v. 10): 'Divisions' is a better translation. After Paul had left Corinth, he heard from 'Chloe's people' (v. 11) that Church members there had split into separate groups. See note on v. 10 below, and notes on 11.17–34 and 12.12–31, where Paul again appealed to his readers to be united.

(b) **'Cross'** (vv. 17, 18, 23, and see also 2.2): After Paul had referred to disunity, he went on to a second thought: the death of Jesus on a cross. He said 'My work among you was to preach about Jesus (and His perfect offering of Himself) rather than to baptize people.' But it seems that he was also thinking: You have split into parties because you have followed people who proudly push themselves forward (i.e. those whom the world calls 'wise'), instead of following Jesus who humbly sacrificed Himself.

(c) **'Wisdom'**: We most often use the word 'wise' to describe a person who uses the intelligence which God has given him. Many old people are rightly called 'wise' because they have discovered by experience that some ways of living are better than others. Some of them have written down what they discovered, and these writings become part of the precious traditions of a nation or tribe. In the same way we say that God has given wisdom to those in modern times who have learnt how to give a plastic heart to a dying man or who design a helicopter by which to rescue sailors from a sinking ship.

Paul did use the word 'wisdom' in this way in 1 Cor. 2 (see note, p. 24). And he himself made use of wisdom of this sort when he spoke (see Acts 17.22–32). But in chapter 1 he gave the word two quite different meanings:

1. God's own wisdom, which He showed in two ways:

(a) By planning to rescue human beings from the results of their sinfulness (1.21).

(b) In Jesus Christ, the only truly wise person (see note on 1.30b below).

2. A false way of human thinking and talking (see 1.17,19,21; and 2.1, 4,5). People who are 'wise' in this false way:

(a) Do not build their ideas upon the actions of God but only upon the ideas of other people (Col. 2.8).

(b) Think and speak as if they did not depend on God. So they foolishly boast about their own wisdom or 'cleverness' (see 3.18 and Matt. 11.25). They are aiming at receiving the praise which should be given to God.

(c) Achieve nothing, because through their way of thinking they do not learn either about God (1 Cor. 1.21) or how to live as human beings (Col. 2.23).

NOTES

1.10. I appeal to you ... be united in the same mind and the same judgement:

1. Why did Paul make this appeal? Why is unity among Christians important?

The reason Paul gave in 3.3 is that if Christians are divided they are no different from other people. In that case, they cannot do the special work to which God has called them.

2. Why were the Corinthian Christians divided?

In this part of the letter Paul referred to the following two reasons: (a) because they had neglected the basic teaching about Jesus's self-offering ('the word of the cross' v. 18); (b) because they paid more attention to their human party-leaders than to Jesus Himself (see note on 1.12 below). We read of other reasons for disunity in chapters 6, 11, 14.

3. What did Paul mean by 'united in the same mind'?

He did not mean that all believers must have the same ideas or that they must all experience the love of God in the same way. But it does mean that they must all share some convictions about God and Jesus Christ. Christians do not become united simply by being well organized.

One of the most difficult questions Christians have to answer is: '*Which* convictions is it necessary for us to share in order that we may live as one Church?' Some people say that the only conviction that is necessary is the conviction that 'Jesus is Lord' (1 Cor. 12.3). Most Christians want to share more than this with other Christians before they are fully united with them.

See also notes on 11.17 in which we study some of the ways in which Christians can have unity.

1.11. Chloe's people: We do not know who Chloe was. She may have been a woman trader who sent her people to Ephesus, where Paul wrote this letter. If so, then her people could bring news to Paul from Corinth.

1.12. I belong to Paul ... I belong to Apollos: The mistake which the Corinthians were making was to put a human leader in the place of God. Each group or 'party' in the congregation used the name of an apostle as their 'war cry'. They gave their loyalty to him instead of to Jesus Christ. It is a mistake which Christians and others have often made. There are many sects or religious groups who honour one human being (usually the person who founded the sect) as if he were a sort of second Christ. They regard him as the one person whom God has appointed to be the interpreter of Christ. For example, we may find that Mormons treat Joseph Smith and that Seventh Day Adventists treat William Miller in this way. Perhaps the big Churches have sometimes fallen into the same error, and have paid more attention to such people as Aquinas, Luther, Calvin and Wesley than to Jesus Christ.

At Corinth some people made Paul their hero. Perhaps they were

'If Christians are divided . . . they cannot do the special work to which God has called them' (p. 12).

By their united efforts, students and labourers in Peru are building a wall as part of a development project.

What are the benefits which come when Christians work together in God's service?

defending him against those who said that he was not a real apostle. Others followed Apollos (of whom we read in Acts 18.2—19.1), perhaps because he was a better speaker than Paul. Another group said, 'We belong to Christ.' Perhaps they had split off from the others, saying proudly that they alone followed Christ properly. But Paul said many times that Jesus is for everyone. Therefore no Christians have the right to think that Jesus belongs to their group rather than other groups.

1.14–16: I baptized none of you except Crispus . . . I did baptize also the household of Stephanas:

1. Was Paul saying that baptism was unnecessary? No. We see from such passages as Acts 2.41 and Romans 6.3,4, that as soon as people had heard the Christians' preaching and believed that it was true, they were baptized. Paul was simply saying that he was glad that he had not started a 'party' of his own by baptizing many people.

2. We notice that Paul had baptized the whole 'household' of Stephanas. This may mean (but it does not prove) that he baptized children as well as adults. (See also Acts 16.31–33 and note on 1 Cor. 16.15.)

3. These verses remind us that Paul wrote this letter by dictating it to his secretary. He spoke as his thoughts came. If he felt that he had said something that was not clear or not accurate, he added another sentence to correct it. (See also note on 15.10 and 16.21.)

1.17. To preach the Gospel, and not with eloquent wisdom: The word which is here translated 'preaching the Gospel' means 'telling good news', i.e. telling the story of Jesus Christ with the hope that those who listen will want to entrust themselves to Him.

'Telling the story' is, of course, not enough. The one who tells the story will fail in his task unless he is also living the life of a Christian. But 'telling the story' in the right way is necessary.

What is the 'right way'? Paul said that for him the right way was to preach without 'eloquent wisdom'. He did not mean that a preacher should not have eloquence, for every preacher needs, for instance, to speak clearly. Nor did he mean that a preacher should not have wisdom. We have seen above that there is a sort of wisdom (or intelligence or common-sense) which is a gift from God.

Paul meant that he preached without drawing attention to his own skill or voice, without drawing attention to his own knowledge or holiness. In this way he was pointing away from himself to what God had done and was still doing. He was aiming at meeting the needs of his listeners rather than at meeting his own need for praise and success (see the note on 2.1).

1.18. The word of the cross is folly to those who are perishing, but to us who are being saved it is the power of God:

1. **Are perishing . . . are being saved.** Some people are on the road to being destroyed, others are on the road to being saved. Paul often looked

back to a past event in his life and in the lives of other Christians, as he did in 1.2. But here he looked ahead. The question he asked here was not 'Were you once sanctified?', but 'Which road are you taking now?'

2. **The power.** Those who are on the right road have 'power' in their lives because they have heard 'the word of the cross', i.e. the good news of Jesus's total self-offering. If we have not heard or accepted this good news, we are without power. We are like the old truck which someone once presented to a theological school. The engine was so weak that if more than one passenger got inside the truck, it would not move!

How can hearing this good news bring us power? There was a schoolboy who cheated in examinations because he was terrified of failing. He was terrified because he did not think he was of any value unless he was successful. One day someone told him and his class the story of the life and death and rising of Jesus, and explained that this was God's action. God did it, he said, 'because He loved us all so much.' From that time the boy began to learn that God loved him as he was and not only 'if he was successful'. The 'word of the cross' gave him the power to change the way he lived, and the way he did his work at school.

Paul said that the wisdom which most people value is false wisdom, because it does not give them power. Although by wisdom we can achieve much in the world, wisdom does not preserve us from being overwhelmed by sin. We may note three other verses in which Paul repeated this:

1.21: 'Wisdom' has not discovered the truth about God.

1.24: It is the message that Christ died for us that gives us power.

1.25: God, by allowing Jesus to die, may seem to be weak. But we have found that this event gives us more strength than any human teachings can.

1.22. Jews demand signs and Greeks seek wisdom:

1. The Jews would not believe that God was at work in Jesus Christ unless Jesus gave them 'signs'. This was not surprising. Throughout the Old Testament we read of Israelites who believed in God mainly because He had done great signs, such as bringing them out of slavery in Egypt (Exod. 13.3) and helping them to cross the Red Sea (Exod. 15.1,2). So when Jesus came they asked Him for signs, i.e. for proofs that He was God's Messiah (see Matt. 12.38; 27.40). Jesus Himself was tempted to do magic to prove that He had the power of God in Him (see Matt. 4.1–11). It is true that He did miracles, but only because he loved and cared for people. He did not do miracles with the intention of making people believe that He was Messiah. He wanted them to follow Him in faith and of their own free choice (but there is no doubt that, as a result of His miracles, they were helped to believe in Him).

We can understand why the Jews asked for signs, because many of us are tempted to ask for signs too, e.g. when we feel that God is 'weak', if the Church is not influential in our country, or if our reading of Bible texts fails to convince others that Jesus is Lord. It is when we no longer

15

trust in God Himself that we begin to look for signs or to call God 'weak'.

2. The Greeks were troubled, not because God seemed to be weak, but because He seemed to be foolish. (In this passage the word 'Greek' refers to anyone who was not a Jew.) It seemed to them that God had wasted a good man's life by letting Jesus die. We can understand why they were troubled. Greek philosophers (the word means 'lovers of wisdom') were careful and profound thinkers. Many of the great and true ideas on which scientists, teachers, and theologians of today base their work came from the Greek philosophers. We can rejoice at these gifts which God has given to human beings. And yet, as we have seen (p. 11), there are two important truths to add:

(a) There is something which that sort of wisdom cannot do: it cannot rescue us from our sinfulness.

(b) If we pay too much attention to human 'wisdom', we become unable to see how much we depend on God (see note below on 1.26).

1.26. Not many of you were wise . . . not many were powerful: This does not mean that the Christians in Corinth were uneducated or starving. Some of them were well-educated (1 Cor. 3.18) and others may have been rich (1 Cor. 11.22). Probably even some of those who were slaves could read. But they did not have influence in the city.

Paul was glad that this was so. He was glad, not because he envied or feared influential or clever people, but because wise and clever and important people often find it difficult to remember that they depend on God and on each other. They are tempted to think that they can earn the love of God by being successful. They are tempted to rely on their own achievements and to boast about them. This is why Jesus said that it was very difficult for rich people to put themselves under the sovereignty of God ('to enter the kingdom of heaven', Matt. 19.23). Little children, He said, do not find it so difficult (Matt. 11.25; see also 1 Cor. 1.17,28).

There are many thousands of Christian congregations today whom other people treat as 'things that are not' and whose members are 'low and despised' (v. 28). We may think of the poorest congregation in the poorest district of Hong Kong or Saõ Paulo and compare it with the congregation of the Cathedrals in those cities, many of whose members are influential and wealthy. We may know of some man or woman who holds no position of authority but whom God uses even more than He uses the official leaders of His Church in that place. Paul's message to the 'poor' congregation and to the individual who has no 'status' is this: 'If because you are "weak", you put your confidence in God, you will have a strength to fight evil which bigger congregations and more well-known individuals may not have.' This does not mean that God has no use for the Cathedrals or for well-known Christians. It means that such 'big' congregations or 'big' people need to be aware of the special temptation that is theirs, i.e. the temptation to rely on their own strength.

1.27. God chose what is weak in the world: For thousands of years people have known that some things and some people which look the weakest are really the strongest. In Africa they tell stories of Tortoise and of Rabbit. All over Asia and Europe they tell the story of Cinderella, the ragged girl who sat among cinders in the hearth, whom the prince chose as his bride. The new teaching that Paul taught was that this is true about God and Jesus and His Church. God does *His* work by choosing what is weak.

Paul wrote because his readers had forgotten this truth, just as Christians have often forgotten it ever since. They forgot it at the time of the Crusades, and at many other times when they have tried to triumph over other people's religions through the power of money or arms.

We see here the difference between what Paul called 'weak' and what most people call 'strong'. For Paul a 'weak' person was someone who had the spirit of the crucified Jesus, who was a willing servant, who pointed away from himself to God who gives power. For most people a 'strong' person is someone who can defeat opponents in an election or an argument, who is willing to do anything in order to get the approval of other people or to hold important positions.

1.30a. He is the source of your life in Christ Jesus: Those who are in Christ (see note p. 7) must remember that God made this possible. So they should boast about Him (v. 31), not about their own cleverness and achievements.

1.30b. Christ Jesus . . . our wisdom, our righteousness, and sanctification and redemption: By using these four words, Paul reminded his readers that Jesus did for us what we could not do for ourselves: He broke down the barriers which we human beings have put up between ourselves and God:

1. **Our wisdom.** When we are 'in Him' we rely on His Wisdom rather than on our own.

2. **Our righteousness.** In the New Testament this word 'righteousness' has two meanings:

(a) living honestly and uprightly (see Eph. 6.14);

(b) being treated by God with as much love as if we were innocent, although we are guilty. This is its meaning here. We are like guilty prisoners in a law-court, said Paul, and God is the judge. When we rely on the righteous Christ and not on ourselves, we share in His righteousness. Then God acquits us, pardons us and treats us as if we were innocent. He has allowed Jesus to 'be righteousness' for us. So God makes a new relationship with us.

People have used illustrations to explain how God could do this. For example, a man is in court because he cannot pay a debt. Just as he is about to be sent to prison, someone in the court pays his debt for him; so the judge lets him go. This illustration, like all illustrations, only points to one side of the truth about God and ourselves. It hides the fact that it was God Himself who, so to speak, 'paid the debt'; that 'the Judge' and not someone

17

else paid it. It fails to show that God enters into a loving relationship with us as the result of Jesus's action.

Instead of looking for illustrations, it may be better to note what Paul was pointing to here:

(a) to the truth that Jesus did for us what we cannot do;

(b) to his own experiences of being at peace, because God had accepted and pardoned him in spite of his sinfulness (see Rom. 5.8).

3. **Our sanctification.** Paul often used this word to mean a long journey or a continuous process, by which Christians grow in holiness as the Spirit of God works in them. 'May the God of peace himself sanctify you wholly' (1 Thess. 5.23).

But here, as in 1.2 and 6.11, the word refers to the beginning of that 'journey', to the time when God pardoned him and others. Thus 'our righteousness' and 'our sanctification' mean very much the same.

4. **Our redemption.** People in the Roman empire used this word 'redemption' when speaking of the freeing of slaves. A slave could become a freeman if money was paid to his owner. Then he could be bought back, i.e. 'redeemed'. So there were two main ideas: (a) someone paid a price, (b) the 'slave' began a new sort of life.

Anyone who was once enslaved, e.g. by a sinful habit, and who has been set free through Jesus Christ will understand why Paul used this word. It was because:

(a) Jesus had paid a price (see 6.20): He had given His whole life, even to the point of dying.

(b) As a result, Paul was free to serve God. He was no longer enslaved (e.g. by feelings of fear or guilt).

In these verses, Paul did not offer his readers good ideas: he told them what had happened to him.

STUDY SUGGESTIONS

WORDS

1. In 1 Cor. 1.10–31, ten of the verses contain the words 'wisdom' or 'wise'.

    (a) Which are those verses?

    (b) Give an example of someone you know who is truly 'wise'. Why do you call him (or her) 'wise'?

    (c) What is the chief difference between a truly wise person and those whose wisdom is false, according to Paul?

2. Which *eight* of the following words are closest to the meaning of the words 'redeem' and 'redemption' as used in 1 Cor. 1.30?

    help   free   release   refresh   rescue   ransom   nourish
    liberate   deliver   save   comfort   unloose

CONTENT

3. Why were there separate 'parties' in the Church at Corinth?
4. Why was Paul glad that he only baptized a few people at Corinth?
5. Why did Paul want to avoid using eloquent wisdom (1 Cor. 1.17)?
6. (a) What did the Jews expect Jesus to do in order to show that He was God's Messiah?
   (b) In what way were they mistaken?
7. Why did the non-Jews think that the story of Jesus's dying on a cross was 'foolish'?

BIBLE

8. 'I belong to Apollos' (1.12). What do we learn about Apollos in Acts 18.24–28?
9. 'Preach the gospel' (1 Cor. 1.17).
   In the following passages in the book of Acts:
   (i) Who preached?   (ii) What was the result?
   (a) 2.14–42 (b) 3.12–4.4 (c) 13.16,26–33,42,43 (d) 17.22–32
10. In each of the following passages we read of those who were neither 'powerful' nor of 'noble birth' (1 Cor. 1.26).
    (i) What words are used to describe such people?
    (ii) What did they receive?
    (a) Psalm 40.17 (b) Isaiah 29.19 (c) Zeph. 3.12
    (d) Luke 1,52,53 (e) Luke 7.22

DISCUSSION AND RESEARCH

11. Aesop told a fable about a fox who wanted some grapes, but could not reach them, so he said that the grapes were sour and he did not want them. A student read 1 Cor. 1.10–31 and said that Paul was like the fox! 'He could not get wisdom and so he said it was not worth having.' What is your opinion?
12. 'Why were the Corinthian Christians divided?' (p. 12)
    (a) What reasons did Paul refer to in 1.10–31?
    (b) In your own experience, what do you think are the two most common reasons for divisions in a congregation?
13. 'Which convictions about God and Jesus Christ is it necessary for us to share in order to be united?' (p. 12). Ask this question of Christians from whom your Church is at present separated. Compare their answers and your own.
14. 'There are religious groups who honour one human being as if he were a sort of second Christ' (p. 12).
    (a) Are there any such groups near you? If so, what are the names of the individuals whom the members honour in this way?
    (b) Do you think that your own Church ever makes the same mistake?
15. 'The word of the cross' (1 Cor. 1.18).

What difference would it make to your beliefs and your behaviour if you thought that Jesus did *not* die on the cross?

16. 'Many of us are tempted to ask for "signs"' (p. 15).
    If you think this is true, give examples.

17. 'God chose what is weak' (1 Cor. 1.27). Give an example, from your own experience or from your knowledge of history, of a group or an individual who seems 'weak', but whom God perhaps used more than He uses those who are 'strong' and well-known.

Special Note A
The City of Corinth

If we know something about Corinth, we can better understand the letters which Paul wrote to the Christians there.

1. The people of Corinth were *rich*, because in two ways the city was a centre for trade. First, it lies on the narrow isthmus which joins northern and southern Greece. So traders from one part of Greece to the other part had to pass through Corinth.

Secondly, most of those who carried cargo by sea between Italy (on the west of Corinth) and Asia Minor (on the east) passed through Corinth rather than sail round the coast of southern Greece, where many ships were wrecked. They unloaded their cargo at one of the small ports near the city, carried it across land on special trucks, and loaded it on to other boats at the other side of the isthmus. (Nowadays there is a canal which ships can sail through.) Because they paid taxes to Corinth for doing this and also brought goods into the city itself, Corinth became rich.

2. It was a fairly *new* city. It is true that there had been an important city of Corinth for many centuries and that Corinth rather than Athens had been the leading city of Greece. (There are very old things in the Corinth Museum today, e.g. jugs which were made there in 3000 BC.) But in 146 BC the Romans completely destroyed it, and it was a ruin for 100 years.

Then in 46 BC the Roman Dictator Julius Caesar founded a new city, including new temples, baths, law courts, shops, etc.

So although some of the city was nearly 100 years old, the inhabitants regarded their city as a 'new' one. As a result they felt free to create their own laws and customs.

3. Its population was very *mixed*. In this respect living in Corinth was like living in Mombasa or Bangkok or other big coastal cities today.

Before the Romans destroyed the old city the inhabitants had been Greek, and Greek was still the main language when Paul went there. The

Isthmian Games (p. 123), which still took place outside Corinth, had been begun by the Greeks in honour of their god Poseidon.

But after Caesar rebuilt the city there were very few Greeks in Corinth. He turned it into a Roman colony and filled it with retired Roman soldiers. It had an amphitheatre where, according to Roman custom, men were forced to fight with wild beasts (p. 46). In 1 Corinthians and Acts 18 we read of people to whom Paul referred who had Roman names: Titus Justus (Acts 18.7), Crispus (Acts 18.8 and 1 Cor. 1.14), Gaius (1 Cor. 1.14), Fortunatus (1 Cor. 16.17). The magistrate Gallio (Acts 18.12) was also a Roman.

There were also a great many Jews in Corinth because the Emperor Claudius had expelled all Jews from Rome (Acts 18.2–4). Naturally, when they settled in other cities, like Corinth, they continued to practise their own religion, e.g. building synagogues, and worshipping in them. The ruins of one of their synagogues are still there today.

In addition to the Greeks, Romans, and Jews, there were people from many other races of Asia Minor, Egypt, and Syria. They passed through Corinth while trading, or came there in order to find work.

Because Corinth was rich and new and had a mixed population, its people experienced those serious difficulties and temptations which the inhabitants of such cities usually do experience, and Paul referred to some of these temptations.

Because the city was rich and important, its people were tempted to think that a good character was less important than the wealth which could buy possessions and pleasure (see 1 Cor. 6.13).

Because the city was new, many of its people rejected old traditions, including the good traditions (see 1 Cor. 5.1).

Because the inhabitants were from different races there was no one God and no one tradition which everyone reverenced. This is why Christians were confused concerning food which had been offered to Roman gods (1 Cor. 8). It is one reason why the Church in Corinth was divided (1 Cor. 1.11).

How was it that Paul had the courage to visit a city of that sort and attempt to found the Church there? He wrote in 1 Cor. 2.3, 'I was with you in weakness and in much fear.' No wonder! What could one man do in such a city? Paul was able to work in Corinth only because he firmly believed that the Spirit of Jesus rather than he himself was in charge (1 Cor. 2.4).

STUDY SUGGESTIONS

1. In what country was Corinth?
2. (a) How far is Corinth from Athens? (See Acts 18.1.)
   (b) Of which Roman Province was Corinth the capital city?

(c) 'Cargo between Italy and Asia Minor passed through Corinth' (p. 20).
Draw a sketch map to illustrate this statement.
3. Why did Corinth become rich?
4. How far is it true to say that Corinth was a 'new' city when Paul went there?
5. Why was Greek the main language of Corinth?
6. What evidence is there in the New Testament that there were Romans in Corinth?
7. Why were there a large number of Jews in Corinth?
8. Why do you think Paul felt 'weak and afraid' when he visited Corinth?
9. When a modern Church leader begins work in a town where many people are rich and belong to different races or tribes,
   (a) What are his chief problems likely to be?
   (b) How far are they the same problems which Paul had to face?

2.1—3.4 True Wisdom

A truly wise man is one who depends on God to give him wisdom

OUTLINE

2.1–5: When I lived among you and gave my testimony about God, it was God Himself who moved you to believe in Him. It was not I or my wisdom.

2.6–8: I do not mean that Christians should not have wisdom or use their minds, I mean that the true wisdom which God gives is different from the wisdom of the world.

2.9–16: True wisdom is, first, knowledge about God and His plans for those who love Him. Secondly, it cannot be understood unless God's Spirit inspires us to understand it.

3.1–4: As for you, you are so divided that it is clear that you are not ready to receive God's Spirit or true wisdom.

INTERPRETATION

In these verses Paul again wrote about the divisions that existed among the Christians at Corinth.

One reason why they were divided was that they had wrong ideas about 'wisdom'. We have seen (p. 11) that Paul used the word 'wisdom' to mean several different things. Here in 2.1—3.4 its different meanings are:

(a) Clever speech. This makes the listeners pay more attention to the speaker and his ideas than to God and to His will. See 'a wisdom of this age' (v. 6). This is false wisdom, as we saw in the note on 1.17.

(b) Knowledge of God's plan to save mankind through Jesus Christ: 'we do impart wisdom'... 'a secret and hidden wisdom of God' (2.6,7). This is true wisdom. We are not born with it. We cannot get it through our own cleverness only.

Those who were truly 'wise' Paul also called 'the mature' (see note on v. 6) and 'the spiritual' (see note on v. 15).

So his message was, 'Until you look humbly to God for your wisdom, and open yourselves to His Spirit, you cannot escape from the quarrels and divisions which spoil the life of your congregation.'

NOTES

2.1. Not ... in lofty words or wisdom: As Paul had said in 1.17, it was not his own clever preaching which led the Corinthians to believe in Jesus Christ. It was the power of God.

What sort of preaching leads the hearers to new or deeper belief? According to Paul it is:

(a) Not words which draw attention to the preacher's own education or cleverness or voice, but words which point to the presence and activity of God ('demonstration of the Spirit' v. 4).

(b) Not words which represent ideas only, but words which also express what the preacher and the Christians have experienced (see Acts 22.2–10).

(c) Not words spoken into the air, but words with which the preacher makes a relationship with his hearers (see 'I was with you' v. 3).

(d) Not words spoken because it is the custom to speak words at that time, but words spoken so that the hearers may turn to God ('My speech and my message were ... in power' v. 4).

(e) Not words that describe rich or successful people but words that refer to Jesus who was killed like a common criminal (see v. 2).

2.2. Know nothing ... except Jesus Christ and him crucified: Paul did not of course mean that the only teaching which he ever gave about Jesus was that Jesus died. See 1 Cor. 15.3–7, where he taught Jesus's resurrection very thoroughly. Nor does this verse mean that a Christian preacher must refer to the death of Christ in every sermon. What Paul meant was that:

(a) We might have expected that when God sent Jesus to set us free, He would have used someone whom everyone praised for His power or eloquence or cleverness. But in fact Jesus did His work for human beings in a way which everyone despised. He was crucified.

(b) This is the truth which Paul had to emphasize because it was the truth which his hearers in Corinth had most seriously failed to understand. They thought that the best Christian was the one who was the most eloquent or the cleverest.

2.3. In much fear and trembling: Paul seems often to have been afraid of being rejected (see Acts 18.9; 2 Cor. 10.1–10; and Additional Note, 'Paul', p. 54). According to a booklet called *Acts of Paul and Thecla*, which was written 100 years after Paul's life, he was 'short, bald, and bow-legged . . .'. If that is true, then this may be one reason why he was nervous among strangers.

But when he reached Corinth there were special reasons for his fears, e.g. the Jews 'opposed and reviled him' (Acts 18.6,13). It could easily happen that a crowd could kill him. He must have been afraid also that he would fail in the work which God had given him to do.

A courageous Christian is not someone who is never afraid. He is someone who has learnt to discover carefully what his real fears are and to tell God about them. In doing this he comes to rely more fully than before on God. Having committed himself into God's hands, he is free to do what he ought to do, and is not held back from action by the weight of his fears.

2.4,5. My speech and my message were not in plausible words . . . that your faith might rest in the power of God: Only preachers who rely on God, as Paul did, can lead their hearers to rely on God.

2.6a. Among the mature we do impart wisdom:

1. 'Mature' Christians are those who are sufficiently fully grown in spirit to know how greatly they need the Spirit of God. They have reached the stage of knowing that they need Him in order to live in love with their fellow human beings. (Note: the AV translation, 'perfect', is misleading.)

2. The word 'mature' has a different meaning here from its meaning in the Greek 'mystery religions' which the Corinthians knew. In those religions 'mature' people were the ones who had passed tests so that they could be initiated into a knowledge of secret traditions and actions. This sort of maturity was unlike the maturity of which Paul wrote, in two ways: (a) people could achieve it simply through their own efforts, (b) it made no difference to the lives of those people, e.g. to the way in which they lived in relation to other people. They could be called 'mature' and yet be uncharitable or dishonest at the same time.

We may compare these two meanings of 'mature' with two ways of preparing adult candidates for Christian baptism. One way (following Paul's teaching) is to say that a candidate is ripe for baptism when he realizes his need for God to control his life and when he knows something about the power of God to do that. A different way (following in some respects the mystery religions) is to say that a candidate is ripe when he has memorized the Ten Commandments and paid his Church contributions.

3. But Paul did not think that true wisdom was unimportant. It is one of God's gifts (see 1 Cor. 12.8: 'To one is given through the Spirit the utterance of wisdom'). Christians are answerable to God for the way in which they use and develop their minds. A theological student who

24

'Mature Christians' (p. 24).

In some countries old people, like this Malaysian woman teaching her grand-daughter to weave, are specially honoured for their long experience and their wisdom. In other places, young people receive greater respect, because of their up-to-date knowledge and technical skills.

To what extent, if any, does people's 'maturity' as Christians depend on their age in years?

organized prayer-meetings during college study-periods would not be following Paul's teaching!

2.6b. Not a wisdom of this age or of the rulers of this age:

1. **This age.** Paul here used the language of most Jews who divided time into 'this age' and 'the age to come'. They thought of 'this age' as a time when people rebel against God (see Gal. 1.4), so in this age what seems to be wisdom is not true wisdom.

2. **The rulers.** Paul may have thought of all rulers who do not acknowledge that they are answerable to God (we remember that Roman Emperors were called 'gods'). Or he may have meant Pontius Pilate who 'crucified the Lord' (v. 8).

But it is more likely that he was thinking of supernatural evil powers, who, for instance, caused Pilate to do what he did (see Eph. 6.12, and note on demons, p. 136).

2.7. Hidden wisdom of God which God decreed . . . for our glorification:

1. **Hidden:** True wisdom, i.e. true knowledge about God, was hidden, (a) from those who lived before Christ, (b) from the immature Christians in Corinth, who were blind to the true wisdom. 'Hidden' does not mean that God intends some people to have this wisdom and hides it from others.

2. **Decreed . . . for our glorification:** NEB 'to bring us to our full glory'.

From the beginning God has intended human beings to share His 'glory', i.e. to enjoy the most complete existence of which we are capable.

The best thing we can do for other people is to help them to see what they are capable of becoming as children of God. There is a West African story about a farmer who kept chickens. A friend looked at the chickens and said, 'One of those birds is an eagle.' The man said, 'No. He eats what the others eat. He is only a chicken.' But the friend gave that bird some meat to eat and its strength developed. One day he put it on his wrist and walked a little way into the bush. As the sun rose he pointed to a mountain and said: 'You are an eagle. Fly!' Then the eagle flew away and the sun lit up its wings.

Writers in the Bible use 'glory' to describe:

(a) The presence and power of God (see Exod. 24.15–17).

(b) The presence and power of God which people could see in Jesus, when He did miracles (John 2.11), and when He gave His life on the cross. See v. 8, 'They crucified the Lord of glory.'

(c) The privilege which God will give to human beings to share His own being. That is what 'glory' means in this sense. It does not mean receiving praise from other people.

2.9. As it is written . . . 'What God has prepared for those who love Him': The words which Paul quoted are like Isaiah 64.4, but not the same. Perhaps he quoted from memory, or from a version of Isaiah which has since been lost. We note:

1. **'Prepared'.** There are blessings which we cannot have now but which

God has prepared for us at 'the end' (see also v. 7). It is important for Christians to remember this truth. When they forget it, they lose hope. But at the same time, they must not pretend to know more about the end than God has shown them (see 1 John 3.2).

2. **'Love'.** The people who will be able to receive those blessings are those who love God, rather than those who work the hardest for Him or 'know' Him or simply wait for Him (see Isa. 64.4).

2.10. The Spirit searches everything: In 2.10–16 Paul said, 'Human beings need the Spirit of God'. If we open ourselves to His Spirit, He can work in us. Then (and not till then) we are able to search out the truth about Him.

2.11. What person knows a man's thoughts, except the spirit of the man? Paul was saying: 'Let me give you an illustration to show that we need God's Spirit. No one knows what another person is thinking except that person himself (except the 'spirit' of the man). In the same way, no one knows the real truth about God except God Himself, and those who are ready to receive His Spirit.

We note that Paul (like other writers in the New Testament) used the word 'spirit' to mean three different things:

1. The real 'personality' of a person. This is the meaning in the first part of this verse (see also Acts 17.16).

Note: In 1 Cor. 14.14,15 'spirit' means something rather different, i.e. the person as he is feeling rather than as he is thinking.

2. An unseen supernatural being (see note on 1 Cor. 10.20).

3. God Himself at work in the world and in human beings, i.e. the 'Holy Spirit' (this is the meaning in the last part of the verse and in vv. 13 and 14). In the RSV the word is printed with a capital S when it has this meaning.

2.14. The unspiritual man does not receive the gifts of the Spirit of God, for they are folly to him: The word which is translated 'unspiritual man' in the RSV does not mean a bad man or an uneducated man. It means someone who does not see that he needs to be filled with God's Spirit. Other translations say 'natural man', i.e. a man who thinks that the most important part of his life is the part which he shares with 'nature', e.g. with animals and plants. This is why he cannot judge the value of ('understand') God's gifts. We think of the friends of Jesus who thought that He was mad (Mark 3.21), or of the family of St Francis of Assisi who thought he was mad because he cared for people whom no one else cared for.

2.15. The spiritual man judges all things, but is himself to be judged by no one.

1. **'The spiritual man':** the person who is willing for God's Spirit to direct him in his daily life, i.e. he is a 'mature' or 'truly wise' person (v.6). It does not mean the man who 'knows' more than others, nor who fasts or who speaks with tongues more than others.

2. **'Judges all things':** tests the real value of things because God's Spirit is with him. He is like the man in a coal-mine deep under the ground

who can test the air to see if it is pure because he carries a special lamp. (The colour of the flame changes if the air is too poisonous for workmen to breathe.)

3. **'To be judged by no one'**: this does not mean that no one should criticize a person who believes that he has opened himself to God's Spirit. It does not mean that no one should test that person to see if he is really open to the Spirit. Indeed, a Church leader who is unwilling to listen to the criticism of other Christians cannot be a 'spiritual' or 'mature' Christian at all (see 1 Cor. 14.29: 'let the others weigh what is said').

The meaning is: 'He is to be judged by God rather than by people. God is the only One who knows how deep is the belief of each person.' 'It is the Lord who judges me' (1 Cor. 4.4).

2.16. We have the mind of Christ:

1. **We:**

(a) We, not I. It is a fellowship of Christians rather than an individual to whom (according to this verse) God gives Himself. (We may follow up this idea by asking what sort of a fellowship is most likely to receive Him, and in what way.)

(b) 'We' means those who are sufficiently ready or 'mature' or 'spiritual' to receive Him. Paul was not here comparing Christians with non-Christians. He was not saying that God is absent from those who are not Christian. He was comparing mature Christians with Christians who were not mature.

2. **Have:** We already have His Spirit. Christians often behave as if they had to fetch the Spirit from somewhere or had to shout 'Lord, hear us' before He will come. A Communist who had begun to study the person of Jesus Christ, and who later became a Christian, said to a Christian minister, 'You've got it, you've got it, but you don't know it!'

3. **The mind of Christ:** In the first part of the verse Paul had said, 'No one can know God so well that he can teach God.' In the second part he added, 'But God gave us Himself when He gave Christ, who is in us in Spirit.' (The word 'mind' here means the same as 'spirit'.)

A mature Christian's thoughts are not, of course, the same as the 'thoughts' of Christ, but he has been given Christ's Spirit.

3.1—4. Not . . . as spiritual men, but as men of the flesh: Here Paul was saying that:

1. It was necessary to express as clearly as possible the difference between 'spiritual' (or 'mature') Christians and those who were immature. The phrase which Paul used for the immature is 'man of the flesh'. Readers often think that these words refer to people who misused their sexual powers, but this is not so.

In other parts of the Bible the word 'flesh' has several meanings, e.g.:

(a) the body (of an animal or person);

(b) a human being: 'The Word became flesh' (John 1.14);

(c) a human being's general sinfulness: 'The works of the flesh are . . . immorality . . . anger . . .' (Gal. 5.19, 20).

But in v. 4 Paul used the word in an unusual way and it does not have any of the above meanings. Here it means 'immaturity'.

2. He himself had not been able to help the Corinthians to grow into 'mature' Christians, because they refused to grow up in the Spirit (see v. 2).

He had preached the Gospel about Jesus who was crucified. That was the 'milk'. But it seems that he had not been able to help them to discover in what way their lives needed to change as a result of Jesus and His cross. That was 'solid food', for which they had no appetite.

3. The Corinthians had showed by their quarrels that they had not received God's Spirit ('there is strife', v. 3). Elsewhere Paul taught that when Christians really open themselves to God's Spirit, there is fellowship, e.g. 'the fruit of the Spirit is love, joy, peace' (Gal. 5.22).

We notice that although Paul described his readers as 'not spiritual', he also called them brethren. In his eyes they did not cease to be Christians because they were unspiritual Christians.

STUDY SUGGESTIONS

WORDS

1. What six different words or phrases did Paul use in 1 Cor. 2.14—3.4 to describe the people (or the attitude of the people) who were not 'mature' or 'spiritual'?

CONTENT

2. 'Among the mature we do impart wisdom' (1 Cor. 2.6a).
   (a) What did Paul mean by 'mature'?
   (b) What was the difference between Paul's idea of 'mature' people and the idea of the Mystery Religions?
   (c) Give an example from your own experience or from what you have read of (i) someone who is truly mature; (ii) someone who is 'mature' in the way in which the Mystery Religions regarded maturity.
3. Whom did Paul refer to when he wrote of the 'rulers of this age' (2.6b)?
4. Complete the sentence: 'No eye has seen what God has prepared for those who . . .'.
5. 'We impart this in words not taught by human wisdom' (1 Cor. 2.13). Did Paul mean that Christians should be less well-educated than other people or less able to use their minds? If not, what did he mean?
6. What made Paul say that his readers were 'babes'?

BIBLE

7. Paul used the word 'spirit' or 'Spirit' to mean three different things:
   (i) The real personality of a person; (ii) an unseen supernatural being;

(iii) God Himself. Which of these three meanings does 'spirit' have in each of the following verses in 1 Corinthians?
(a) 2.4   (b) 2.11   (c) 3.16   (d) 5.5   (e) 6.19   (f) 7.34   (g) 12.10   (h) 14.2   (i) 16.18

8. Writers in the Bible refer to the 'glory' of (i) God, (ii) Jesus, (iii) Christians (see p. 26). In which of those three ways does the writer of each of the following passages use the word 'glory'?
(a) Num. 14.10   (b) Isa. 6.3   (c) John 1.14   (d) 1 Cor. 2.7
(e) 1 Cor. 2.8   (f) 1 Cor. 15.43   (g) 2 Cor. 4.17   (h) Heb. 2.9

DISCUSSION AND RESEARCH

9. How can an 'unspiritual' Christian become a 'spiritual' Christian?
10. 'I was with you . . . in much fear' (1 Cor. 2.3).
(a) Why do you think Paul was afraid?
(b) Read Ps. 27.1 and Mark 6.50. Do you think Paul ought not to have been afraid? Give reasons for your answer.
(c) What difference does trusting in God make to us when we are afraid?
11. Four preachers were asked what they replied on the last occasion when someone thanked them for a 'good sermon'. One had replied: 'Thank you very much'; the second, 'That is a wonderful text, isn't it?'; the third, 'The devil said that to me as I came to the end of the sermon'; the fourth, 'What part did you find helpful?' Judging from their replies, how far do you think each of them avoided the dangers to which Paul referred when he wrote, 'That your faith might not rest in the wisdom of men but in the power of God' (1 Cor. 2.5).
12. 'A Church leader who is unwilling to listen to the criticism of other Christians cannot be a spiritual or mature Christian' (p. 28).
(a) Is that true? Or do you think that a leader cannot allow people to criticize him without losing some of his authority? Give your reasons.
(b) What makes it difficult to accept criticism from others?
(c) How can a Christian learn to accept criticism?
13. 'In Paul's eyes, his readers did not cease to be Christians because they were unspiritual Christians' (p. 29).
Was Paul right? Or should he have broken off fellowship with the Corinthians because they were 'not real Christians'? What is your opinion? Give your reasons.

3.5–23 Leaders as Partners

The leaders in the Church are partners, not rivals

OUTLINE

3.5–9b: We who have been the leaders of your congregation are like labourers who work together on a farm. You are the farm and God owns it.
3.9c–15: Or you could compare us to the workmen who lay foundations or build the walls of a house. We know that not all those who build the wall are equally good workmen, and that those who spoil a building lose their wages.
3.16,17: Those who spoil a congregation are like people who destroy a temple. In both cases they are seriously punished.
3.18–20: Some of your leaders hold those false ideas about wisdom which I have already written about.
3.21–23: Beware of subjecting yourselves to such leaders. They are only human beings. The truth is that in so far as you are 'in Christ', everything is subject to you.

INTERPRETATION

1. LEADERS

In these verses and in chapter 4 Paul wrote about leaders in the Church. Here (3.5–23) he was chiefly writing about the way in which members should regard their leaders. In chapter 4 he was thinking of the work which the leaders did.

Why was it important that his readers should regard their leaders in the right way? It was important for two reasons:

(a) It made a difference to the way in which they regarded God. If they were always drawing attention to the 'wisdom' of their leaders, they could not pay proper attention to God.

(b) It made a difference to the unity of their congregation. If the members followed 'party' leaders, the congregation became divided. (Paul had said this before, e.g. 1.10.)

Concerning the leaders themselves Paul said two things in verses 5–23: (1) they are the servants, not the masters of their members (see notes on vv. 5 and 21); (2) they need a true idea of 'wisdom', so that they may draw attention to God rather than to themselves (see p. 11).

What Paul said here is important for all those who work as Church leaders today, whether they have been appointed and 'ordained' or not.

2. PICTURE-LANGUAGE

Paul gave his teaching here mainly through picture-language. He compared the congregation to three different things. Through each of the three pictures he was teaching one special lesson:

1. The congregation is like a farm (vv. 5–9a). Lesson: 'You will be united if you remember that God has given to each leader in the congregation his own special job to do, just as a farmer gives work to each of his labourers.'

2. It is like a building (vv. 9b–15). Lesson: 'The bad leaders and the congregation all suffer because of their mistakes, just as a bad builder (and those who live in the house) suffer.'

3. It is like a temple (vv. 16, 17). Lesson: 'Anyone who comes to a temple comes to the God of that temple. In the same way, leaders are answerable to God and will be punished by Him if they harm the congregation.'

Writers and speakers often use 'picture-language', but it is dangerous. It can easily be misinterpreted (see notes on 11.24b; 12.13b; and 15.52). In these verses, for example, we notice that:

(a) When Paul compared the congregation to a building, he meant that it was like it in one or two ways only: i.e. a congregation, like a building, is good in so far as it has good builders. We should be wrong to search for too many other lessons and to say, for instance, that the members of a church should always stay in the same place and do the same job because the stones of a building stay in the same place.

(b) Paul was not always careful in the way he used picture-language or 'metaphor'. Builders do not really use gold and silver, as he said in vv. 12 and 13, and if they did, the gold and silver would not be tested by fire. They would melt. Because Paul was not careful in using 'metaphors', we need to be especially careful in interpreting them.

NOTES

3.5a. What then is Apollos? What is Paul?: One reason for the quarrels in the congregation in Corinth was that some people said they followed Apollos, and others said they followed Paul (see note on 1.12). They treated Apollos and Paul as if they were rival candidates in an election. So in vv. 5–9 Paul explained that they were not rivals. What did he say about them?

1. That God had given each of them different work to do. Paul 'planted', i.e. he was the first evangelist to reach Corinth. See Acts 18.1 and 11. Apollos carried on the work that Paul had begun (Acts 18.24; 19.1). But the difference between them was not that one was superior to the other, only that they did different work.

2. That Paul and Apollos were equally used by God. They were a team

or partnership. They had the same reasons for working and the same aims. The Greek words in v. 8 mean 'he who plants and he who waters are one.'

What Paul said here about himself and Apollos he said more fully about all active members of Christian congregations, in 1 Corinthians 12.4–31. Such people, he said, will work in harmony and will avoid jealousy only if they share the following beliefs:

(a) That God intends people to do different jobs;

(b) That God does not regard the doer of one job as 'superior' to the doer of a different job;

(c) That everyone should give the praise to God rather than to those who work for Him, because it is only God who gives the growth (3.7).

So the senior member of the 'staff' of a congregation is not superior to his younger assistant: they have different jobs to do. A bishop is not superior to those women who in many Churches give up their time on a Saturday to clean the floor of their church building. The bishop and the women are equally the servants of Christ, with different jobs to do.

3.5b. Servants through whom you believed:
Servants:

1. The Greek word *diakonos* is here translated 'servant'. In the AV it is 'ministers'. In the NEB it is 'agents'. The words *diakonos*, *diakonia* (service), *diakoneo* (serve), occur 100 times in the New Testament (see notes on 12.5 and 16.15). In ordinary conversation people used the word for an attendant in a shop or a waiter in an inn.

(a) God had not called Paul and Apollos to be masters of the Corinthian Christians, but to serve them and to attend to their needs. See also Luke 22.26: 'Let the leader be as one who serves', and Mark 10.45: 'The Son of man came not to be served but to serve.'

(b) They served the Corinthians because they first of all served Jesus Christ. See 'as the Lord has assigned to each'. It was Christ who had given Paul and Apollos the authority they had, just as a very important person with an official car gives the driver whatever authority that driver has. Paul and Apollos depended on Christ, as an assistant in a shop depends on the shopkeeper. See 1 Peter 4.11: 'Whoever renders service (i.e. whoever is a *diakonos*), renders it by the strength which God supplies; in order that in everything God may be glorified.'

In these verses (5–9) and in 93 other verses in the New Testament the word refers to the service which a Christian gives and the way in which he gives it, not to the position and rank which that Christian holds in the Church.

2. However, there are a few (seven) verses in the New Testament where the word does mean the position which a Christian holds, and to which those in authority in the Church have appointed him, e.g. Phil. 1.1: 'To all the bishops and deacons' (where 'deacon' is a translation of *diakonos*). There, and in 1 Tim. 3.8–13, the word referred to people officially

appointed to be personal assistants to bishops. So today in some Churches a 'deacon' is a person who holds a special position in the Church.

Through whom you believed: God used Paul as His 'agent'. Through him God had made Himself known to some of the people of Corinth. We may ask, 'How far does God use such "agents" and how far does He communicate with human beings directly?'

1. God usually seems to communicate with us through other people. Most children begin to know that God loves them because they have discovered that their parents love them and because their parents have told them about God's love. We do not always know the people through whom God has reached us. The Mexican terrorist, Juan Chavez, found a Bible in a box he had stolen. He had never seen a Bible before, but after reading parts of it he felt that God had a claim on his life. He never knew the 'agents' whom God used, i.e. the Bible writers and those who translated it into Mexican, or the owner of the box from whom he stole it.

But there are dangers when God uses agents. There have been agents who made themselves too important, like the young priest who said, 'You cannot be forgiven by God unless I declare that He has forgiven you.'

2. God does sometimes make Himself known to us directly. See, for example, the stories of dreams and visions of which we read in the New Testament (see note on 1 Cor. 15.8). But there is danger here, too. As we saw in studying the word 'call' (1.2), the man who feels certain that God wants him to be an ordained minister because of a dream he has had may be wrong. He needs to compare what he feels with what other Christians feel.

3.8. Each shall receive his wages: See also v. 14: 'he will receive a reward', and 9.17: 'I have a reward.'

1. What sort of wages did Paul mean? Perhaps it was the reward of seeing people growing in faith to whom he had preached the Gospel. Or perhaps he meant the reward of eternal life and salvation.

2. Is it possible to earn such rewards? No. As we have seen in the 'Interpretation' above, it is easy to misinterpret picture-language, and 'wages' is part of Paul's picture-language here. Receiving wages is one of the things that a farm-labourer does. But the meaning is clear from Paul's other writings. He did not think that anyone could earn salvation by hard work. See Ephesians 2.8: 'By grace you have been saved, through faith; and this is not your own doing, it is the gift of God.'

3. Why did Paul write about wages or reward at all? Because when someone follows Jesus Christ, he does receive a better sort of life than he was living before. He experiences eternal life. He finds that it is 'worth' being a Christian. The merchant in Jesus's parable knew that it was 'worth' selling everything he had in order to buy the pearl of very special value (Matt. 13.45,46).

3.9a. We are God's fellow-workers: This probably means, 'We are God's servants, working together'.

But we could also translate it 'we work together with God'. Paul believed that. See 15.10 (and the note on p. 195).

3.9b. You are God's field: This is the first of the three things to which Paul, beginning at v. 6, compared the congregation at Corinth. They were like a field, or a garden, or a farm, whose owner employed workmen. But God Himself is the owner. The words mean: 'You are not our field, but God's.' The Corinthians must not treat any of the workmen in the congregation as if he, rather than God, was the owner.

3.9c. You are God's building: Again it means 'you are not our building, but God's'.

In vv. 9–15 Paul compared the congregation to a building, and said four things about them:

(a) They had a firm foundation. His own preaching was the foundation (vv. 6, 10).

(b) Other builders followed him. These were Apollos and their present leaders (v. 10c).

(c) Some of the builders were good and used gold and silver and fine stone. These represent the good teachers (vv. 12a and 14).

(d) Other builders used hay and straw. They represent the bad teachers; and these teachers would be punished (vv. 12b and 15).

Paul had said that those who work for God are all equal and that no one is more important than another. But he did not mean that all the Corinthian Christians were equally useful to God. Some of them were hindering His work. This is why it is necessary for each leader to examine what he is doing to build up the Church, and to take seriously the advice and criticism of other members.

3.11. No other foundation than ... Jesus Christ:

1. Paul was here referring to his own work. Some Christians in Corinth had said that they preferred to follow other leaders instead of him. So he said here, 'Even if you reject me, you cannot reject the preaching which I brought you, because my preaching is the foundation of your life as Christians.'

His 'foundation-preaching' was about Jesus Christ, the crucified One, as he said in 1.17 and 2.2. Jesus Himself, rather than His followers, is the foundation. This is why Christians need continually to study the story of Jesus's life and death and resurrection in the Gospels, and the story of His Spirit at work in people's lives in Acts and the Epistles. There is no substitute.

2. The purpose of any foundation is to uphold a building. So Paul wanted others to build on the foundations he had laid, and Apollos had done so. The Gospel which Paul preached in Greek and Hebrew has had to be translated into other languages spoken in other parts of the world and by later generations. The interpretation of the Gospel which Paul gave in his letters has had to be followed by other interpretations, such as those

'Those who work for God are all equal . . . no one is more important than another' (p. 35).

In Hong Kong a government official consults passengers on one of the harbour ferryboats, in preparation for planning a traffic improvement scheme.

What opportunities do Church leaders in your country have, for consulting with local congregation members?

which show the meaning of the Gospel for this generation. In these ways we 'build on the foundations'. There have been Christians who have mistakenly wanted to do nothing except what the first Christians did, like a certain Mr Peachey, who used tape instead of buttons on his clothes. He said 'I do not use buttons because I do not read that Paul used buttons.' Such Christians are unwilling to *build* on the foundations.

But it must be on the *original* foundations. If anyone tries to put down new foundations alongside the original ones, he can no doubt build a Church, but it will not be the Christian Church. This has, of course, happened, and is one reason for the large number of sects today.

3.13. The Day will disclose it . . . it will be revealed with fire: The 'Day' means the day when God will judge the world and when each man's work will be examined (Rom. 2.16). See notes on 1.8 and 15.24.

In the Bible fire is usually the sign that God judges and tests people, as it is here (see also 1 Pet. 1.7). In other passages it is the sign that God purifies those whom He judges (see Zech. 13.9). But Paul was not thinking of purification in this verse.

Although Paul told his readers to distinguish the good leaders from the bad ones, he reminded them here that they themselves were not the judges. Their opinions about other Christians might often be wrong. The only judge is God, and He will make His judgement when He chooses. See Jesus's parable of the 'Weeds in the Wheat': 'let both grow together until the harvest' (Matt. 13.30). There would be greater harmony among Christians if, for example, the revolutionaries and the conservatives in the Church both remembered this when they met each other.

3.15. He will suffer loss, though he himself will be saved: The bad leader will not receive the rewards which Paul wrote about in vv. 8 and 14. But, because God is generous, it is his work and not he himself which will be destroyed (Paul was still referring to those at Corinth who were leading the congregation astray).

The picture which Paul had in mind was of a builder who used poor materials. While he was building a house, it caught fire and was destroyed. The builder himself just managed to run through the flames and escape. According to this picture, those who lead a congregation astray see their work destroyed. We see this happening, but usually the congregation becomes disheartened and diminished, rather than totally destroyed.

3.16. You are God's temple: The third thing to which Paul compared the congregation at Corinth was a temple. His thoughts were probably as follows: 'If you were non-Christians worshipping at a temple or shrine, with the image of the god inside the shrine, you would take care not to damage the shrine. Because you are Christians, the shrine is the congregation and "God's Spirit dwells" in it. Do not imagine that because your God is invisible you can take less care of your shrine than non-Christians take of theirs.'

Christians have often tried to answer the question, 'Where is God?' especially when they are worshipping Him. Some of them have answered, 'He is wherever the Bible is read aloud'; others: 'He is wherever bread and wine are shared in a service of Holy Communion'. Paul's answer here is: 'He is in the whole congregation. You are the temple where He dwells.' See also Romans 8.9. (We note that in 1 Cor. 6.19 it was the individual Christian whom Paul called God's temple.)

3.17. If anyone destroys God's temple, God will destroy him:

1. **Destroys God's temple:** Is this possible? According to Jesus (Matt. 16.18) no one can destroy the Church. But here Paul was talking not about the Church, but about a congregation. It is certainly possible for a congregation to be destroyed, e.g. when leaders and members refuse to forgive each other, or when leaders give false teaching and as a result there is confusion and division in the congregation. We read in Revelation 1.11 of seven congregations, but all of them came to an end. One of them was already dead when that book was written (Rev. 3.1).

2. **God will destroy him.** Does God destroy bad Church leaders? Do not these words contradict what Paul said in v. 15, that such leaders would be 'saved'?

Some people say that these words do contradict v. 15, that in this verse Paul wrote like a Jewish rabbi rather than as a Christian, that he was remembering the Jewish tradition that Uzzah touched the holy Ark and that 'God smote him' (2 Sam. 6.7). See notes on 5.5; 10.11; and 16.22.

In whatever way we explain this verse, we are faced with the question: 'Does God destroy any human soul?' We find different answers in the New Testament, not one only. From a verse such as Mark 9.43, the answer seems to be 'Yes'. From a parable such as the Lost Coin (Luke 15.8), the answer seems to be 'No', for that story suggests that God in His love will never cease to call on human beings to repent.

3.18. If any one . . . thinks that he is wise in this age: In vv. 18–23 Paul repeated some of the ideas which we saw in chapters 1.18 to 2.5.

First he referred again to those who were causing division in the congregation. He said:

1. They were deceiving themselves (v. 18a).

2. They were drawing attention to their own achievements, and were proud of being 'wise by the standards of this passing age' (NEB). They were allowing members to give honour to them rather than to God. This was 'false wisdom'.

3. This sort of person had to give up false wisdom before he could have true wisdom. The further he went along the road of false wisdom, the further away he was from true wisdom. He had, so to speak, to go back to the starting-point, 'let him become a fool' (v. 18b).

3.21. Let no one boast of men. For all things are yours: This refers to the ordinary members of the congregation. Some of them were following the different 'party leaders' so blindly that they were making the same mistakes as their leaders. They were proud of them rather than of Jesus Christ. They obeyed them as if they were their masters instead of obeying their true Master Jesus Christ. As a result, the congregation was divided.

This can happen in any small group of Christians. There was one group in which a woman member had a sick child, and the group prayed for the child regularly. When the mother said that she was taking the child to hospital the leader of the group said that the mother should not do that. She should have more faith in the Holy Spirit. At first the mother did not feel able to disagree with the leader. But the child became weaker. Then the mother had to leave the group altogether before she could take him to hospital.

Paul said to the Corinthians, 'You have misunderstood the position of your leaders in the Church. You think that the members belong to your leaders and serve them and exist for their benefit, and that your leaders in turn serve God. But the truth is, first, that we, your leaders, are here to serve you. We belong to you and exist for your benefit. Secondly, you belong to Christ. Thirdly, Christ belongs to God.'

This teaching agrees with what Paul had already said about leaders being 'servants'. It is important for our understanding of the ordained ministry today.

After saying that he and the other leaders existed to serve the ordinary members, Paul added a further thought in v. 22. It is a great statement of his faith in God. 'Everything serves you', he said: 'In the end, everything which you experience will turn out to be for your good. You are not helplessly under the control of people or things.' We find a similar statement in Romans 8.35–39.

3.23. Christ is God's: These words do not mean that Christ is less than God (see note on 11.3a, p. 145). In saying that Christ belonged to and served God, Paul was probably thinking of what Christ had done, not what Christ was. Christ had offered His whole life to His Father God. He had shown that He 'belonged to' God in a practical way.

STUDY SUGGESTIONS

WORDS

1. 'In chapter 3.5–9 the word *diakonos* refers to the service which a Christian gives. . . . However, there are a few verses in the New Testament when the word does mean the "position" which a Christian holds . . .' (p. 33).

   Which *five* of the following words refer to 'service' and which *five* refer to the 'position' of a *diakonos*?

   office   work   task   grade   class   job   rank   duty   post
   function

CONTENT

2. Why did Paul write 1 Corinthians 3.5–23?
3. (a) To what three things did Paul compare the congregation at Corinth?
   (b) What lesson did he want to teach in each case?
4. 'Paul did not think that anyone could earn salvation' (p. 34). Why then did he say, 'Each shall receive his wages'? (1 Cor. 3.8)?
5. (a) While writing about a 'building' in 3.9–11, who or what did Paul say the 'foundation' was?
   (b) In what practical ways can the leaders of a modern congregation make sure that they are building on that foundation?

BIBLE

6. 'The words *diakonos* (servant), *diakonia* (service), *diakoneo* (serve) occur 100 times in the New Testament' (p. 33).
   (i) How are they translated in the RSV in each of the following verses?
       (a) Acts 11.29 (b) Acts 21.19 (c) Rom. 15.25 (d) 1 Cor. 16.15 (e) 2 Cor. 9.1
   (ii) Whom did the servant serve in each of the following:
       (a) Mark 1.31 (b) John 12.26 (c) Rom. 11.13 (d) Rom. 16.1 (e) 2 Tim. 4.11.
   (iii) What sort of service did the 'servant' give in each of the following passages?
       (a) Acts 6.4 (b) Acts 11.29 (c) 1 Cor. 3.5 (d) 2 Cor. 5.18 (e) Philemon 13.
7. We have said (p. 39) that Romans 8.35–39 is in some ways like 1 Corinthians 3.22,23.
   (a) In what way are the two passages alike?
   (b) In what way, if any, do they contain good news for us today?
8. What is the connection between Matthew 13.24–30 and 1 Corinthians 3.13?
9. 'In the Bible, fire is usually the sign that God judges and tests people. In other passages . . . that God purifies' (p. 37). In each of the following passages is fire a sign of (i) judging and testing, or (ii) purifying?
   (a) Ps. 12.6 (b) Amos 7.4 (c) Zech. 13.9 (d) Mal. 3.2 (e) Matt. 3.10 (f) 1 Cor. 3.13 (g) 1 Pet. 1.7 (h) Rev. 3.18?

DISCUSSION AND RESEARCH

10. (a) Why do writers and speakers often use 'picture language'? (see p. 34).
    (b) What would be the advantages and disadvantages in each case of comparing a Christian congregation to (i) a flock? (ii) a family?

(c) (i) To what other thing could you compare a congregation in order to show what kind of a life it should lead? (ii) What dangers would there be in using this 'picture-language'?

11. 'How far does God use agents. . . ?' (p. 34).
    Give examples of (a) God using 'agents' (perhaps mentioning people through whom you yourself came to believe in Jesus Christ), (b) God communicating directly with someone whom you know or about whom you have heard.

12. 'Christians have often tried to answer the question "where is God", especially when they are worshipping Him' (p. 38).
    (a) Do you think that Christians think of God as being more in one place than another during a service of worship? If so, in what place?
    (b) How can worshippers show by their actions and words that they believe, as Paul did, that the whole congregation is the temple where God's Spirit dwells (1 Cor. 3.16)?

13. 'God will destroy him' (1 Cor. 3.17). 'Does God destroy any human soul?' (p. 38).
    What is your own answer? Give reasons for it.

14. 'Let no one boast of men' (1 Cor. 3.21).
    Consider a Christian congregation which you know well.
    (a) How do the members regard the leader (or leaders)? Do they want him to be their master (and to accept all the responsibility), or do they want him to be their servant (one who can help them to accept responsibility)?
    (b) How does the leader think of himself – as the master or the servant of the congregation, or in some other way?
    (c) In what way do the leader and members avoid the mistake into which the Corinthians had fallen, of giving more honour to their leaders than to Jesus Christ?

4.1–21 Leaders as Servants

We, your leaders, are servants of Christ and caretakers of the congregation

OUTLINE

4.1–5: Apollos and I are like caretakers of your congregation. But we are answerable to God, the owner, rather than to you (vv. 1, 2). Since God is our judge, do not let us judge each other unfairly (vv. 3–5).

4.6–7: Remember that God gave you your gifts, you did not make or earn them.

4.8–13: Are you so self-satisfied that you imagine that you already know everything and already have everything that you need? (vv. 8–10). Apollos and I certainly do not have everything that we need (vv. 11–13).

4.14–21: Without me you would not be Christian, so listen to what I say (vv. 14–16). I have sent Timothy to you and I shall soon visit you myself (vv. 17–21).

INTERPRETATION

In 3.5–23 Paul was writing about the leaders of the congregation in Corinth. His chief aim was to show how the members ought to regard those leaders, but in chapter 4 it was the leaders' own life and work to which he drew special attention. He also referred to the criticism which he and Apollos had received.

Although the leaders he referred to in chapters 3 and 4 were himself and Apollos, what he wrote is true about all Church leaders in any country at any time. Their work, according to this chapter, is to look after the members and see that they receive the true Gospel.

THE LEADERS' WORK

There are five words and phrases in 4.1,9 and 15, which Paul used to describe the Church leaders' work. (Further comment on these words also appears in the notes below.)

1. **Servants** (v. 1): This is not a translation of *diakonos* (see p. 33), but of another word which refers to the galley-slaves who rowed the huge ships of the Greek fleet in obedience to their captain. As Corinth was a sea-port, the Corinthians knew about such work.

2. **Stewards** (v. 1). They were not the owners of the houses, but the 'housekeepers' who were responsible to the owner.

3. **Apostles** (v. 9a). See note on 9.1a, p. 109.

4. **Spectacle to the world** (v. 9b). Slaves who had been condemned to death were sometimes made to fight wild animals as a 'spectacle' or entertainment.

5. **Father** (v. 15). See also v. 14 'my beloved children'. This word refers only to Paul, not to Apollos. It was through Paul's preaching that they had been 'born again' and become Christians. In this sense he was their father.

NOTES

4.1. Servants of Christ and stewards of the mysteries of God: Although Paul was writing about Church leaders, he began by pointing away from the leaders themselves to the One whom the leaders served. To show this clearly we could translate this, 'It is Christ whose servants we are and it is God's mysteries for which we are the stewards.'

LEADERS AS SERVANTS

1. **Servants:** We have seen that Paul was here comparing a Church leader to a slave who rowed in a ship, of which the captain is Christ. Could he have written like this unless Jesus had first shown, by the way he lived that the leader is also the servant? (Mark 10.45)

2. **Stewards:** The Greek word translated 'stewards' is the word from which we get the English word 'economy'. The leader is like a housekeeper (the head-slave) who is responsible to the owner for the careful distribution of the food in the house. The leader is responsible to God as he distributes amongst members God's 'mysteries', i.e. the truths about God, which were once hidden but are now revealed. The congregation is God's, not his.

Jesus used the same picture-language to teach His followers that God had, so to speak, lent them their lives. They were answerable to Him (Luke 12.41–48). So all Christians are stewards who are answerable to God as they use their possessions, their bodies, their time, and their friendships.

4.3. It is a very small thing that I should be judged by you: In chapter 4 Paul referred to three sorts of judgement: (1) Other people judge us, (2) We judge ourselves, (3) God judges us.

1. *Other people judge us.* One reason why Paul wrote this chapter is that some Corinthian Christians had been judging or criticizing him. Perhaps some said that he was not a real apostle, or that he was not such a good speaker as Apollos. We do not know all the reasons. But we do know his chief aim in referring to it here: it was to say, 'In this matter you have judged me in such a way that you have forgotten God. He is the only judge who knows all the facts.'

We may note further:

(a) Paul himself frequently judged and criticized others, including the Christians at Corinth. See vv. 6b, 14, and 18 of this chapter.

(b) All leaders need to be criticized by those whom they lead. This is true in a family. After the father of one family had rebuked his daughter, his son said, 'Father, you were unfair to my sister.' When the father thought about it, he agreed with his son, and put matters right with his daughter.

(c) Leaders find it difficult to accept criticism. Paul probably found it very difficult (see Special Note, p. 54).

In many countries Government leaders forbid people to speak freely, because they fear the people's criticism. They fear that if people criticize the Government, the Government will lose its power. So they resist the criticism which they need. Church leaders have special temptations, e.g. to resist criticism by simply saying: 'God has shown me that what I say is true.' The question arises, 'When, if ever, should a leader prevent those whom he is leading from criticizing him?'

2. *We judge ourselves.* When Paul wrote 'I am not aware of anything against myself', he surely meant, 'Concerning the matter you have raised, I was not to blame.' Elsewhere we see that Paul looked carefully at his own conduct and judged himself when he had done wrong. See 1 Timothy 1.15:

43

'I am the foremost of sinners': Romans 7.15: 'I do the very thing I hate.'

No one can overcome his faults unless he is able to judge himself. This is the reason why in some Communist countries 'self-criticism classes' have been held in every community in the land. Real self-criticism has not always taken place in such classes, where people are sometimes forced to make a confession. But often the self-criticism is real. And this can happen among Christians.

3. *God judges us.* This is the sort of judgement to which Paul was especially referring in chapter 4. See note below on v. 4.

4.4. It is the Lord who judges: Paul's thought here was: 'I am God's steward. My Master is the One who knows best whether I am faithful or not. He, and not someone else, is the proper person to judge.'

Some readers feel afraid when they think of God as judge, because they think of a judge as someone who punishes people, sometimes unjustly. But to Paul and to other writers in the Bible it was good news that God is the judge. It is good news because it means that: (1) Someone is in control of the world; things do not simply happen by chance; (2) Someone knows the truth about us, even if other people and even we ourselves do not know it; and He is just and fair.

Paul was also saying that any judgements which we make here are imperfect. God will make perfect judgements at the Judgement Day, 'when the Lord comes'. But alongside this Paul also said that God was already judging him (v. 4). God is both our present and our future judge.

4.6. Learn by us not to go beyond what is written:

1. **What is written:** These words probably refer to the Jewish Scriptures, i.e. the Old Testament. When Paul wrote these words there was no other part of the Bible 'written'. It was the Old Testament which (as we saw) he quoted in such passages as 1.19; 1.31; 3.19.

2. **'Not to go beyond'** means not to add to the teaching which we obtain from reading Scripture. Probably the Corinthians were treating the teaching of some of their leaders as if it was as important as Scripture itself. See note on 15.3c.

How do we know whether our own teaching goes beyond the teaching which we obtain from reading Scripture? Even if we interpret 'what is written' to mean the whole Bible, it is not a simple matter. However closely we want to follow Scripture, we still have to interpret it. We must not, for example, follow it as the old man did who said, 'Abraham had two wives and, thank God, I have been able to follow his example.'

4.7. What have you that you did not receive? Paul wrote this because some of his readers were 'puffed up' (v. 6) and 'boasting of men' (3.21). The sort of thing that Paul referred to was that one group in the congregation had said to another group, 'We, under our leader, have received more of God's Spirit than you have. We are the real Christians here.'

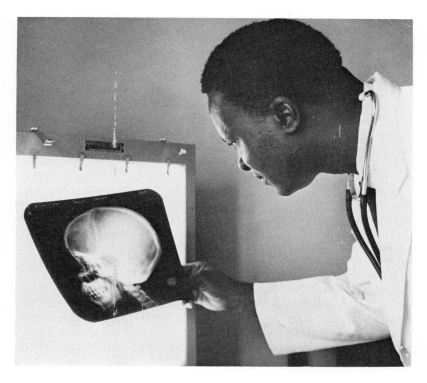

'God knows best whether I am faithful or not . . . He is the proper person to judge' (p. 44).

As this Nigerian doctor examines the evidence which an X-ray photograph provides, he can judge whether the patient is fully cured, or needs further treatment.

On what sort of 'evidence' does God make His judgements?

This is the sort of mistake which Christians have always been tempted to make after experiencing revival. And it can happen whenever two groups of Christians both feel they are the more important, e.g. when Church members have a Christian school on their land, and the congregation and the school each want to be the more important.

So Paul said, 'You have indeed received God's Spirit, but it was a gift. Thank God for it, but don't think that it makes you better than other people. Don't cut yourselves off from the other people because of it.'

This verse points to the real meaning of a 'humble' person. A humble person is not someone who pretends that he is a less loving parent or a less skilful preacher than he really is. He is the person who gives the praise to God for whatever gifts he has. The verse also tells us about 'grace'. 'Grace' is God giving us gifts because he loves us and not because we have deserved them.

4.8. Already you are filled . . . have become rich . . . have become kings: In vv. 8–13 Paul compared (a) the Corinthian Christians who were self-satisfied and longing to be superior to other people, with (b) the Apostles who were ill-fed and treated as inferior to everyone else. Paul did not really think that the Corinthians were already 'filled' or 'rich' or 'kings'. We could translate his words, 'Do you really think that you have everything that you need? How absurd!' It was his readers who thought that they were 'filled'. They thought that because they had 'knowledge' they already had special power to overcome all evil. In this way they were following the 'Gnostic' philosophers (see p. 100). They did not understand that overcoming all evil is what God will do 'when the Lord comes' (see 4.5; 6.2).

We do not know whether Paul, by making fun of his readers in this way and saying the opposite of what he *really* thought, was successful in making them change their minds. Teachers and preachers are not usually successful when they speak to their listeners in this 'sarcastic' way.

4.9. A spectacle to the world: 'Spectacle' is a picture-word which Paul's readers well understood. The Romans had a huge empire to govern, and therefore were often at war. When a general won an important battle, he arranged a procession through the streets of Rome, and afterwards there was an entertainment. At the back of this procession (see 'last of all', v. 9) some slaves walked who had to fight armed men or wild animals as part of the 'spectacle' when the entertainment began. They were usually killed.

By this word Paul referred to the sufferings of the apostles, and, as we have seen, of all who lead the Church. One of the five 'tasks' of the Christian leader to which Paul referred in this chapter (see Interpretation, p. 42) is to endure suffering. It is not 'bad luck' when suffering comes to him. When he accepts a position of leadership, he accepts the task of suffering. One of the bishops in an African country was studying in Europe recently, when the government of his own country began to persecute Christians. Someone asked him if he was going to return home. He said,

'Of course I shall, that is if the Church and my family need me.' Sometimes other Christians know about the leader's sufferings and can pray for him and write letters to him. Sometimes no one except himself knows.

There are of course, many different reasons why we suffer. We may suffer because we are leaders, but we may on the other hand suffer as the result of our own mistakes or sins.

4.12a. Working with our own hands: Educated Greeks paid so much attention to the use of the mind that many of them despised those who earned their living by using their hands. (If we today find that people who 'work with their own hands' receive less honour than those who do not, it may be because the teachers in our schools have been trained to follow the tradition of the Greeks in this matter.) The Corinthians seem to have despised manual workers. So when Paul earned money by making tents (Acts 18.3) so as to keep himself while preaching and teaching, some people despised him. In chapter 9, he said more about this (see p. 113).

4.12b. When reviled, we bless: The Apostles did not simply endure suffering. They went further and gave a blessing to those by whom they had been cursed or injured. So they followed the teaching of Jesus (Luke 6.28). See note on 13.5, p. 173.

4.13. We have become the refuse of the world: It may be that Paul only meant that people despised the Apostles. But it is more likely that the words 'refuse' and 'off-scouring' were picture-words. In some parts of Greece where there had been a great disaster like an earthquake or a flood, people thought that the 'gods' had sent it. Then the authorities asked for someone to offer himself as a sacrifice to the gods. This was done so that the land should be 'made clean'. These volunteers were well-treated and well-fed before they died. But only the most despised and unhappy people offered themselves. They were called by these words: 'refuse', 'off-scouring'.

If Paul had this in mind, then he was regarding his sufferings as a sort of sacrifice which he was offering up for the sake of others. We know, however, that Paul did not think that God was like the gods to whom the Greeks sacrificed. He did not, for example, believe that God would send disease or other disasters on the country unless His apostles endured suffering. The 'sacrifices' which Paul made were the result of the service he gave to his fellow human-beings; they were not made in order to satisfy an angry God.

4.15. You have countless guides . . . I became your father:

1. The word which is translated 'guides' means the attendants or slaves who looked after the children in a rich Greek's household, and took them to school. ('Tutor' and 'schoolmaster' are not good translations.) Paul meant, 'your congregation is like a family which has plenty of slave-attendants (the leaders of the rival parties) but only one father. I am your father, so listen!'

2. Paul called himself their 'father' mainly because it had been through him that the members of the Church in Corinth had been 'born' as Christians, and had begun life 'in Christ Jesus'. Because of his preaching their lives had become so different that it was like being born again (see John 3.3 and 1 Cor. 6.11).

But Paul was not only looking back to what had already happened. He still had the same sort of love for his readers and felt as responsible for them as a father for his family. For this reason he could 'admonish' (warn) them (v. 14).

Since that time it has often happened that the leader of a Christian congregation has regarded himself as the 'father' of the members, and they have regarded him in the same way. In some Churches they actually call their leader 'Father' – or 'Padre'. But Paul made no rules about this, and there are many different names and titles which congregations give their leaders, e.g.: 'shepherd' or 'pastor', 'vicar', 'priest', 'minister', 'elder', 'clergyman'. See note on 12.5 (p. 164).

4.16. Be imitators of me: See the note on 11.1 (p. 138). The important word here is 'me', i.e. 'follow *me* rather than the guides I referred to in v. 15.'

4.17a. I sent Timothy, my beloved and faithful child: Paul not only wrote this letter to the Corinthian Christians, but sent Timothy to explain the letter to them. But there were difficulties. First, it seems Paul had already heard that the Corinthians, knowing that Timothy was coming, were saying that Paul was afraid to come himself (v. 18). So Timothy, as Paul's messenger, had a difficult job to do (see also 1 Cor. 16.11).

Secondly, there was delay before Timothy could reach Corinth, according to 1 Corinthians 16.10.

From the words 'faithful child' it is likely that Timothy became a Christian as a result of Paul's preaching. From Acts 18.5 and 2 Corinthians 1.19 it seems that he had been one of Paul's assistants when Paul first went to Corinth. After that time he was Paul's companion.

4.17b. To remind you of my ways in Christ: Paul sent Timothy to the Church at Corinth to remind them of the 'ways' of living as Christians, and not only of the teaching which Paul had given them.

According to Acts 9.2, when someone belonged to the Church people said that he 'belonged to the Way'. They could see that he had accepted Christian teaching and that he believed in Jesus Christ by the 'way' he lived. Paul was referring to this 'way' when he used the word 'power' (v. 20), 'life' (1 Cor. 7.17), and 'practice' (1 Cor. 11.16). In many of his letters Paul began with his teaching. Then came the word 'therefore', e.g. in Philippians 2.12. This meant, 'This is the truth about Jesus: therefore live it.'

4.20. The Kingdom of God does not consist in talk:

1. The 'Kingdom of God' does not refer to a territory or piece of land such as a nation or state possesses. It means 'God ruling like a king over

men's lives'. Paul usually thought of this as happening in the future, when all beings will accept His rule (see 1 Cor. 6.9; 15.24–28; 15.50). But sometimes (e.g. Col. 1.13) he said that some people had already allowed God to rule over their lives, as Jesus said in Matthew 12.28.

2. This verse refers to the Church leaders. Their task is to bring people to place themselves under the ruling of God. Paul said that they could not do this by 'talk'. They certainly could not do it if they were arrogant (v. 19), i.e. pointing to their own importance. They could only do it if they humbly opened themselves to receive power from God, so that people could see the 'way' they lived.

STUDY SUGGESTIONS

WORDS

1. Which *four* of the following words have the same or nearly the same meaning as 'steward' (1 Cor. 4.1)?
   Employer   director   housekeeper   governor   agent   caretaker   master   warden

2. Which *five* of the following words have the same or nearly the same meaning as 'trustworthy' (1 Cor. 4.2)?
   faithful   perfect   wonderful   reliable   dependable   clever   active   loyal   responsible   popular

3. 'Spectacle' is one of the words in 1 Cor. 4.9–13 by which Paul referred to the sufferings of Church leaders. What *twelve* other words did he use in these verses to refer to their sufferings?

CONTENT

4. (a) What *three* sorts of 'judgement' did Paul refer to in 1 Cor. 4?
   (b) Which of them did he regard as the most important?

5. How does 1 Cor. 4.7 help us to understand the meaning of 'humility'?

6. (a) Why did Paul call himself the 'father' of the Christians of Corinth (1 Cor. 4.15)?
   (b) What is (i) the *value*, (ii) the *danger* of Church members regarding their leader as their 'father'?

7. (a) Why did Paul send Timothy to Corinth?
   (b) What would you have found the most difficult part of your work if you had been in Timothy's place?

BIBLE

8. 'God will make perfect judgements. . . . Alongside this Paul also said that God was already judging him' (p. 44).
   Which of the following verses suggest: (i) that God will judge at the Judgement Day, (ii) that God is already judging now?

49

(a) Matt. 10.15   (b) Matt. 12.36   (c) John 5.30   (d) John 8.16
(e) John 12.31   (f) Rom. 2.5   (g) 1 Pet. 4.17   (h) 1 John 4.17

9. In 1 Cor. 4.11,12 we read of some of Paul's sufferings. Which of those sufferings do we read of in each of the following:
(a) 2 Cor. 4.7–10   (b) 2 Cor. 6.4–10   (c) 2. Cor. 11.23–27

10. Read the following passages.
Which two verses in 1 Cor. 4 show most clearly that Paul followed the teaching of those passages?
Prov. 15.1; Matt. 5.44; Rom. 12.14; Rom. 12.21; 1 Pet. 2.23; 1 Pet. 3.9

11. What do we find out about Timothy from the following passages?
(a) Acts 16.1–3   (b) Acts 17.14   (c) 1 Thess. 1.1

DISCUSSION AND RESEARCH

12. (a) There are five words and phrases 'in 1 Cor. 4.1,9,15 which Paul used to describe the Church leaders' work' (p. 42). Give an example from the present time of Church leaders showing their leadership in each of those ways.
(b) 'There are many different names and titles which congregations give their leaders' (p. 48). Does it matter what names and titles are used for Church leaders? Give reasons for your answer.

13. 'All leaders need to be criticized by those whom they lead' (p. 43). When is it wise and when is it unwise for a Church leader to invite others to criticize him? Give examples.

14. 'Abraham had two wives, and thank God, I have been able to follow his example' (p. 44).
(a) How would you answer someone who said that?
(b) What guidance could you give him as to the right use of the Bible?

15. 'Paul was making fun of his readers by saying the opposite of what he really thought' (p. 46).
(a) Give an example from your own experience of someone doing that.
(b) In what circumstances is it wise for a Christian teacher to do that?

16. 'The sufferings of those who lead the Church' (p. 46). What do you think are the *two* ways in which the leader of your own congregation suffers most?

17. 'Working with our own hands' (1 Cor. 4.12).
(a) Why do you think that in many places those who work with their hands receive less honour than other workers?
(b) What signs, if any, do you see around you that this happens?

Special Note B
Paul

1. HE WAS A JEW

Paul's parents were Pharisees (Acts 23.6b), and he belonged to the tribe of Benjamin (Phil. 3.5). After attending Synagogue school in his home town of Tarsus, he went to Jerusalem to study Jewish law under Gamaliel (Acts 22.3). He could probably speak and read Hebrew, but his vernacular was Aramaic.

In his studies he learnt both the 'law' contained in the Old Testament, and such Jewish beliefs as the following: that salvation is obtained through keeping the law, that God is one, that there are spiritual forces for good (angels) and for evil (demons), and that there will be a day of Judgement when the Messiah will rule supreme.

Although Paul became a Christian and changed some of his beliefs, he continued to use his mind in a Jewish way. He continued to interpret the Old Testament in the way that the Pharisees interpreted it, e.g. by treating it as 'allegory' (see p. 112).

2. HE LIVED AMONG ROMANS AND GREEKS

Although Paul was born a Jew, he was also born a Roman citizen, and thus had a position of honour in the Roman Empire (Acts 22.25–28).

But throughout the Empire the first language was Greek, and Paul could speak Greek and wrote his letters in Greek. Tarsus, where he was born, was a Greek city. He had also studied Greek philosophy, and when he referred to 'nature' in 1 Corinthians 11.14 he was using the language of Greek Stoic philosophy.

3. HE EXPERIENCED 'ÇONVERSION' OR 'TURNING'

Although Paul did not actually use these words, they are a useful way of saying that there was a special time when he was turned from his old life to a new sort of life. The most important part of this experience was that he was turned *from* believing that he could be saved by keeping the Jewish law *to* accepting salvation by trusting that God through Christ had forgiven him (Gal. 2.16). He was also turned from following human leaders to following Christ (Acts 9.1–5), from persecuting the Church to being an Apostle in it (1 Tim. 1.15,16).

As Paul saw it, this event was the reason for everything that he afterwards did and taught. For example, it was the reason why he had authority ('Have I not seen Jesus our Lord?' 1 Cor. 9.1), and why he was able to do his work: 'I was not disobedient to the heavenly vision' (Acts 26.19).

4. FOR HIM LIFE WAS CHRIST (see Phil. 1.21)

All his life Paul had believed in God, but since his conversion the most important truth about God was that He comes to us in Jesus Christ. Paul expressed this truth in the phrase above and in ways such as the following:

It was Christ who had met him and turned him round at his conversion; Paul had not turned himself round (Acts 22.7). It was through Christ that Paul had received God's forgiveness (Rom. 5.1). It was the risen Christ who had met him (1 Cor. 15.8), so that for him there was no doubt that the Resurrection was true. Christ was the new life which Paul found in himself: 'Christ lives in me' (Gal. 2.20). Christ was all that he needed: 'He said to me, "My grace is sufficient"' (2 Cor. 12.9).

For Paul Jesus Christ was not an idea but a person, a personal friend, rescuer, and Lord, whom he could trust completely. Paul experienced Christ in this way while still believing, like other Jews, that there is only one God.

5. HE WAS AN OUTSTANDING WORKER

When we think of all the congregations which developed as the result of Paul's work in Asia Minor and Europe, we see what an extraordinary amount of work he did. We read in Acts of his preaching to strangers, disputing with his opponents, teaching and supporting new congregations, and writing letters to older congregations (he probably wrote far more letters than we have in the New Testament). In addition to that, he was all the time working out the truths about God and man ('theology') which had to be formed because of the coming of Jesus. In order to do these things he needed to travel, and he often suffered great hardship on these journeys (see 2 Cor. 11.23–33).

From the following outline of Paul's life as a Christian, we see how much of it was spent in travelling.

Event	Date AD
Conversion (Acts 1–9)	32
In Arabia (see Gal. 1.17)	32–46?
First Journey (Acts 13.4—14.28)	47–49
Second Journey (Acts 15.36—18.22)	49–52
Living in Corinth for $1\frac{1}{2}$ years (Acts 18)	50–51
Living in Ephesus, where he wrote to the Corinthians in AD 54 or 55 (Acts 19.1—21.16)	53–56
Third Journey (Acts 18.23—21.16)	53–56
Second visit to Corinth (see 2 Cor. 13.2)	56
Arrest in Jerusalem (Acts 21.27—23.30)	57

Journey to Rome (Acts 27.1—28.16)	59 or 60
In prison in Rome (see Acts 28.17–20)	62–64

6. PRAYER WAS VERY IMPORTANT TO HIM

According to Galatians 1.17 Paul went into the desert country of Arabia immediately after he had been converted, and it is likely that he spent the time in stillness with God.

According to Acts there were many times when in prayer Paul received guidance from God in a special way (see Acts 16.9,10; 18.9,10; 22.18–21; 23.11; 27.23,24). In 2 Corinthians 12.3,4 he referred to another experience which he had while he was praying. In nearly every letter which he wrote he assured his readers that he was praying for them (1 Cor. 1.4). In most of his letters he gave teaching about prayer and asked his readers to pray for him (see Rom. 8.26,27; 15.30; 2 Cor. 1.11; Phil. 4.6; Col. 1.12; 1 Thess. 5.16–18; 2 Thess. 3.1). Then in 1 Corinthians 11—14 he showed that congregational prayer was as important as personal prayers.

7. HE WAS A PIONEER

Paul did what no one else had done before. Since the coming of Jesus and the beginnings of the Church people were asking new questions, and it was useless to answer them merely by saying, 'See what is written in the Old Testament.' So in his letters Paul did his best to answer these questions in the power of God's Holy Spirit. Such questions were:

'What place do Gentiles have in the Church?' (See Gal. 2.11–21 for Paul's reply);

'What is the relation of Jesus to God?' (see p. 104 below);

'What should be the position of slaves and women in the Church?' (see pp. 91, 92, and 141–146 below).

Paul did not write his letters in order to lay down laws, but to give the guidance which, he believed, would at that time help those Christians who had asked the question.

8. HE WAS A HUMAN BEING

This needs to be said because some people have treated Paul as if he were God. We see that he was a human being, although a very remarkable one, from the following:

He was limited in his understanding of God's creation, e.g. he did not know about or enjoy plants and birds in the way that Jesus did. He understood much less about life in the country than about life in the town (a countryman would not have written 1 Cor. 9.8–10 or Rom. 11.17–24).

He continued to grow and develop in his understanding, as all healthy human beings do. He said in Philippians 3.12: 'Not that I am already perfect, but I press on.' For example, he seems at first to have regarded Jesus as in some way less than God, but later revised this belief (see p. 145).

He seems at first to have expected that the end of the world would come very soon, but later changed his opinion (see p. 202).

He was not able to understand all people equally well. He understood men better than he understood women.

He seems sometimes to have quoted the Old Testament incorrectly. Compare 1 Corinthians 10.8 with Numbers 25.9.

In some parts of his letters he was so excited about his ideas that he wrote them down in a confused way (e.g. in Ephesians 3.1–3). But we have to remember that Paul did not think that any one except the addressees would read his letters.

He sometimes gave way to feelings of self-pity and humiliation (see 2 Cor. 10.10; 12.11), and self-glory (2 Cor. 10.8). As a result he was quick to see and criticize such feelings in other people, and was less loving than he ought to have been (Gal. 2.6). But at other times he was glad that he was weak, because his weakness showed how much he needed Christ's strength and what a difference Christ's strength made to him: 'When I am weak, then I am strong' (2 Cor. 12.10). See note on 2.3 (p. 24).

We do not note these examples in order to speak ill of Paul, but in order to show how marvellously God can use a human being. Perhaps the best way to describe Paul is to use his own words in 2 Corinthians 4.7: 'in earthen vessels . . . to show that the power belongs to God and not to us'.

STUDY SUGGESTIONS

1. What words or phrases in the New Testament show that Paul:
   (a) Was a Jew?
   (b) Received advanced education?
   (c) Was a Roman citizen?
   (d) Turned from one sort of life to another?
   (e) Prayed?
   (f) Was a human being?
2. In what language did Paul write his letters?
3. What do you think were the two most important results of Paul's conversion?
4. 'To live is Christ' (Phil. 1.21):
   (a) What made it possible for Paul to say this, considering that he believed there is only one God?
   (b) What language do you use to describe your own relationship to God? To what extent is it the same language which Paul used in Philippians 1.21?
5. (a) Which *two* activities of Paul do you think you would have found most difficult if you had been alive then and had been chosen to do Paul's work?

(b) Which of the dangers which Paul described in 2 Corinthians 11.23–33 do present-day Church leaders experience?

6. (a) 'In prayer Paul received guidance from God' (p. 53). Do you think that the experiences which Paul had according to Acts 16.9 and 10 (and the other passages listed on p. 53) came to him because he was an unusual person, or can ordinary Christians today have similar experiences? Give reasons for your answer.

(b) 'In most of his letters Paul gave teaching about prayer' (p. 53). Which of the following passages is the most important at this moment, (i) for you, and (ii) for the congregation to which you belong?
Rom. 8.26,27; 15.30; 2 Cor. 1.11; Phil. 4.6; Col. 1.12; 4.2; 1 Thess. 5.16–18; 2 Thess. 3.1.

7. 'Paul was a human being' (p. 53).
(a) Did the paragraph with this heading make you feel glad, sad, or angry? What were your feelings? Give reasons for your answers.
(b) If you had met Paul, would you have liked him? What do you think you would have felt about him?

5.1–13 Discipline in the Church

When members do wrong, you must discipline them

OUTLINE

5.1–2: Why are you not taking seriously the behaviour of the man who is living immorally with his step-mother?

5.3–5: The only way to save that man's soul is to separate him from the congregation.

5.6–8: You must do this not only for the man's sake but for the sake of the congregation. Just as the Jews purify their houses at the time of the Passover, so must you purify your congregation.

5.9–13: In saying this, I am not referring to the way you treat people of other religions. It is a Christian from whom I am telling you to be separate.

INTERPRETATION

WHY DID PAUL WRITE THESE VERSES?

He had heard that a member of the congregation of Corinth was having sexual intercourse with a woman who was not his wife. He was troubled to hear this, but he was far more troubled to hear that the other members were not taking any notice of this sin. Evidently they were forgetting the newness of life to which Christ had called them. They were forgetting that unless they were different from the people of other religions there was no reason for them to exist as a congregation. So he raises the question: 'How can a small congregation, living among neighbours who follow different customs, remain distinctively Christian?'

The answer which Paul gave here is 'when members go astray, deal severely with them.'

This is only one of the answers to that question which Paul gave in his letters. For another answer, see 2 Cor. 2.5–8. But all Christian congregations since that time have found it necessary to discipline offenders in some way.

DISCIPLINING OFFENDERS

(a) *For what sin should Christians exercise discipline?*
The answer seems to be: 'whenever someone is leading other members astray'.

The sin Paul referred to in chapter 5 concerns the wrong use which a man made of his sexuality. This has often been the reason why members have been 'disciplined'. Indeed in some Churches, this has become the only reason for disciplining members. As a result, many people have wrongly thought that such behaviour as committing adultery or marrying a non-Christian or taking a second wife or getting a divorce were more serious offences than cruelty, malice, or dishonesty. Paul did not make this mistake. See note on v. 10a (p. 61).

We notice today that there are many other reasons for which Christians in different parts of the world are 'disciplined'. Some examples are: drunkenness, witchcraft, taking a fellow-Christian to court, preaching what is not true, dancing, smoking, wearing short skirts, parting hair in the middle, and keeping a pet dog. It is clear that different Churches have different ideas as to which sins are serious.

(b) *What sort of discipline is used?* In this passage Paul referred to a very severe sort of discipline: to 'remove' him (v. 2), to 'deliver him to Satan', i.e. so that he may suffer physically (v. 5). Sometimes Christians have read these verses as if they were rules for all to follow, and as a result have behaved cruelly towards offenders. In Europe in the thirteenth century and later years some Church authorities (in what is called 'the Inquisition') tortured and even burnt to death those whom they accused of holding false doctrine. In some cases they handed the offender over to the State authorities to do the work for them. It was done, they said, 'that their spirits may be saved' (1 Cor. 5.5). This is an example of the wrong ways in which Christians can behave when they use the Bible in the wrong way.

At the present time, Church authorities discipline offenders in such ways as forbidding them to share in the Holy Communion for a period of time, or preventing them from holding official positions in the Church or from voting in Church meetings.

(c) *What is the purpose of such discipline?* Paul expressed the purpose in v. 7: that the whole congregation may be purified; i.e. so that the other members may not be corrupted by the offender.

In the first place, then, offenders are disciplined for the sake of the whole congregation; in the second place, for the benefit of the member who has sinned (see v. 5 and note below, p. 59). Discipline is not the same as punishment.

Although Paul said nothing in these verses about loving and caring for the offender, he believed that the congregation should do so. See 2 Thess. 3.15: 'Warn him as a brother'. He may also have known the teaching of Jesus in passages such as Matthew 18.15–17. Certainly Christians should only discipline an offender if they have warned him, called on him to repent, forgiven him, and gone on caring for him.

Paul's teaching in 1 Cor. 5 referred to a Church congregation, but what was true for them is also true for other Christian groups. For example, if the principal of a training college finds that a student is secretly (illegally) trading in drugs, he has the same question to ask: 'Should I expel him? If I do, is it for the sake of the other students or for the man himself? If I expel him, who will now help and support him?'

(d) *Who disciplines offenders?* According to chapter 5, it was Paul who decided what should be done to the offender. It was he who called on the members to meet together (v. 4) to carry out his plan. Similarly today, it is the rule in many Churches that someone who is outside the congregation must exercise such discipline, e.g. a bishop, after receiving a report from the leader of the congregation. When the members themselves discipline offenders, they may be tempted to do so for the wrong reasons. e.g. they may do it because they enjoy acting as judges, and not in order that the offender may repent.

The one who disciplines offenders runs the risk of making enemies. The leader of one congregation learnt that a member who was rich and who regularly gave the Church a lot of money, was secretly living with someone else's wife. He consulted with another leader and then told the man that he must stay away from Holy Communion unless he left the woman. Instead of repenting the man did everything he could to remove the leader from his position.

NOTES

5.1. A man is living with his father's wife: We have said that Paul was less troubled about this man's sin than he was about the attitude of the other members. But we should notice what his sin was:

(a) He was probably having sexual intercourse with his step-mother.

'Remove him.' 'Deliver this man to Satan' (1 Cor. 5.2,5).

A Ghanaian potter checks newly-made water-coolers, and throws out those which are faulty.

What is the chief reason for 'removing' offenders from a congregation? What are the reasons *against* doing so?

(Not his own mother. Paul would have called her 'his mother' if that is what she was.)

(b) It had not been only a single act; he was continuing in the sin.

(c) It is likely that his father was still alive. If he had not been alive, Paul would probably not have regarded the sin as so serious.

(d) The woman does not seem to have been a Christian. Paul did not make any judgement of her.

The sin was serious for two reasons:

1. *The truth about our bodies:* Many Christians of that time were saying that since they had received the Holy Spirit in their spirits, it did not matter what they did with their bodies. The passages in 1 Corinthians which concern sexuality (this chapter and chapter 6) are important, not because the wrong use of sexuality is worse than other sins, but because in such chapters we learn that we are answerable to God for the way in which we use *the whole* of ourselves (see Rom. 12.1 and note on 'Body' p. 65).

If we consider our sexuality by itself, its wrong use is serious chiefly because others are concerned and not only we ourselves.

2. *The truth about God's eternal 'laws':* Others were saying that since they had received the Holy Spirit they no longer had any need of any of the laws by which they had lived before. It is not surprising that they said this because when they became Christians it was like starting a completely different life. But there are some laws by which God rules over us in every generation and Jesus did not cancel them. See Mark 10.6–9; Luke 10.26–28. Whether we live in the first century or the twentieth century, whether we live in Tokyo or Tunis, it is always true that loving God and our neighbours is the best sort of life and is God's will for us. It is the task of the Church to interpret these unchanging laws of God in each generation and in each country.

5.5. Deliver this man to Satan for the destruction of the flesh:

1. Deliver to Satan: Paul was instructing the congregation at Corinth to meet together ('when you are assembled' v. 4) and to pronounce a sort of curse upon the offender, so that he would be under the control of Satan. Paul and his readers believed that everyone was controlled by a number of invisible spirits. When people became Christians they were no longer under Satan's spirit, but under the Spirit of Jesus. In v.5 Paul told them to hand the man back to Satan.

Many readers find it extraordinary that Paul, a Christian, should tell his readers to do this. They notice that Jesus did not deliver sinners to Satan, but sat down and ate with them (Luke 5.29–32). Perhaps we can understand why Paul wrote this if we remember that the Church to which he was writing was very young and very weak. Probably he thought that unless Church leaders disciplined offenders severely, Christian congregations throughout the world would become just like the rest of the world, and so would soon cease to exist. What Paul wrote there he wrote for the Corinthian Christians at that time. He nowhere said that he was making rules for all future Christians.

2. Satan:

(a) Most writers of the Old Testament regarded Satan as the 'accuser', an angel who was useful to God. He discovered evil people and accused them in God's presence (see Job. 1.6–12).

(b) But in the New Testament, writers use the name for the leader of the evil spirits who are against God and who lead people to oppose God. Jesus used the word in this way (e.g. Mark. 3.22–27).

(c) Some Christians today talk of 'evil' rather than 'Satan' because, they say, talking about Satan leads us to think of two Gods, one God and the other Satan. Others talk of 'Satan' or 'the Devil', chiefly because Jesus did.

(d) The important thing is not what name we use for 'evil' or 'Satan', but whether we know how to obtain God's Spirit to fight such evil (see Eph. 6.11).

3. For the destruction of the flesh: Most Jews believed that Satan was a sort of servant of God who punished people by sending them suffering (see Job. 2.6,7). So Paul meant, 'Send the offender away so that he may suffer physically.'

Paul did not explain how the man's spirit, because he had suffered physically, would 'be saved in the day of the Lord'. But these words show that Paul wanted the man to be saved in the end, not simply to suffer. (For the words 'day of the Lord' see note on p. 8.)

5.6. A little leaven leavens the whole lump: One man who has sinned affects the whole congregation. Paul said that if the other members had understood this they would not have been arrogant (v. 2) or have boasted (v. 6). They would have removed the man, 'cleansed out the old leaven' as Paul said.

Most writers in the Bible used 'leaven' or 'yeast' as a sign of evil, as Paul did here and as Jesus did in Mark 8.15. But note that Jesus also used it as a sign of goodness – see Matthew 13.33. Leaven is like an explosive. When we put a little into bread, it changes the whole loaf.

The lesson which Paul wanted to teach was that the congregation was 'one lump'. He explained it more fully in chapter 12 (see especially v. 26). What each member is and does affects all the other members.

5.7b: Christ, our paschal lamb, has been sacrificed: Paul had called removing the offender 'cleansing out the old leaven' (v. 7a). Here he added another thought about leaven: that it was at Passover time that the Jews removed all leaven from their houses. When they had done that, they could sacrifice the Passover ('paschal') lamb. By this sacrifice they remembered how God has set them free from the Egyptians (Exod. 12.5,6).

By reminding them of the Jewish Passover, Paul meant:

1. 'The Jews, by sacrificing a lamb at Passover, remember that God had set them free.' So Christians, because Jesus willingly offered Himself to do God's will and as a result was killed like a 'lamb', are set free from the overwhelming power of sin.

2. 'Let us Christians celebrate this fact', i.e. let every day be like a festival, when we rejoice that Christ has set us free (see v. 8).

We note that in this verse Paul did not simply tell his readers what to do. He first reminded them what God had done, and only after that told them what to do: (a) God has given you forgiveness and freedom through Jesus, (b) therefore show in your life that you have accepted these gifts. This is the usual order of events when Christians worship. They first celebrate what God has done (by readings and hymns, etc.), and after that they are ready to consider what sort of lives they should lead.

5.9. I wrote to you in my letter: We see from these words that Paul had already written one letter to the Corinthians. What we call '1 Corinthians' is really his second letter to them.

It is likely that Paul wrote four letters to the Corinthians, as follows:

1. The letter which he referred to in this verse. It may be that part of that letter is now in 2 Corinthians 6.14—7.1.

2. Then, after he had heard about troubles in the Church at Corinth, he wrote the letter which we call 1 Corinthians.

3. Then, when the troubles increased and he had made another visit to Corinth, he wrote 2 Corinthians 10—13.

4. Lastly, when things had improved, he wrote 2 Corinthians 1—9.

5.10a: The immoral . . . or the greedy and robbers, or idolaters: In this chapter Paul was telling his readers to discipline a member who was 'immoral', i.e. who had offended against the customs concerning the use of sexuality. See note on 6.13b. If we only read vv. 1–8 we might think that Paul was too much troubled about those who, like this man, misused their sexuality, and that he was not troubled enough about other sorts of wrong-doing. But from vv. 10 and 11 and from chapters 6, 9 and 10 we see that this is not so. Alongside 'immorality' Paul referred to other sorts of sin as being equally serious. In v. 10 we read of:

(a) 'The greedy and robbers': those who value material possessions so highly that they refuse to share them with other people and even take them from other people.

(b) 'The idolators': those who put other things and other people in the place of God. See note on p. 102. These three sorts of wrong-doing are all equally serious.

5.10b: You would need to go out of the world: It seems from v. 9 ('I wrote to you'), that some time before this Paul had told the Corinthian Christians to avoid 'immoral' people. They had thought that it was the non-Christians whom they should avoid. So he now wrote, 'No. It was Christians to whom I was referring. You cannot avoid the immoral of the world (i.e. those people who do not accept God as their Lord). That would mean that you would have to go out of the world.'

This verse shows clearly the situation in which God placed the Corinthians, and in which he has placed most Christians since that time. On the one hand they are 'holy', i.e. God has set them apart from others so that they can do His special work (see note on p. 6). On the other hand, He has placed them in the world. As Jesus said, 'They are not of the world . . . (yet) I do not pray that thou shouldst take them out of the world' (John 17.14,15).

This is not an easy situation in which God has placed Christians. Some of them are so much in the world that they forget the special sort of life to which God has called them. Others mix with non-Christians as little as possible (like the 'Strict Brethren' who do not eat food with anyone who does not belong to the 'Strict Brethren'), with the result that they do not take their share in the life of the local community. Nor do they have many opportunities of sharing with non-Christians what they believe about God. See notes on chapter 8 (Interpretation) and 10.27.

This verse has reminded some readers of monks and nuns who have 'gone out of the world' by forming religious communities, and some have thought Paul was here advising Christians not to form religious communities. But he was writing about disciplining offenders, not about monks and nuns. If we want to know if it is God's will that some Christians should be monks and nuns today, we shall not look for rules in this verse. Instead we shall study the story of how God has used such communities in the past, study the circumstances that exist today, and ask God to show us if this is His will for us at this time.

STUDY SUGGESTIONS

WORDS

1. The word 'discipline' does not occur in 1 Cor. 5 but appears many times in the notes above. Which *four* of the following words are most like 'discipline' in their meaning?
   persecute   control   torture   educate   correct
   terrify   train   punish
2. What is the meaning of 'paschal'?

CONTENT

3. Why did Paul write 1 Cor. 5?
4. What sin had the offender committed?
5. What six words or phrases did Paul use in 1 Cor. 5 to show how his readers ought to behave towards offenders?

6. For what two reasons did Paul tell his readers to discipline the offender?
7. (a) What is leaven?
   (b) Why did Paul mention it in chapter 5?

BIBLE

8. Compare (a) 1 Cor. 5.2–5 with (b) Matt. 18.15–17; Luke 5.29–32; and 2 Thess. 3.15. How do you explain the difference between (a) and (b)?
9. (i) What names did the writers give to Satan in each of the following passages?
   (a) Matt. 4.3   (b) Matt. 6.13   (c) Luke 4.2   (d) Luke 22.3   (e) John 12.31   (f) 1 John 2.13
   (ii) Following the note on 'Satan' (p. 60) read the following passages and say in each case whether the writer regards him chiefly as (1) Useful to God as an accuser, (2) The leader of all evil spirits, or (3) The evil which Christians must fight:
   (a) Job 1.6–12   (b) Zech. 3.1   (c) Eph. 6.11   (d) 1 Thess. 3.5
   (e) James 4.7   (f) 1 Pet. 5.8   (g) 1 John 3.8   (h) Rev. 12.9

DISCUSSION AND RESEARCH

10. What sort of help and guidance do you think your own congregation can obtain from reading 1 Cor. 5?
11. (a) In your Church do the authorities discipline their members in any way?
    (b) If they do:
     (i) Who decides to discipline a member?
     (ii) In what ways do they discipline members?
     (iii) For what offences are members chiefly disciplined?
    (c) Find out what is the custom in a Church which is different from your own.
12. In the notes above (e.g. on 5.5 and 5.10) we have said that Paul was not laying down rules for all future Christians to follow.
    (a) Do you agree?
    (b) If so, what is the value of our reading this chapter?
13. Some Christians talk about 'evil' . . . others talk of 'Satan' (p. 60). Does it matter whether we talk of 'evil' or of 'Satan'? Give reasons for your answer.
14. 'Deliver this man to Satan for the destruction of the flesh' (v. 5). A hospital chaplain once told a patient whom he had never seen before, 'God has sent Satan to punish you for your sins.' What would you want to say,
    (a) to the chaplain?
    (b) to the patient?

15. 'That his spirit may be saved' (v. 5). When a Church disciplines a member, e.g. by forbidding him to share Holy Communion:
    (a) how far does this help the member to reform?
    (b) in what other ways can the member be helped?
16. 'It might seem that Paul was too much troubled about those who misused their sexuality, and not troubled enough about other sorts of wrong-doing' (p. 61).
    (a) Do you think that Paul was 'too much troubled about such sins'? How does v. 10 help us to answer that?
    (b) Do you think that your own Church is too much troubled about such sins? If so, what action can you take? If not, what sort of sins do trouble the Church most?
17. 'On the one hand God has set Christians apart . . . on the other hand He has placed them in the world' (p. 62). In what ways can members of a congregation
    (a) show that they are 'set apart'?
    (b) take their proper place in the world?

6.1–20 Members of Christ

You are members of Christ's Church: be loyal members

OUTLINE

6.1–6: Because you belong to Christ's Church, settle your disputes within the congregation.

6.7–8: But it is much better not to have disputes at all. Forgive one another.

6.9–11: The reason I say this is that you are a new and holy community.

6.12–20: Again, because you belong to Christ, you must have nothing to do with prostitutes.

INTERPRETATION

In the whole of this chapter Paul was continuing the teaching he had begun to give in chapter 5 (see note, p. 56). He was reminding his readers that they were a special community, separated out by God to serve Him. Although they lived and worked alongside the other citizens of Corinth (see 5.10), they themselves belonged to a different master, their Lord Jesus Christ. If they really believed that, they would show it by the way they behaved.

There are two parts to this chapter:

In *Part 1* (vv. 1–11) Paul said, 'Because you are "saints", i.e. a special community, settle your disputes among yourselves.'

In *Part 2* (vv. 12–20) he said, 'Show that you are a special community in the way that you use your bodies and your sexuality. Have nothing to do with prostitutes.'

Note on the word 'body' and its meanings:

1. '*Whole person*'. In modern English we use the word 'somebody' to mean 'some person'. So in the New Testament 'body' usually means the whole 'person' or 'personality' or 'self'. It does not only refer to flesh and bones, but to mind and spirit as well. 'Glorify God in your body' (6.20) means 'Glorify Him with your whole personalities.' Greek philosophers said that the flesh was separate from the soul. New Testament writers did not believe this, and used 'body' to describe the unity of flesh and soul (see note on 6.13a).

Occasionally New Testament writers did use 'body' to mean flesh (e.g. 1 Cor. 13.3), but far more often they used the Greek word *sarx* for 'flesh'.

2. '*Means of expression*': In 1 Cor. 15.35–50 Paul used 'body' chiefly to mean 'the means we have of expressing ourselves.' If we want to express our pleasure at seeing someone, we move towards him and give him our attention. We have used our whole person to express ourselves (see notes on 12.27 and 15.38).

3. '*A congregation of Christians*': Because 'body' means (a) a whole or unified person, and (b) the means of expression, Paul found that it was a suitable 'picture-word' when he was writing about a congregation (see chapter 12, Interpretation p. 160).

NOTES

6.1. Does he dare to go to law before the unrighteous instead of the saints?
Christians in Corinth were taking other Christians to court before non-Christian magistrates, instead of finding a Christian to help them to settle the dispute. We see the same thing happening today.

At a public revival meeting a Christian student confessed to a sin which he had committed and gave the name of a Church leader who had joined him in that sin. The Church leader was so angry that he refused to meet the student, in spite of the advice of his friends, and sued him for slander in the public courts.

When the leaders of all the Protestant churches in one country had agreed to join together as a united Church, after twenty-five years' preparation, two members of one congregation took the Church Union Committee to court to prevent the Committee from taking possession of their church building. They did this although their congregation had a representative who had served on that Committee for many years.

A new leader was appointed by the authorities to a congregation. One of the members complained to the authorities that the new man's teaching was not 'scriptural'. When they rejected his complaint, the member took them to court.

The governors of a Christian College planned to sell the land on which the college was built in order to build larger buildings in another place. The local Church leaders said that the land belonged to them and took the College governors to court.

The bishops in one country agreed that one of them should retire (since he had reached the age when, according to the rules of that Church, bishops do retire). They appointed someone else in his place. The old bishop refused to retire. Even though each of the other bishops in turn tried to persuade him, he rejected their advice and took the newly-appointed one to court.

Three questions arise:

1. *Why did Paul tell his readers not to use the public courts?* Mainly because Christians are a distinctive community and because they need to behave in ways which are different from the ways of other people. If they take each other to court they would be making themselves the same as other people. They would also be saying (by their behaviour) that they would get more justice in the public non-Christian courts than in the meetings of Christians.

By speaking of 'unrighteous', Paul did not mean that magistrates in the public courts were wicked men, but that they did not acknowledge the rule of God (in v. 4 he called them the 'least esteemed by the church'). Paul himself had experienced that a non-Christian judge could be just, e.g. when they took him before Gallio (Acts 18.12–17). God's wisdom is not only given to Christians.

2. *Are Paul's words a rule for all Christians?* It would be unwise to say that Paul laid down a law of that sort, or that it is always wrong for Christians to take other Christians to court. In some present-day situations people may need to go to court in order to find out what the law is, for example if the dispute concerns land-boundaries, and neither party has documents to show where the boundary should lie. Then, justice may be better done by both of them going to court. This is quite different from someone who habitually tries to increase his own wealth by taking people to court who are too poor to defend themselves.

What are the results of Christians taking other Christians to court? It is clear from Paul's words that:

(a) People outside the Church are less likely to see the Church as a special community, and less likely to want to join it.

(b) The Church itself is weakened.

3. *What should Christians do when they have a dispute?* As far as possible, they should settle it among Christians. Usually members ask one

person, such as their leader or their bishop, to be judge. (But such a person is not only 'judge' among Christians, he is their counsellor as well.) Or, they appoint a group such as a 'Church Court' to settle the matter. Such judges need to treat offences as seriously as the public courts do. If they do not, Christians will not want to use them.

Paul referred to another way of settling disputes in v. 7.

6.2. The saints will judge the world: Paul was probably familiar with Daniel 7.27, where it was said that God's saints would be given 'the kingdom and the dominion' (and perhaps Jesus was also quoting this verse in Matt. 19.28).

Paul's thought was, 'since Christians will one day share with God Himself the carrying out of perfect justice in all the world, surely they can do a much simpler thing, namely, see that justice is carried out among themselves here and now.'

6.3. We are to judge angels: Christians will not only share in judging people; they will judge angels. Then surely they can settle matters 'pertaining to this life', e.g., concerning property and money.

Most writers in the Old Testament and New Testament refer to angels as spirits whom God created: (a) to be His messengers to human beings (see Ps. 91.11), and (b) to join in His fight against evil (see Matt. 25.31). In this verse (6.3) Paul said that God had given Christians a special fellowship with Him which He had not given even to angels (see also 1 Pet. 1.12).

6.7. To have lawsuits at all with one another is defeat for you. Why not rather suffer wrong? In vv. 1–6 Paul said, 'If someone has ill-treated you, bring the matter to a Christian to settle.' In v. 7 he said, 'But, there is something still better than that: forgiving, and if necessary, suffering.'

Being a Christian means forgiving those who have wronged you. So if Christians have lawsuits between themselves it shows that they have been 'defeated', i.e. they have failed to forgive. (We do not know whether Paul knew the words of Jesus in Matthew 5.39,40.)

6.9a The unrighteous will not inherit the kingdom of God. Do not be deceived: In v. 8 Paul said that the people who failed to forgive those who had wronged them were themselves treating others wrongfully. They were 'unrighteous'. Now in v. 9 he gave them a warning that, if they continued in this way, they (together with the sort of people he referred to in vv. 9, 10) would not share in God's rule or 'kingdom'.

1. **The unrighteous:** In vv. 9 and 10 Paul made a list of people who were very commonly found in large cities such as Corinth. (They were the sort of people amongst whom his readers were living and whom the Christians had to be careful not to imitate.) The list is: 'immoral' (the Greek word used here means 'male prostitutes'), idolaters, adulterers, sexual perverts (see note below), thieves, greedy people, drunkards, revilers (i.e. slanderers) and robbers.

2. **The kingdom of God:** This 'kingdom' is not a place, but refers to the fact that God is King over the lives of people (see note on 4.20).

3. **Do not be deceived:** This means, 'Do not let anyone persuade you that the way you behave does not matter. You may lose eternal life because of evil behaviour.'

6.9b. Sexual perverts: The Greek phrase Paul used means homosexuals, i.e. those who use their sexuality in relation to people of their own sex.

1. It was a very serious problem in Corinth that there were so many homosexuals, and it is a serious problem today in many places, e.g. it is especially serious when adult homosexuals cause ordinary children to become homosexuals in order to make money from it.

2. But it is not right to label all homosexuals as 'unrighteous' or 'outside the Kingdom of God'. Of course homosexuals may be sinful, just as, indeed, very many people use their sexual instinct in wicked ways. But we now know more of the reasons why some people are homosexuals than anyone knew at the time when Paul was writing. Many of them are born as homosexuals. They cannot make a relationship with people of the other sex, just as a person born with blue eyes cannot change them to brown ones. It is therefore better to call such people 'different' rather than 'sinful'.

3. Thus there is a difference between people who are born homosexuals and the idolaters and other groups to whom Paul referred in vv. 9 and 10. When people are born homosexuals they cannot turn away from it. But when someone is born into a family which practises idolatry (i.e. is 'born idolater') he can turn away from idolatry later on, and 'repent and be baptized'.

6.11. Such were some of you. But you were washed: Paul had given a warning in vv. 9 and 10. Now in v. 11 he appealed to his readers and encouraged them: 'Remember what sort of people you really are. You once knew nothing better than the life of sinfulness, but now you have been given new life by God. You have been made into a new and special community. Live the new life!'

The three words that Paul used to describe people in this new community are:

1. **Washed:** They had been baptised with water and God had washed away the old sort of life.

2. **Sanctified:** They had been made 'holy' members of His special People (see note on 1.2, p. 6).

3. **Justified:** They had been treated by God as He treats innocent people, in spite of their sinfulness. God had done this, not because of any effort which they had made, but because of Jesus ('in the name of the Lord Jesus . . .'). The word which is translated 'justified' here is the same as the word Paul used in 1.30 ('Jesus . . . our righteousness': see note on p. 17).

These three words referred to a great turning-point in their lives, which

Paul wanted them to remember. So Christians of all generations are strengthened by thinking about their baptism and renewing their promises. Many do this, for example, at a special service on the day before Easter.

6.12a. 'All things are lawful for me' — but not all things are helpful. This verse is the beginning of the second part of the chapter (vv. 12–20).

In the whole chapter Paul was reminding his readers that they were a new community. In this part his chief teaching is: '*Show* that you are a new community; show that God has given you new life by the way you use your bodies and your sexuality.'

In order to follow Paul's thoughts in vv. 12–20, we need to notice that he was partly referring to false ideas which some of them held, and partly giving them his own thoughts.

Their false ideas were:

1. They said that when they became Christians they were free to do anything. 'All things are lawful', they said. 'We are even free to have sexual intercourse with prostitutes.'

2. They probably thought that Paul had actually told them that there were no longer any laws which they must obey. If they thought this, it was because of what Paul had said in verses such as Galatians 5.18: 'If you are led by the Spirit, you are not under the law.'

3. They said 'What we do with our bodies does not have any effect on our "personalities" or "souls". Therefore, it does not matter how we use our bodies, whether for eating food or for committing adultery.'

Paul's teaching is in vv. 12–20, and we study it under the notes for each verse.

In v. 12 he explained that the Corinthian Christians had not understood the meaning of being free of the law. He seems to have two chief thoughts here:

(a) *Attitude to the law:* 'It is true that we are "free" from Moses's regulations. But being free from them means that we do not depend on them as we once did. It does not mean that we can do what we please. We no longer depend on the old law because we now have a new spirit in us which God has given us through Jesus Christ. It is this spirit which moves us to do right. The law has no power to do that: it could only show what was right and what was wrong.' (A student reading this note said, 'When I began to take part in debates and preaching, I followed a book called *How to Speak in Public*. But the more I speak in public the less I depend on the book.') See note on 9.21b.

(b) *Attitude to other people:* 'It is absurd to say that what we do only concerns ourselves and has no effect on anyone else.' (Note that what Paul said here he said more fully in chapters 8 and 9, i.e. 'you can tell if an action is right or wrong by seeing what it does to other people, as well as what it does to yourself'.)

'Show that you are a new community. Show that God has given you new life' (p. 69).

At an outdoor baptism service in the USA, a boy reads a hand-out urging the new Christians to depend on the Spirit of Jesus, and give up the drug-taking which has enslaved them.

What are some of the most important ways in which Christians can show that they are a 'new community'?

6.12b. I will not be enslaved by anything:

1. 'I might say that I was free from the law and that, therefore, I was free to do what I liked. But I must not do just what I like. If I did, I should form habits which would gradually enslave me.'

Paul's readers might think, for example, that they were free to have sexual intercourse with prostitutes. But if they did that they would soon find that they could not escape from the prostitutes even when they wanted to. They would not be able to escape from the habit of misusing sexuality in that way.

As we read this, we shall think of other habits which can enslave human beings.

2. We may also ask, 'What is true freedom for a Christian?' To be truly free means opening ourselves to receive the Spirit of Jesus so that we are no longer enslaved by habits and are, therefore, free to choose the way of living that seems best.

6.13a. Food is meant for the stomach! Paul's readers seem to have said this: 'We satisfy our hunger by putting food into our stomachs, so why should we not satisfy our sexual hunger by having intercourse with prostitutes, or anyone else? Neither action affects our souls.'

Paul said that the two actions were different. Eating mainly affects the stomach, but sexual intercourse concerns the whole personality or 'body' (see note in Interpretation, p. 65).

Then he added that God will 'raise up' the whole personality. Therefore, the way we use it will make a difference to the way we exist in the future (v. 14).

The Christians in Corinth were expressing an opinion which they had probably learnt from Greek thinkers. These Greeks (a) regarded a human being as 'a soul added to a body'; (b) regarded someone's 'soul' (or 'spirit') as so important that they thought that the body of flesh and bones did not matter.

But the truth is that a human being is a whole person. What a person does with his body affects what he thinks and feels (e.g. if he wastes his body by over-working, his thinking is damaged). What he thinks and feels affects what he does with his body (e.g. if he is afraid, his body sweats or shakes). We cannot split a person into parts. 'Healing' a person means helping him to have wholeness and completeness in himself, i.e. health, so that he can eat and think and feel and pray rightly.

6.13b. 'The body is not meant for immorality, but for the Lord'.

1. Immorality:

(a) Paul used this word to refer to someone having a sexual relationship with another person in a way that is wrong. The Greek word is *porn-eia*, and is translated in the New English Bible in this verse as 'lust' and in v. 18 as 'fornication'. But there are many ways in which human beings misuse their sexuality in relation to others and the word *porneia* refers to them all, whether the people concerned are married or unmarried. It refers not only to wrongful intercourse, but also to actions which result in wrongful intercourse, e.g. the writing of magazines and books which encourage readers to use their sexuality wrongly, and the printing, selling, and reading of this sort of literature; making, showing, and seeing films of the same sort; drinking so much alcohol or taking other drugs or dancing so violently that we can no longer control our sexual powers.

(b) What makes such behaviour 'immoral'? People often give as a reason, 'Because from such behaviour come children who are not wanted'. This is indeed one reason why such behaviour is wrong, but it is not the main reason (we can use contraceptives in order to prevent children being conceived).

Others say that such behaviour is wrong 'Because it often leads to venereal disease'. This also is true. But it is not the main reason for calling behaviour 'immoral' (we can partially cure venereal disease by using such medicines as penicillin).

The following are some of the reasons why we call such a person 'immoral' (these reasons apply equally to men and women):

(1) He is treating another person as a thing, not a person.

It is of course possible for married people to 'use' each other, and to use their sexuality wrongly.

(2) He is using the other person rather than committing himself and giving himself wholly to her. This is why Christians should not have sexual intercourse with strangers or friends to whom they are not married.

If one of the two people are married we should add two further reasons:

(3) He is destroying the wholeness of his sexual relationship with his wife (and probably making her jealous and unhappy).

(4) He is damaging the wholeness of his relationship with his children and family (they are likely to become filled with hatred and bitterness).

Note: The customs of all Churches are not the same. For example, in some parts of the world the Church allows a man and a woman who are 'betrothed' or 'engaged' to have sexual intercourse before they are actually married. In most parts such intercourse is not allowed. But everywhere the Church gives some guidance concerning the right use of a person's sexuality in relation to other people.

2. **For the Lord:** Instead of using their bodies 'immorally', Christians should use them to carry out the will of God. When God made us He planned that we should put the whole of ourselves at His service: our physical strength, our thinking, our ability to make things, to make music, to paint pictures, our pleasure in making relationships with others, including people of the other sex.

As we shall see in chapter 7, Paul sometimes wrote as if he was sorry that God had given human beings sexuality. But in verses 13b and 20 he was not saying that at all. He was saying that our whole body, including our sexuality, is something with which we are to praise, glorify, and serve God. In saying this he was following Jesus Christ. Although Jesus was not married, it is clear that he believed it was right and good for people to marry and bring up a family (see for example Mark 10.6–9).

6.15a. Your bodies are members of Christ: We should read vv. 15, 16 and 17 together. In these verses Paul was saying:

1. When someone becomes a Christian, his 'body' ('personality') is joined to Christ. (In other places Paul describes Christians as being 'in' Christ, see 1.30; 3.1 and note on p. 7.)

2. Someone who is joined to Christ takes into himself Christ's Spirit: 'he becomes one spirit' with Him (v. 17).

3. It is like what happens when a man and woman happily and successfully marry each other. 'The two shall become one' (v. 16b). See Gen. 2.24.

4. Therefore, if a Christian has sexual intercourse with a prostitute he is choosing to have her spirit in him instead of Christ's Spirit. No one can belong to Christ and also to a prostitute (see notes on vv. 16 and 19a).

6.15b. Shall I . . . make them members of a prostitute? Never! By 'prostitute' we usually mean a woman who, in return for money, offers her body to people who want to have sexual intercourse with her. Paul probably meant this when he used the word *porne* in this verse.

But there are other sorts of prostitutes, e.g. male prostitutes, and women who in some religions live in a place of worship and have intercourse with the worshippers (this took place in Corinth).

It is clear, then, why Christians should not join themselves to prostitutes: because someone who pays a prostitute is not using his body in the way in which God intended. God intended a man to commit himself to a woman with the whole of himself (by means of his body); and He intended a woman to commit herself to a man in the same way. This 'committing' is giving oneself wholeheartedly and for life. But in the case of a man and a prostitute, each is half-hearted towards the other and uncommitted. Both are using the other to get what they want, without committing themselves.

6.16. He who joins himself to a prostitute becomes one body with her: Although a man does not commit himself whole-heartedly to a prostitute, their action has a great effect on him. It affects him far more than the action of eating (see v. 13). They become 'one body' and share one spirit. But this spirit is the spirit to get something (she gets money, he gets pleasure). So this is the spirit with which he is filled. This is very different from the 'Spirit of the Lord' who 'gave Himself' for us (Gal. 2.20). That is the character of the spirit with which we can be filled when we are 'united to the Lord' (v. 17, see also v. 19).

6.18a. Shun immorality: This does not simply mean 'avoid the wrong use of sexuality' but 'run away from it'. So many people in Corinth had wrongful sexual relationships that Christians needed to be active in resisting the temptations.

6.18b. Every other sin which a man commits is outside the body: This may refer to another sentence which the Corinthians had written to Paul. If so, they meant, 'Every sin which a man commits, whether it is over-eating or wrongful sexual relationships with another person, only affects the outside of him. It does not affect his real "self".' Paul repeated what he had said in v. 13: 'No. Anyone who has a wrongful sexual relationship with another person does harm to his own "personality" or "body".'

6.19a. Your body is a temple of the Holy Spirit: In 3.16 Paul said that the whole congregation was the 'temple' where the Spirit was present. Here in v. 19 he said that it was in each Christian that He, God the Holy Spirit, was present.

He was saying, 'You must choose which spirit you will receive and serve, the spirit which comes from your relationship with a prostitute or God's Spirit.' God's plan is that you receive His Spirit. Compare Matthew 6.24: 'No one can serve two masters', and Joshua 24.15: 'Choose this day whom you will serve.'

6.19b, 20. You are not your own; you were bought with a price:

1. **Not your own.** They had said, 'My body is my own. I can do what I like with it.' But here and in all the New Testament we learn that this is not so. Our bodies (i.e. our whole personalities) belong to God. So do our children and our friends, our time, our abilities and our possessions. So we are answerable to Him, who is the owner, for the way in which we use them.

2. **Bought with a price:** i.e. set free, as slaves could be set free if someone bought them from their master (see note on 'Redemption', p. 18). Once they were the slaves of their sin (1.30). Then they were set free to serve the true God. They were set free by the self-offering which Jesus Christ made. He 'paid the price'.

A reader of this verse once said, 'But I did not ask to be set free or to be bought or to belong to God or to be answerable to Him: Why should I be grateful? I would prefer to be answerable only to myself.' The truth is that, although it is difficult to be always answerable to God, it is far more difficult to live on our own, without God's commands or His support or His forgiveness or His presence.

STUDY SUGGESTIONS

WORDS

1. Which *three* of the following words mean the same or nearly the same as 'Kingdom' as Paul used it in 6.9,10?

   empire   sovereignty   rule   territory   country   supremacy

2. Which *three* of the following words mean the same or nearly the same as 'body', as Paul used the word in 6.13–16?
   person   corpse   corporation   personality   self   flesh
3. (a) What sort of behaviour did Paul refer to when he used the words 'immorality' and 'immoral' in 6.9,13,18?
   (b) How are these words translated in those verses in another language known to you?

CONTENT

4. For what two chief reasons did Paul tell his readers to find a Christian to settle their disputes?
5. What was Paul's purpose in saying that Christians would one day judge the world and angels (vv. 2 and 3)?
6. Why did Paul call it a 'defeat' (v. 7) if Christians had lawsuits with one another?
7 (a) Apart from the general word 'immorality', what *four* words or phrases did Paul use in chapter 6 to refer to *wrong* ways of using physical powers, including sexuality?
   (b) What *two* phrases did he use to refer to the *right* use of those powers?

BIBLE

8. What are the *two* chief thoughts which occur in 1 Cor. 6.4,20, and which also occur in Exodus 6.6 and Isaiah 43.1?
9. What teaching do we find in 1 Cor. 6.7 and also in Matthew 5.38–42?
10. (i) What did Paul mean by saying that his readers had been 'justified' (6.11)?
    (ii) In which *four* of the following passages do we find the same or similar teaching?   (a) Luke 10.29   (b) Rom. 5.1   (c) 1 Cor. 1.30   (d) 2 Cor. 6.1   (e) Gal 2.16

DISCUSSION AND RESEARCH

11. Paul was reminding his readers that they were a special community (p. 64). How can Christians be a 'special community' without cutting themselves off from others or feeling superior to them?
12. There are five stories on pp. 65, 66 about Christians taking other Christians to law in a public court. What do you think (from the small amount of information given) the injured people should have done in each case?
13. In your experience, why do Christians take other Christians to law in a public court rather than to a fellow-Christian? Give examples.
14. What can the leader of a congregation do to prevent disputes among the members?

15. 'All things are lawful for me' (1 Cor. 6.12a).
    (a) Why did some of the Christians at Corinth say this?
    (b) What is the difference between 'doing what you like' and 'Christian freedom'?
16. 'I will not be enslaved' (1 Cor. 6.12b).
    (a) What do you think are the *two* habits which are most likely to enslave your neighbours and yourself at this present time?
    (b) What can you do to be free from them and to help others to be free from them?
17. 'There are many ways in which human beings misuse their sexuality in relation to others' (p. 71). What are some of these many ways?
18. Is it 'immoral' for someone to have sexual intercourse with:
    (i) the person to whom he or she is betrothed or engaged?
    (ii) any friend or stranger who is willing? (See note on 6.13b.)
    (a) What do your Church authorities say in each case, and what reasons do they give?
    (b) What do you say, and what are your reasons?
19. 'Shall I make them members of a prostitute? Never!' (6.15b).
    (a) What sort of prostitutes exist in your country?
    (b) What laws (if any) exist concerning them?
    (c) If there are laws, how effective are they?
    (d) Who, if anyone, is trying to help prostitutes to lead a different sort of life, and in what ways?
20. 'Glorify God in your body' (6.20). Give *two* examples to show how a Christian can do this.

7.1–16 Marriage

If you get married, do so whole-heartedly

OUTLINE

7.1,2: You say that it is good if a man does not have sexual intercourse with a woman. I agree. But most men and women should get married.

7.3,4: You ask if married Christians should have intercourse together. They should indeed. And in this and in other matters each should respect the wishes of the other.

7.5,6: They may both agree not to have intercourse for a time, but that time should not be long.

7.7: I wish that you were all like me. But I realize that God has given us different gifts.

7.8,9: Those who are unmarried and widows should stay as they are. But if they cannot resist the desire to have sexual intercourse, it is better for them to get married than to spend their energy in fighting against that desire.

7.10,11: You ask if married Christians should now cease to live as husband and wife. No, there must be no divorce, as Jesus said.

7.12–16: Similarly, Christians who are married to non-Christians must not divorce them or leave them (vv. 12–14). But if non-Christian partners wish for a separation, let them have it (vv. 15, 16).

INTERPRETATION

A NEW SECTION

Chapter 7.1 is the beginning of a new section of Paul's letter. In the earlier chapters (1.10—6.20) he had chiefly written about the way in which Christians should treat each other. Now, in 7.1—11.1, he was mainly answering the question 'How should we Christians behave in a city where most people are not Christians?'

A REPLY TO LETTERS

In these verses (vv. 1–16) Paul was replying to a letter or letters which the Christians in Corinth had sent him on the subject of marriage. He used the words 'Now concerning . . .' to show that he was replying to them, not only in 7.1, but also in 7.25; 8.1; 12.1; and 16.1.

FALSE IDEAS

Two false ideas about marriage which many non-Christians and some Christians held at that time were:

1. That, 'since it is the soul (not the body) that is important, it does not matter what we do with our bodies. We can get married or have sexual intercourse with anyone we choose.' Paul had referred to this idea in Chapters 5 and 6.

2. That, 'since it is the soul that is important, we should avoid marriage and all bodily pleasures altogether.'

The Christians in Corinth were living among people who held ideas like these, and so it is not surprising that some of them began to think the same thoughts. When this happened, some members of the congregation wrote to Paul and asked for his opinion.

PAUL'S REPLY

Paul was, as we have already seen, against both those two ideas. His chief teaching was: 'Commit yourself either to remaining single or to being married. But if you are married, don't behave as if you were single.' Thus they had to make a choice between:

(a) Remaining unmarried and avoiding sexual intercourse (vv. 1, 7, 8),

(b) Marriage, in which partners had sexual intercourse (vv. 2–5a, 9a) and which was permanent (vv. 10–16).

If they did one of those two things, they would avoid having sexual intercourse with people in a wrong way ('immorality' v. 2a, see note on 6.13b).

PAUL'S REPLY AND OURSELVES

How far are Paul's words a guide for our own behaviour? They will be a strong guide if we remember that:

(a) Paul was replying to one or two questions which the Corinthians had asked. He was not writing a full statement about Christian marriage, nor making a list of marriage laws.

(b) Paul wrote out of his own experience and feelings about women and about sexuality, just as we who interpret what he said do so out of our own experience. If he was unmarried, for example, that would make a difference to what he wrote about marriage. This does not mean that what he wrote is not inspired by God. It means that we gain most from it if we remember who he was and what he had experienced. See note on 7.25a, p.93.

(c) Paul was expecting Jesus to return to the earth very soon (see 7.29 and 31). Thus the words, 'Remain single', do not show that Paul regarded sexuality as sinful. The words probably mean, 'Do not get married just at the moment when all human activities such as marriage are coming to an end.'

(d) Paul is not the only guide whom we have. When we read what he wrote in 1 Cor. 7, we should also read what God guided others to write in other parts of the New Testament, and what He has guided other Christians in each generation to say about marriage.

NOTES

7.1b: It is well for a man not to touch a woman: These words seem to have been part of a letter which a group of Corinthian Christians had written to Paul (see 'the matters about which you wrote' (v. 1a)). They had probably said, 'We think that now we are Christians we ought not to have sexual intercourse ('not to touch a woman'). So some of us are not getting married and others (who are married already) are not having sexual intercourse with their partners.'

Paul must have been glad that they were so keen to show that they had left the old life and were living a new life as Christians. By deciding not to get married they were certainly departing from the Jewish custom which was based on Genesis 2.18: 'It is not good that the man should be alone.' Secondly, he agreed that it was good not to marry. (Concerning this and the question whether Paul himself was married or not, see note on v. 7a.)

But he felt that some of these Corinthians were making serious mistakes.

First, they were too confident of their own powers. They were living in a city where there were a great many temptations. They ought not to remain unmarried unless they could stand up to those temptations. Secondly, as we saw above (p. 77), they seem to have been mistaken in their reasons for remaining single, e.g. saying that 'the better Christian you are, the less you concern yourself with material things such as your body, and the more you are concerned with the activities of the spirit'.

7.2b. Because of the temptation to immorality, each man should have his own wife:

1. Most of the Corinthian Christians should get married because there were so many temptations in Corinth for single people. Paul was *not* saying that in every generation the chief reason for Christians to get married is to avoid temptation. We have to notice this because people have so often misinterpreted both this verse and v. 9.

2. What, then, is the chief purpose of Christian marriage? Paul has not clearly told us in these verses, nor in any of his letters, but we can discover some of his teaching from vv. 3 and 4 below, from 6.16. 'the two shall become one', from 1 Cor. 11.11,12, and from Ephesians 5.33: 'Let each . . . love his wife . . . and let the wife see that she respects her husband'.

3. In this verse, however, there is a further thought: that when a Christian gets married, he marries one wife only. See 'his own wife'. Most Christians have said that if we read these words along with Mark 10.7 it is clear that a Christian should marry only one wife. The chief reason why they have said this is that God's purpose for marriage is 'to bring men and women to a new relationship with each other in Christ' (see TEF Study Guide No. 9, chapter 9, 'Polygamy'). If this is so, then monogamy is not a harsh law. Nor is it merely a custom which suited the people of Europe in the first century AD. It is God's invitation to a man and a woman to commit themselves to each other and to experience the best possible relationship together. Such a relationship cannot exist between more than two people.

7.3. The husband should give to his wife her conjugal rights: Paul was pointing here to the spirit of Christian marriage:

1. To *complete* and fulfil the marriage. No one was forced to get married, but married people should take marriage seriously, e.g. by having sexual intercourse together (see note on v. 5).

2. To *share* the marriage. In vv. 2–4 Paul repeatedly said that each partner in a Christian marriage has an equal right, e.g. to ask the other to have intercourse or to expect the other to be faithful. We see the same sort of teaching in Ephesians 5.21–25 and Colossians 3.18,19. It was new teaching for his readers, and Paul could not have given it unless Jesus had first shown what 'loving' really means. But we are right to ask how far Christians today are putting it into practice. (See also the notes on 11.3–9, where Paul seems to say something different about the position of women in marriage.)

'God's invitation to a man and a woman to experience the best possible relationship together' (p. 79).

This Land Dayak couple in Sarawak no longer live in the traditional village 'longhouse' of their people, but have built a small house of their own.

Do you think that this will help them to 'commit themselves to each other'?

3. To be *considerate*, e.g. a man who wants intercourse with his wife must consider her wishes. If she is menstruating, or if she has just had a baby or is breast-feeding a baby, she may not want it at all. On the other hand, no wife or husband should refuse the other unless there is a good reason for refusing (see v. 5 'by agreement').

Although Paul was teaching both partners to consider the wishes of the other, it seems that it was the men who especially needed this teaching. Then (as now) too many men expected their wives to remain faithful but claimed the right to be unfaithful themselves. Some years ago a Christian chief in Zaire who had learnt to read used to call his wives together every morning to listen to the Bible. He very often used to read Ephesians 5.22: 'Wives, be subject to your husbands'. The time came when one of his wives learnt to read, and she discovered v. 25: 'Husbands, love your wives as Christ loved the church and gave himself up for her.' The next time he read Ephesians 5.22, 'Wives, be subject to your husbands', she asked him to continue the passage. He did so, but after that time he did not choose Ephesians 5 so often!

If it is true that most men find it more difficult than women to be faithful in marriage, why is this so? Is it because men have a stronger urge for sexual intercourse? Because they remain for a much longer time capable of being a parent? Because men travel more?

See Study Suggestion 14, p. 86.

7.5. Do not refuse one another except perhaps by agreement for a season:

1. **'Do not refuse,'** i.e. do not refuse to have sexual intercourse. So Paul clearly taught that Christian husbands and wives should use their bodies, each for the sake of the other. As we have seen, there were many false teachers who taught that the spiritual part of a person was important and that their physical part was not important. There were Christian husbands and wives who said, 'Now that I am a truly spiritual Christian, I can only have spiritual intercourse with you, not sexual intercourse.' So Paul said 'Do not refuse . . .'.

In saying this he was following the teaching and behaviour of Jesus, who treated the physical body as a very important part of the whole person. He did not want to separate the physical part from the spiritual part. He came to bring 'wholeness' to people. That is why some people criticized Him, e.g. 'Why do your disciples not fast?' (Mark 2.18), and called Him 'a glutton' (Luke 7.34).

There is misunderstanding over the interpretation of this verse, for example:

(a) Some people have said that according to these words Paul was against parents controlling the number of children which they have. But Paul, who expected the Coming of Jesus very soon, could not have intended to give guidance to all future generations on the subject of birth control. In fact Christian parents are responsible for controlling very carefully the number of children they have.

(b) Others have said that Paul taught that Christians should have intercourse only in order to have children, and not in order to enjoy each other's bodies. But Paul did not say this. Sexual intercourse is a sign of two people sharing life, and the joy which comes from sharing life is a gift from God.

2. **'Except for a season.'** In saying this Paul was referring to a Jewish custom, by which husbands and wives did not have intercourse on the Day of Atonement. So in this verse he probably meant any plan by which husband and wife agreed, for example, to put aside the night for prayer.

But he said that it was 'unwise' to withhold from intercourse for a long time (see 'lest Satan tempt'). Husband and wife should soon 'come together again'. If they remained apart for too long one of them might say, 'I could not pray. I spent all the time struggling against the wish for intercourse.' Or one of them might be tempted during this 'season' to have intercourse with someone else. Paul evidently understood how powerful the sexuality of most people is. He was writing for ordinary people. (See note on p. 60 for 'Satan'.)

7.6. I say this ... not of command: 'This' refers to what Paul had suggested in v. 5. It means, 'I do not say that you should abstain from sexual intercourse. I am telling you to do so only if you both agree that there is a good reason for abstaining.' He did not want anyone to think that he regarded the physical activity of intercourse between husband and wife as wrong.

7.7a. I wish that all were as I myself am: This could mean, 'I wish that you were all unmarried, as I am' (see note on 7.25,26). But it is more likely that Paul was saying, 'I wish that you were all as free as I am to make the right choice, to remain unmarried if you believe that is God's will for you, free to get married if you believe that is right.'

7.7b. Each has his own special gift from God: The meaning is, 'God has given to each of you the gift of His grace which is suited to your own situation, e.g. if you are unmarried He has given you the gifts which an unmarried person needs. Whatever situation you are in, you can rely on Him to meet your need.'

7.9. It is better to marry than to be aflame with passion: As we have already seen, Paul wrote this because there were unmarried Christians in Corinth who were burning with a desire to use their sexuality in relation to another person. Some people had told them, (a) that it was not 'spiritual' to get married, (b) that the end of the world was coming soon and that it was too late to get married. So some of them were having intercourse with prostitutes and strangers.

So Paul here said, 'get married'. But neither in this verse nor in 7.1–16 was Paul describing the chief purpose of marriage for all Christians. He was advising one group of Christians in Corinth. Christians do not get married in order to avoid evil, e.g. the evil use of sexuality (see note on 6.13b). They get married chiefly in order to create something, e.g. a loving relationship between two people who are committed to each other, and a home where children may be supported and grow up, and where relatives and friends may be welcomed.

7.10,11. I give charge, not I but the Lord, that the wife should not separate from her husband:

1. *Their question.* It seems that the Christians in Corinth had put another question to Paul, 'Should married Christians cease to live as husband and wife in order to prepare themselves for the Coming of Jesus?'

2. *His answer* (vv. 10–12). 'No, they should not. What Jesus said about marriage applies to you.' In connection with this reply, we note:

(a) Paul based his reply on what 'the Lord' had said. This probably refers to Jesus's words according to Mark 10.9: 'What God has joined together, let no man put asunder.' Paul had not read Mark's Gospel, which was not written until ten years after he wrote to the Corinthians. But it must be that Christians had handed down by word of mouth some words of Jesus which contained the teaching, 'No divorce'.

(b) Paul may not have known the rather different teaching which Matthew has recorded. In Matthew 19.9 we read 'Whoever divorces his wife, except for unchastity, and marries another, commits adultery'. See also Matt. 5.32. Thus, according to Matthew, Jesus (like most Jewish teachers) allowed divorce if one partner had been "unchaste", i.e. unfaithful.

(c) Paul gave the same teaching to husbands which he gave to wives, as he had in vv. 2–4. This was different from the Jewish tradition, by which a man could divorce his wife but the wife could not usually divorce him.

(d) Paul knew that some married people find it impossible to live together, and to such people he said, 'Either separate and live apart like two single people, or work to restore the relationship which you once had.'

(e) Paul used two words 'separate' and 'divorce' in vv. 10 and 11, but in this passage both words mean 'divorce'.

3. *Paul's teaching and ourselves.* How far do Christians today follow Paul's instruction, 'No divorce'?

Roman Catholics try to follow it (and Mark 10.9) closely. They do not follow Matthew 5.32, and do not allow members to divorce and marry again, even if one has committed adultery. But there are special reasons why divorce may be allowed to Roman Catholics (e.g. if husband and wife have never had sexual intercourse.)

Other Christians also teach that when two Christians marry they do so in order to stay together for the whole of their lives. But they do not want to reject the words in Matthew 5.32 or to be stricter than Jesus was Himself. So most Protestant Churches allow divorced people to continue as full members, and are willing to remarry in church someone who has been divorced.

In some areas there is no divorce, because the problem is dealt with in other ways, e.g. in one West African Church, if a man want to be separated from his wife, he may be allowed to take a second wife, provided that he has made arrangements for the first one to live near-by or with her parents.

7.12. If any brother (i.e. a Christian) has a wife who is an unbeliever . . .: Here Paul was again answering a question which the Corinthians had put to him. It seems that they had asked, 'If one of us became a Christian after marrying a non-Christian, should he divorce his non-Christian wife?' (Perhaps such Christians were already divorcing their non-Christian partners, and perhaps people were accusing the Church of breaking up family life.) Again Paul answered, 'No, he should not divorce her' (v. 12). And again he said that what was true for the husband was equally true for the wife (v. 13).

Paul was referring to mixed marriages between Christian and non-Christian. But there are other sorts of mixed marriages, e.g. between members of different nationalities or tribes or castes, or of different races, or between Protestants and Catholics, or between members of two other parts of God's Church, or when one partner joins a sect which tells him or her to neglect the other partner. Marriages like this are increasing, as: (a) more people live in cities and meet people from different groups, and (b) more people feel free to choose their own partner. The partners in such 'mixed' marriages need support from their fellow-Christians in order that they may remain together.

7.14. The unbelieving husband is consecrated through his wife: The question which Paul was answering here seems to have been, 'Surely mixed marriages should be broken up, because the non-Christian partner will have a bad effect on the Christian?' Again Paul's answer was, 'No, let the partners stay together, unless the non-Christian asks for a divorce' (v. 15). 'You treat the children of a mixed marriage as "holy" and you let them belong to your congregation because one of their parents is a Christian' (see the last part of v. 14).

In this reply we may note:

(a) *The family.* Paul showed in this verse that he believed that a family should be united. He may have been thinking of a 'close' family, father, mother, and their children, or perhaps he had an 'extended' family in mind – a family which also includes cousins and uncles and aunts and grandparents, etc. But he did not want anyone to think that the Church was encouraging any sort of family to break up.

He seems to have thought of the family as if it were a single personality. What one member did had results for the rest of the family. See Acts 16.25–34. In this passage we read of the jailer 'believing in the Lord' and 'all his family' being baptized with him. Yet today when an individual decides to become a Christian, his family is sometimes divided, e.g. if the new Christian spends so much time with his Christian friends that he neglects his family.

(b) *Consecration and salvation.* Paul was not able to describe clearly the relation to God of the non-Christian partner in such marriages. On the one hand he said that the non-Christian was 'consecrated', i.e. had already been made 'holy', was already 'someone whom God had marked out for the special purpose of doing His work in association with Christ' (see note on p. 6).

On the other hand he wrote in v. 16 that such people would perhaps be 'saved' in the end because of their Christian partner (see note on p. 190 for the meaning of 'saved'). So in his opinion they were not yet fully consecrated.

Some readers are troubled to find that Paul was not able to describe clearly someone else's relation to God. But is this so surprising? How far can any Christian describe accurately the spiritual condition of another person? Perhaps the best thing that Christians can do, whose marriage partners are not Christians, is to give themselves increasingly to do the will of God and to pray that the other person may do the same.

STUDY SUGGESTIONS

WORDS

1. From the following list put together in pairs the words or phrases which have the same or nearly the same meaning in 1 Cor. 7.1–16;
   (a) touch (v. 1)   (b) conjugal (v. 3)   (c) unmarried (v. 8)   (d) be reconciled to (v. 11)   (e) unbeliever (v. 12)   (f) single   (g) have sexual intercourse with   (h) non-Christian   (i) restore fellowship with   (j) of a married person

CONTENT

2. What words from 7.1–16 show that Paul was answering a letter from the Corinthians?
3. What were the two wrong ideas about marriage which were common in Corinth?
4. What was the chief piece of teaching which Paul gave in 7.1–16:
   (a) To unmarried Christians?
   (b) To married Christians?
5. From which verse does it seem likely that Paul taught that a Christian should marry one wife only?
6. Why was it unwise, according to Paul, for a husband and wife to withhold from sexual intercourse for a long time?
7. Paul's chief teaching was, 'Commit yourself either to remaining single

or to being married. But if you are married, don't behave as if you were single' (p. 77).
In which two verses in 7.1–16 do you find this teaching most clearly expressed?

BIBLE

8. (a) What single piece of teaching concerning Christian marriage do we find in all the following passages: 1 Cor. 7.3,4; 1 Cor. 7.10,11; Eph. 5.21–25; Col. 3.18,19?
   (b) In which *two* of those passages is the teaching given most clearly?
9. What is the chief difference between the accounts of Jesus's teaching on marriage and divorce in (a) Matt. 19.9, and (b) Mark 10.11,12?

DISCUSSION AND RESEARCH

10. 'In 7.1–16 Paul was replying to questions which the Corinthians had asked' (p. 78). Since this is so, to what extent are his words a guide for Christians of today?'
11. 'Neither in 7.9 nor in 7.1–16 was Paul describing the chief purpose of marriage for all Christians' (p. 82).
   What do you think is the most important truth about Christian marriage which is *not* referred to in these verses?
12. 'When a Christian gets married, he marries one wife only' (p. 79).
   (a) How far is this a rule for all Christians to observe?
   (b) What is your opinion of the statement on p. 79 that monogamy is 'God's invitation to a man and a woman to commit themselves to each other and to experience the best possible relationship together', and that 'such a relationship cannot exist between more than two people'?
13. 'Each partner in a Christian marriage has an equal right' (p. 79).
   (a) Can each partner in practice exercise that right?
   (b) What encourages it to happen, or makes it *less* likely?
14. 'Men find it more difficult than women to be faithful' in marriage (p. 81).
   Do you agree? If so what other reasons, if any, would you add to those suggested on p. 81?
15. If you know of a Church in which there is a rule that all Church leaders must be unmarried, ask why the authorities made this rule.
16. 'The wife should not separate from the husband' (7.10).
   (a) For what reasons, if any, is it right for one partner to divorce the other?
   (b) Do members of the Church divorce each other, in your experience?
   (c) If they do, in what way, if any, does the Church discipline them?
17. 'The partners in mixed marriages need support from their fellow-Christians' (p. 84).
   (a) What sort of mixed marriages are the most common among Christians in your area?

(b) What difficulties do the partners in such a marriage face?

(c) How can fellow-Christians help them?

18. 'Paul showed in 7.14 that he believed that a family should be united' (p. 84). Compare this with Mark 10.28–31. Do we have to choose between the teaching of Jesus and the teaching of Paul? Or were each of them pointing to a different truth? Give reasons for your answer.

7.17–40 Contentment

Serve God where you are

OUTLINE

7.17: Do not try to change the position which you had in the world when you became a Christian.

7.18–20: I say this both to those who are circumcised and to those who are uncircumcised, because serving God matters much more than belonging to either group.

7.21–24: I say it to slaves, because all members of the Church are, in an important way, free already.

7.25–31: I say it to unmarried people because the way we live in this world is already passing away –

7.32–35: – and also because I believe that unmarried people are more free than married ones to serve God.

7.36–38: I say it to married people who have vowed not to have sexual intercourse;

7.39–40: And I say it to widows.

INTERPRETATION

In 7.1–16 Paul had said, '*Either* remain unmarried *or* get married. But don't have dealings with prostitutes.' Why did Paul add verses 17–40 to what he had clearly written in vv. 1–16?

It seems that Christians at Corinth wanted to change their position in the world: they wanted a new 'status' or 'rank'. Many unmarried women naturally wanted to get married. Slaves, who had experienced the change of leaving their old religion and now following Christ, naturally wanted the change of becoming free citizens. Paul did not say that they ought not to wish for such changes, but that there was something even more important than these changes, namely learning how to serve God in the position in which they were when they became Christians (see especially vv. 17, 20, 24).

Paul gave two reasons for saying this:

1. God would very soon bring such great changes into the world that it was unwise to try to make lesser changes now. (We have already met this teaching: see note on p. 78). Paul was probably referring to two sorts of changes which God would bring: (a) changes in the way that people behaved in society: 'the form of this world is passing away' (v. 31). (b) the greatest change of all when Christ would come again and the whole created world would come to an end. See the note below on v. 25b.

2. When someone becomes a Christian he experiences an inward change, i.e. a change in his relationship to God. This sort of change is so important that changes in 'outward' circumstances, e.g. his position or 'status' in the world, are less important by comparison.

Most present-day readers of Paul's words have wished at some time to change their existing position in the world and to get a better position, e.g. through being promoted in their job. Most lively and active Christians have this wish, and it is not a sinful wish. But for such people there is important teaching in Paul's words, e.g.:

(a) It is possible to be Christians in the position in which they are already (see note on v. 17 below). Even slaves could fully enjoy the love of God while still remaining slaves.

(b) God has done us the honour of making us members of a Church in which everyone is equally loved by Him and equally in need of His grace. The more we realize that we all have an equal share of God's love, the less anxious we shall be to obtain greater 'status' in society.

(c) There are some places in the world where you are more likely to get a better job and better pay if you belong to the Christian Church. A few years ago a Japanese could learn English more easily by belonging to the Protestant Church than in any other way, and people in Japan who knew English could get well-paid jobs. Whenever this is true, people may be tempted to become Christians in order to become more important or to earn higher wages. In many parts of the world this temptation does not exist, but in some it does exist.

Having noticed some of the teaching which Paul was giving here, we should also notice what he did *not* say. First, he did *not* say that Christians must accept things as they find them. We must admit that Christians have often been against changes, e.g. because they misinterpreted Paul's words such as v. 24: 'In whatever state each was called, there let him remain'. They have quoted these words, for instance, in order to maintain slavery, or to refuse to educate girls, or to keep apart people of different castes or classes. See note below on v. 21 concerning the teaching which Paul did give. Secondly, he did *not* say that if a Christian is offered a more responsible and a better paid job, he should refuse it.

'Do not try to change the position which you had in the world when you became a Christian.' But Paul 'did *not* say that Christians must accept things as they find them' (pp. 87 and 88).

What, if any, are the things in this picture of Jamaican children playing outside their homes, that you think a Christian should try to change?

NOTES

7.17. Let everyone lead the life which the Lord has assigned to him, and in which God has called him:
1. **Lead the life:** i.e. Let Christians live their lives instead of thinking how they might live them if their 'status' in the world was different. Let them be content to have the same position in the world which they had when they became Christians.

Many people think that they could be better Christians if they were in different surroundings; as a result they are sometimes restless and discontented. A builder made a long journey to the head of a theological school, and said, 'I became a Christian two years ago. So I want to leave my job and to enter your school.' The head said, 'It may be right for you to do that; on the other hand, God may want you to be a Christian builder where you are now.'

2. **The life which the Lord has assigned:** This does not mean that God has created some people to work with their hands and others to work with their minds, or that He has intended some to starve and others to grow fat, or that He wants some nations always to rule other nations and others always to be ruled over. The words simply mean, 'The life which God has given you to live at present.'

3. **In which God has called him:** See the note on 'call' on p. 4. God's 'calling' in this verse and in vv. 18, 20–22, 24 refer to His calling human beings to be Christians. Christians do sometimes believe (and say) that God is calling them to be a lawyer or a parent or a choirmaster, or they say that they have a 'vocation' (calling) to be a priest. But, generally speaking, writers in the New Testament do not use the word 'call' in that way. The reason is that when people believe that God is calling them to be Christians, it is so important that by comparison it is unimportant whether they are Christian bicycle-repairers or Christian bishops.

7.19. Neither circumcision counts for anything nor uncircumcision, but keeping the commandments of God: One of the important differences between Jews and non-Jews was that Jews were circumcised. In the Church in Galatia, some non-Jews were circumcised when they became Christians, in order to be like the Jewish Christians (see Gal. 2.3). On the other hand there were some Jews who 'removed the marks of circumcision' (see v. 18) in order that when they took part in the Greek public games (where the athletes were naked), they looked like Greeks. But Paul said to both circumcised and uncircumcised, 'Do not change these outward signs.'

Why did Paul say this? Because when someone makes the big change from another religion to the religion of accepting Jesus as his Lord, other changes (like being circumcised) are no longer very important to him. The important thing is whether or not he is 'keeping God's commandments', of which the central part, according to Jesus, is loving Him 'with all the heart and with all the understanding' (Mark 12.33). This is what 'counts' most.

When the wrong things 'count' most among Church members, divisions appear in the Church, just as there was division in Corinth between the circumcised and the uncircumcised. If the most important thing in life for one Christian is attending Holy Communion very frequently, or keeping the Church accounts correctly, then he will perhaps be separated from those who do not attend Holy Communion very frequently or keep Church accounts correctly.

It is a very difficult task for Christians to find out together what things really 'count' for most in God's eyes (i.e. what 'keeping God's command-ments' really means). But that is what Christians need to do afresh in each generation.

7.21. Were you a slave when called? Never mind:

1. *Paul's thoughts* in vv. 21–23 were as follows:

(a) If you are a slave, remain a slave (v. 21a).

(b) If anyone offers you freedom, accept it (v. 21b).

(c) But a slave who is a Christian already has one sort of freedom because (through Jesus) he has been set free from the overwhelming power of sin and evil over his life (v. 22a).

(d) And a Christian 'free man' is in one way a slave, because he owes total loyalty to Christ (v. 22b).

(e) Whether you are a 'slave' or a 'free man' in the world, obey Christ, because you belong to Him (v. 23a).

(f) Obey Christ before you obey any human being; e.g. do not let anyone (friend or political leader or husband or wife) take away your freedom to hold your own opinions – 'Do not become slaves of men' (v. 23b).

2. *Why did Paul not attack slavery?* First, because he believed that very soon there would be no slaves or slave-owners in the world, because all existing customs among human-beings were about to come to an end (v. 31b).

Secondly, because he believed that at that time in Corinth it was more important to lead people to believe in Jesus Christ who could change them, than to change the laws.

Paul's special work was to help people to change their relationship to God. He was a revolutionary, but the revolution he took part in was to overthrow the power of sin which prevents people from doing God's will. He was not engaged in a revolution to overthrow governments or the laws concerning the owning of slaves.

Thirdly, Paul did not attack slavery because there were very few Christians in the Roman Empire, and it was therefore impossible for them to have the laws changed.

People sometimes quote v. 21a in order to show that Paul (and

Christians since Paul) did not care about the conditions in which slaves and poor people live. In reply to this we may note that:

(a) Paul was saying what he believed to be the most important truth to state at that time to those Christians;

(b) Christians have often misinterpreted his words and are still doing so;

(c) Paul was in fact sowing the seed which in the end led to the abolition of slavery. When he reminded Philemon that he and his slave Onesimus were now brothers because they both belonged to Christ, he was giving the teaching which (after a very long time) put an end to the trade in the slaves who were taken from Africa. See Philemon vv. 15, 16.

3. *What should be the attitude of Christians to slavery today?* First, they should understand that many different forms of slavery exist. We usually label it 'slavery' when one person, because of his power, buys another human being and uses him. The Greek philosopher Aristotle said, 'A slave is a living tool, just as a tool is a lifeless slave.' But all customs and laws under which people use their power to deprive other people of freedom are forms of 'slavery', e.g. when one man because of his power allows someone else to work for him for insufficient wages, or when the staff of a hospital let poor people who cannot pay bribes stand in queues for many days before receiving treatment.

Secondly, Christians should work to change the conditions under which people live, if those conditions need changing. They should work to change those laws by which some human beings are allowed to treat other human beings cruelly and unjustly or simply to neglect them. So Christians are concerned with the wages which workers receive, the buildings in which they work, and the laws by which their employers employ them.

Thirdly, Christians should understand that it is not enough to change laws and conditions of work. They should work to let the Spirit of Christ come into the hearts and wills of the law-makers and the employers and the employed (and into themselves). Unless there is a change in people's hearts, changes in the laws will not benefit anyone very much.

So Christians should be concerned for the outward conditions under which people live and also for the spiritual condition of those people. A group of theological students found that this was true. They had been preaching the gospel for some weeks in villages in South East Asia. One had found that the people were so exhausted from lack of food that what he said did not seem to be 'good news' to them at all. Another had gone to preach in a prison and discovered that several of the prisoners were there only because they had voted against the local Police Chief at a recent election. A third found no women or girls to speak to because the men had forbidden them to leave their houses because they did not want the women to get new knowledge.

In their report the students said, 'We believe that we must care both for the souls and the bodies of the people to whom we go.'

7.25a. Concerning the unmarried: In verses 25–38 Paul said that most unmarried people should remain unmarried. His chief reason for saying this was that he believed the 'end of things' was near (see note on v. 25c). He gave other reasons which we study in the notes on v. 32 (p. 95).

What other reasons were there?

Some people think that Paul had never been married and therefore did not know how good a gift from God marriage is. This may be so. When Paul referred to a married apostle in 1 Cor. 9.5 he mentioned Peter and others, not himself. On the other hand, he had been a member of the Jewish Sanhedrin Council, and its members were probably all married. If so, then Paul was a widower who had experienced marriage.

Others think that Paul had to remain unmarried because only in this way could he do the work which he did. Is this perhaps one reason why Jesus did not get married? It is certainly one reason why some Christians become monks and nuns, and why some Hindus become Sanyasis. They are not escaping the duties of human beings, but are using a special 'gift'. They are showing that you can be a fully developed human being without getting married.

7.25b. I have no command of the Lord, but I give my opinion: Paul felt that he had no very clear answer to give to the unmarried. He had a clearer answer for widows in v. 40, 'I think I have the Spirit of God'. Paul, like other Christian leaders, felt that he saw God's will more clearly on some matters than on others.

The question is asked: 'How can we know on which matters Paul saw God's will clearly and on which he saw less clearly?' When we compare vv. 25–38 with v. 40 it is not difficult, but on other matters it is very difficult.

1. We can say that Paul saw God's will most clearly on any matter when his teaching agrees with: (a) what other writers in the Bible have said, especially writers in the New Testament; (b) what most Christian leaders have taught; (c) what seems to be true to ourselves (who have been promised the gift of the same Spirit who guided Paul).

For example, when Paul said in chapter 6 that a Christian should not have dealings with a prostitute, we regard what he said as an expression of God's will because other writers in the Bible and other Church leaders have said the same, and because we ourselves feel that his teaching is right.

2. Therefore we have to distinguish between different parts of Paul's teaching. Paul did so himself in this verse, as we have seen, and nearly all Christians do so. God has given us His Spirit in order to 'guide us into all the truth' (John 16.13), and He guides us to distinguish between things that are different. See 1 Corinthians 12.10 and Philippians 1.10, in which the words usually translated 'approve what is excellent' really mean 'distinguish between things that are different'. So also we have to distinguish those parts of the Bible which are of special value, from the other parts. Nearly all Christians do this, e.g. they find that a chapter from

one of the Gospels is more helpful to them than a chapter from the Book of Esther.

3. In doing so, we are always in danger of 'pleasing ourselves rather than God', i.e. of calling teaching 'good' when it agrees with our own ideas, and calling it 'less good' when it disagrees with the ideas and customs of ourselves and our friends. In spite of this great danger and temptation, we cannot escape the duty of 'distinguishing between things that are different'.

7.26. In view of the present distress, it is well for a person to remain as he is: Paul had advised slaves to be content to remain slaves. He also advised unmarried people to remain unmarried (and in v. 27a advised married people to stay married). He expressed the reasons for giving this advice in three ways:

1. Because of the 'present distress' (v. 26).

2. Because the 'appointed time has grown very short' (v. 29). (NEB has: 'the time we live in will not last long').

3. Because 'the form of this world is passing away' (see note on v. 31).

These phrases are like the words in Mark 13.8: 'This is but the beginning of the sufferings', i.e. of the sufferings which must take place before 'the end' (see also Mark 13.14–20).

Paul believed so strongly that this 'end' was close that he urged his readers to prepare themselves for it rather than to change their circumstances.

What should be the attitude of present day Christians? They must both:

(a) Be ready for the end of life as we know it, whether the end means the end of all life on earth coming through the sin of man and the explosion of nuclear bombs, or whether 'end' means the end of the present way of living.

(b) Do their work faithfully in the present world.

Christians are like farmers who hear that the State has plans to buy up their land for a new road at some time in the future. They must be ready to move to another part of the country, but until that time comes they must farm their present land as well as possible.

7.29. Let those who have wives live as though they had none: At first this seems to contradict vv. 2, 10, and 27 of this chapter, in which Paul told married people to stay married and to enjoy marriage to the full. But it is not a contradiction. He was saying, 'It is so important to prepare for the end that everything else becomes less important by comparison, even marriage (v. 29), mourning and rejoicing, and trading (v. 30).

7.31b. The form of this world is passing away: The ways in which human beings behave towards each other are always changing. (We may compare the way children spoke to their parents, or the way people treated the mentally sick or the way they travelled, fifty years ago, with the way we do these things today.) Paul probably did think that the whole created world would soon come to an end (see note on 1.7 and 3.13). But he was not saying that in this verse. Here he was thinking of the Corinthians' customs, e.g. concerning slavery and marriage, and saying that these customs would soon change. Therefore it was foolish to treat them as if they were everlasting.

Christians, like other people, sometimes treat customs as if God had intended the customs to last for ever, e.g. they may think the way in which a country is governed or the way in which parents bring up their children or the way in which a Church leader leads his congregation are never to be changed. But it is God alone who is unchanging. (See Psalm 103.15–17.)

7.32. I want you to be free from anxieties: In this verse and in vv. 33 and 34 Paul used the same word 'anxieties' (or 'anxious') with two different meanings:

1. In v. 32a the word means 'worrying' with the fear which shows that we do not trust God enough (see also Matt. 6.25–34). Paul, using the word in this way, said that a married person worries about such things as pleasing his wife (v. 33) so that he becomes divided within himself, not knowing how to please God as well as his wife (see also v. 34b).

2. In vv. 32b and 34a the word means 'having a keen interest in something or someone'. Paul said that unmarried people had a keener interest in the 'affairs of the Lord' than married people had.

There is teaching in these verses which we all need:

(a) That when we let worry overwhelm us, we are lacking trust in God.

(b) That 'pleasing the Lord' is our first duty, and that we must not put anyone in the place of the Lord.

But Paul also expressed other ideas with which most of us cannot agree:

(a) We cannot agree that unmarried people are keener than married ones to please the Lord (v. 32b). Happily married Christians can 'please the Lord' by the way they love each other. One newly married man said recently, 'When I received the love of my wife as we came together I discovered in a fresh way how greatly God loved me. I realized that it was God's love coming to me through her.' They do not have to choose between pleasing each other and pleasing God.

(b) We cannot agree that unmarried people are less 'divided' (v. 34) than married people. There are many other things besides marriage which may 'divide' people, and may draw their attention away from pleasing God, e.g. politics, sport, business, and so on (see v. 19).

Some readers are deeply troubled to discover that Paul expressed ideas with which they cannot agree. But we do not read Paul's letters because he wrote without error. We read them because Paul, inspired by God, was passing on to the Corinthians what was true for them at that time as far as he saw it. This is what a modern Church also tries to do. And, as we have seen, Paul was not God!

7.36. If anyone thinks that he is not behaving properly towards his betrothed . . . let them marry: The word translated 'betrothed' simply means 'virgin'. So who was Paul referring to in vv. 36–38? Probably to a

95

man and a woman who had married but who had vowed not to have sexual intercourse. See the NEB translation. So his advice was, 'If the man feels that he cannot keep this vow, then he should break it and have intercourse. But it is better if he can keep the vow.'

Readers may feel that so few Christians make vows of that sort that there is no teaching in this verse for us today. But that is not so. From Paul's words it is clear that:

(a) Self-control, which we can exercise in many different ways, is important.

(b) For married people, sexual intercourse is good and important – 'let them marry' (see note on p. 79).

(c) The vows which Christians make are their servants, not their masters. There was a Christian who made a plan to attend a daily prayer-meeting every day. He kept to this plan even when his wife was desperately ill and needed him to bring her water. His plan had become his master. Someone who is open to God's spirit is able to discover when it is right to keep a vow and when it is right to break it.

Note. There are two other ways of interpreting vv. 36–38:

1. According to the RSV, Paul was referring to a man and a woman who were betrothed to each other but who were not yet married.

2. According to the AV and RV, Paul was writing about fathers helping their daughters to find a husband.

But neither of these interpretations is likely to be correct. The word which is translated 'betrothed' in the RSV and 'virgin daughter' in the RV simply means 'virgin'.

7.39. A wife is bound to her husband . . . If the husband dies, she is free: In vv. 39 and 40 Paul added a note to what he had already said about widows in vv. 8 and 9:

(a) It is best if a widow remains a widow. Why re-marry since the end of the present life is so near?

(b) But she is free to marry.

(c) If she does marry again, she must remember her duties as a Christian ('marry in the Lord').

STUDY SUGGESTIONS

WORDS

1. Give an example to show what it means to have 'position' or 'status' or 'rank' in the world. (These three words are used on p. 87.)

CONTENT

2. For what two reasons did Paul tell his readers not to change their position in society?

3. To what *five* special groups of people did he chiefly write in 7.17–40?
4. (a) In which verses do we read that God 'calls' people?
   (b) To what does God call them?
5. Are the following statements 'true' or 'untrue'? In each case, give a reason for your answer:
   (a) According to 1 Cor. 7.17 God does not like Christians to change their jobs.
   (b) Christians should be concerned with the material conditions in which other people live.
   (c) Unmarried Christians are anxious to please God, but married Christians are anxious to please their wives (or husbands).
   (d) The ways in which human beings behave towards each other in society are always changing.
   (e) A Christian should never break a vow which he has made.

BIBLE

6. According to (a) 1 Cor. 7.19; (b) Gal. 5.6; (c) Gal. 6.15, it does not matter whether a Christian is circumcised or not. Express in your own words what *does* matter according to each passage.
7. Paul taught in 7.22 that all Christians are in one sense 'free' and also, in another sense, 'slaves'. What do we learn about being 'free' and being 'slaves' in each of the following passages?:
   (a) John 8.32–36   (b) Rom. 6.22
8. (i) What are the two different meanings of the word 'anxiety' which we find in 7.32–34?
   (ii) Which of those two meanings did the writer refer to in each of the following passages:
   (a) Matt. 6.25–34   (b) Luke 10.41   (c) 1 Cor. 12.25
   (d) Phil. 2.20   (e) Phil. 4.6
9. (a) Why do you think the note on 7.21 makes a reference to Paul's letter to Philemon?
   (b) After reading the letter, what difference do you think it made to the way Philemon treated Onesimus?

DISCUSSION AND RESEARCH

10. 'There are some places where you are more likely to get a better job if you belong to the Christian Church' (p. 88).
    Invite some friends in your congregation to tell you what difference (if any) joining the Church made to their 'position' in the world.
11. 'Paul did *not* say that Christians must accept things as they find them' (p. 88).
    A group of young Christians were asked what in their opinion was the most important change that should take place in the world during

the next ten years. One said 'sharing the world's grain', another 'abolishing nuclear bombs'.

(a) What would you say? Give a reason for your choice.

(b) What action (if any) could your group take to make the change happen?

12. 'When the wrong things "count" most among Church members, divisions appear in the Church' (p. 91).

(a) Give an example of a practice which in your opinion wrongly counts for a great deal in the Church and which therefore divides Christians.

(b) What action could you take to help to correct this error?

13. 'Do not let anyone . . . take away your freedom to hold your own opinions . . . Do not become slaves of men' (p. 91). Give two examples from your own experience of people becoming 'slaves' in this way.

14. 'Christians should be concerned about the outward conditions under which people live and also about the spiritual condition of those people' (p. 92).

(a) Give an example of (i) a Christian congregation; (ii) a Christian person being engaged in that two-fold 'concern'.

(b) When (if ever) is it right for Christians to use violence to change the outward conditions under which people are living miserable lives?

15. 'Concerning the unmarried' (7.25a).

(a) If you can visit some Christians who have decided never to get married, or write to them, find out why they took that decision.

(b) What difficulties so you think such people face?

16. 'Paul believed that this "end" was close' (p. 94).

(a) Do you (and your friends) expect that life on this earth will come to an end before 2000 AD? Give reasons for your answer.

(b) What difference does it make to the way you live whether you said 'Yes' or 'No' to question 16(a)?

8.1–13 True Knowledge

A Christian who truly 'knows' is one who truly loves

OUTLINE

8.1–3: (True and false knowledge) You who say that you have 'knowledge' have asked me about eating food which has been offered to idols. If you have true knowledge, you will not feel superior to other members, but will build them up by loving them.

8.4–6: (Paul's own belief about 'gods') You and I know that idols are only stones or wood. We know that they are not the shrines of real gods, because there are no gods, except the one God. There are many spirits or 'gods', but only one God, the Father, and one Lord (Jesus).

8.7–13: (Consideration for fellow-Christians) But some members are less certain about this than you are. They feel that if they eat such food it would be disloyalty to Christ (vv. 7–8). What will be the effect on them if you eat this food? That is what you must consider, because you and they are brothers. If you sin against them, you are sinning against Christ (vv. 9–13).

INTERPRETATION

1. *Why did Paul write this?* At that time many Greeks had ceased to believe seriously in their traditional gods, such as Zeus and Hermes (Acts 14.12) and Artemis (Acts 19.24). But they still held public festivals in the name of these gods, which all citizens were expected to attend. In the same way, many people today keep Christmas as a festival although they no longer believe that at the first Christmas 'God was in Christ'.

Christians in these Greek cities found it difficult to decide what part to take in such festivals. They found it difficult because during the festival animals were sacrificed to idols. Part of the meat which had been sacrificed was eaten in a temple (see 10.14–22), part of it was eaten in people's homes (see 10.27), and part was sold in the public market (see 10.25).

Some Christians in Corinth were certain that the gods (which the idols were supposed to represent) did not really exist. But others were less certain, and were afraid that by eating such food they might be disloyal to Jesus Christ.

Eventually those who were certain that idols were only stone or wood wrote to Paul and said, 'Surely it is all right to eat this food?'

2. *Paul's answer was:*

(a) The question is not a simple one. It is not only whether you should or should not eat that food.

(b) The important question is 'what is knowledge?' If you have true knowledge, you will have enough love to know what your fellow-members' needs are, i.e. if your eating that food spoils their awareness of God and causes them to return to their old gods, then you know you must not eat it. In this way you will 'build them up'.

(c) Your attitude to fellow-members, i.e. whether you love them or not, affects your attitude to God. You cannot separate the two.

3. *Living in the world:* The question arose because the Christians in Corinth were a minority in the city, and because they took part in the life of the city (see note on 5.10b). Modern Christians have similar questions to answer.

At the Hindu festival of Diwali in India, little trays of food called *prasad* (wheat flour) are offered to villagers who belong to other religions. Some of the food has been placed before a Hindu shrine. Many Christians do not accept it because they are afraid that if they did so they might be tempted to mix Hindu beliefs with Christian belief, or perhaps to give up Christian belief and to become Hindus again.

African Christians who sincerely want to serve their people sometimes have the opportunity of becoming chiefs. But the ceremony of installing a chief often includes prayers and sacrifices to the gods who were worshipped before there was a Church there. What is the result for those men and for their fellow-Christians if they take part in such ceremonies? What should they do?

Christians in most countries of the world ask the same question when they are invited to join such groups as a political party in which most of the members are anti-religious, or a secret society whose ceremonies include anti-Christian worship or whose members make promises to each other which prevent them from doing their duty to the nation as a whole.

From the above it is clear that there are two questions for a Christian to answer, not one only.

(a) The first concerns his loyalty to God. He must ask, 'If I attend this ceremony or join that society, shall I be giving to something else the loyalty which I owe to God Himself?'

(b) The second concern is love for his fellow-Christians; e.g. 'What ought I to do, knowing that my behaviour will affect other Christians? If I become a member of that club, will it hinder my fellow-Christians in their loyalty to God?' In chapter 8 Paul was chiefly drawing attention to this second question. We find further teaching about Christians 'loving' each other in 10.14–33 and chapter 13.

4. *Some words:* We should study the meaning which Paul gave to some of the words he used in this part of the letter:

Idol (vv. 1, 4, 7, 10): see note on v. 4.

Knowledge (vv. 1, 7): True knowledge includes loving other people. See note on v. 1.

Love (vv. 1, 3): Wanting the best things for other people. See p. 171.

Liberty (v. 9): Not 'doing what you like', but 'being free to do what is best for the whole Christian community.'

Conscience (vv. 7, 10, 12): Being conscious of God and aware of Him. See p. 105.

NOTES

8.1. 'Knowledge' puffs up, but love builds up.

1. *The letter from Corinth.* The group of Christians who had written to Paul had said, 'All of us in this group possess knowledge', i.e. about God. In this verse Paul was saying, 'I agree that we all have knowledge, but many of you have not yet found the true knowledge.'

2. *The 'gnostics'.* Having special knowledge or *gnosis* was so important

for some Christians that people called them 'gnostics'. For such people their minds and spirits were so important to them, that they regarded as unimportant what they did with their flesh (their physical bodies). As a result, they took little notice of the action of God in coming to this world in the flesh, as Jesus. Here Paul did not refer to gnostic beliefs in general, but to special ways in which this group at Corinth has misunderstood 'knowledge'.

3. *False knowledge.* Paul referred to someone who had a false idea of knowledge as follows:

(a) He concentrates chiefly on his own powers and on the fact that it is he who has the knowledge.

(b) He feels superior to those who do not have it. He is 'puffed up'.

(c) He is so interested in himself that he is not concerned with 'building up' the other members of the congregation. He lacks 'love'. (For further notes on 'building up' see notes on 10.23 and 14.4.)

(d) He thinks he is an advanced Christian but really he is only a beginner. Verse 2 means, 'If anyone thinks that the knowledge that he has makes him superior to other people, it shows that he has not yet found real knowledge.'

(e) He knows *about* God, but has not yet entered into a relationship with Him. See note on v. 3.

8.2. Know as he ought to know: Paul did not fully explain what true knowledge was, but he was referring to it in these words. Someone who 'knows as he ought to know' is someone who is learning the truth about God's will for man and for His universe, and who receives it humbly and gratefully as a gift from God, through Jesus Christ.

Readers may ask, 'Are not other forms of knowledge also "true", such as a knowledge of farming or radio or ancient history or law? People have obtained such knowledge through hard work and through it they are useful citizens.' To this we must reply that all such information and skill are certainly good and 'true', but that they are *not the same* as the knowledge to which Paul was referring. Perhaps people who have received many years of schooling and training are always in danger of forgetting this, e.g. they may easily forget that in the matter of discovering God's will concerning faithfulness in marriage or how to forgive one another or how to care for one's children, they are on a level with those who have not had that schooling. They may forget that because they have obtained a certificate or degree they are not for that reason better people than those who have no certificate. (This is because possessing anything, whether it is money or a Diploma or special knowledge, can easily make the owner less aware of the value of those around him or less sensitive to their real needs.)

8.3. If one loves God, one is known by Him: This does not mean that if we go on loving God, He will in the end reward us by putting us on the list of His friends. Paul meant:

1. If we have both 'knowledge' and 'love', and if we love both other people and God, it is a sign that God has accepted us. See also 1 John 4.19: 'We love because he first loved us.'

2. A truly knowledgeable person is one who not only knows facts about God (such as Paul referred to in vv. 4–6), but who also enters into relationship with Him. Writers in the Bible often use the phrases 'to know' and to 'be known', when they are referring to close relationships between people, including sexual intercourse, e.g. 'Adam knew Eve his wife' (Gen. 4.1).

8.4b. 'An idol has no real existence': The group at Corinth had written these words in order to explain why they ate food which had been offered to 'idols'. Paul in this verse agreed with these words, and in vv. 4–6 stated clearly that there is only one true God.

He did not mean that idols did not exist. He saw them, for instance, in Athens (Acts 17.16), which was full of stone idols of the traditional Greek gods and goddesses. He meant that the gods which the idols represented were not real.

What did he mean by an 'idol'?

1. Something (an image, a pillar, or a figure) which people make out of stone, wood, or metal (Judg. 17.3).

2. People made it in the belief that a god will live in it or will give power to it (Isa. 44.17).

3. By means of it people put their trust in something which they themselves have made, instead of trusting in God who has made them. This is why Israelites and Christians could not truly worship one God in addition to worshipping idols (Exod. 20.4,5).

4. It has no power to save people, because it represents nothing (Isa. 46.6,7).

5. Paul added (1 Cor. 10.19–21) that although it could do no good, it might do harm. See note p. 136.

Note: There are of course many things which are not really idols but to which some people pay the same respect which is paid to an idol, e.g. political parties, family advancement, success in business, progress through science. (A young works manager in Tokyo said, 'I will do anything to get to the top'.) We are treating such things as idols if we put them in the place of God, if we let them fill our life, if we rely on them above everything else.

8.4c. 'There is no God but one': In these verses Paul used the two words 'Gods' and 'gods'.

Gods. He simply said 'they do not exist'. There is only one God, and He has no rivals. This is what the Jews had said in their daily prayer (Deut. 6.4), and what we hear from every Muslim minaret. So the idols are in honour of nothing!

Today we see idols, fetishes, and shrines all over the world which are in

'People put their trust in something they themselves have made, instead of trusting God who has made them' (p. 102).

For nearly 900 years country people in Korea have believed – and some still believe – that these two stone statues have power to affect the lives of those who offer prayers to them. And in many places today people put all their trust in material possessions and modern technology, as, for example, this atomic energy establishment in India.

What 'idols' are you yourself tempted to trust in, instead of God?

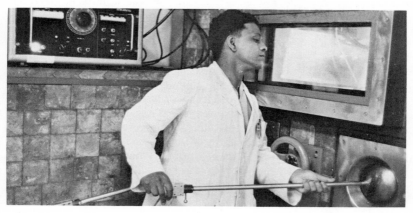

honour of gods which have names. Do their worshippers believe that those gods are real, or *only* names? The people of Bangkok maintain the Golden Buddha which weighs 6 tons and whose gold could be sold for many millions of dollars. Why do they maintain it? Hindus in Puri and many other places in India arrange for a huge chariot to be pulled through the streets at the festival of Jagat Nath, the 'lord of the Universe' (called Juggernaut by visitors). What sort of power do educated Hindus believe that Jagat Nath possesses?

gods (spelt with a small 'g'). Paul believed that invisible spiritual beings existed whom he called 'gods' or 'lords' in v. 5. He also called them 'rulers of this age' (1 Cor. 2.8), 'demons' (1 Cor. 10.19–22), 'elemental spirits' (Gal. 4.9). He did not believe that they were rivals to God, but that they were real and could cause harm to human beings. See note on 1 Corinthians 10.20, p. 136.

In comparing the one true God to the 'gods', Paul was not referring to an idea. He was thinking of behaviour, the behaviour of someone who shows that he believes that there is only one God by the way he is loyal to God, and by the way he gains strength and hope from God. This is the meaning of 'I believe in one God'.

8.6a. The God, the Father, from whom are all things and for whom we exist: The three truths Paul pointed to here are:

1. God is not unknowable. This is part of what Paul meant when he used the words 'Father' and 'Son' in writing about God. Jesus (the 'Son') has shown us what the 'Father' is like: 'He who has seen me has seen the Father' (John 14.9).

2. God is our creator on whom we depend. He did not only create the world in the past but gives life to the world continually: ('from whom are all things').

3. The chief aim of life is to serve Him ('for whom we exist'). People have all sorts of aims, e.g. to bring up a family, to make a lot of money, to defeat political enemies, and so on. It is a satisfying experience to have a clear aim. Life is miserable for anyone who has no aim. But the person who is most fully satisfied is one whose chief aim is to serve the one God (see note on 9.24–27).

8.6b. And one Lord, Jesus Christ, through whom are all things and through whom we exist: At this time of his life Paul was not yet able to call Jesus 'God'. He was still thinking out the relationship of Jesus to God. But already he felt that when he spoke of God he must also speak of Jesus.

Lord: The word does not here mean 'God', even though Greek translations of the Old Testament had used the word in referring to God. To Paul's readers in Corinth the word would mean someone to whom one owes loyalty and obedience.

Through whom: Jesus has been and is God's unique 'agent'. This is what a Christian means when he ends a prayer with the words 'through Jesus

Christ our Lord'. Jesus is the one through whom God showed Himself to the world, and through whom we exist as forgiven Christians. (It may be that Paul was also saying here what he said in 10.4: that Christ existed before He became man in our world. See note, p. 128.)

8.7. Their conscience, being weak, is defiled: In this section (vv. 7–13) Paul was addressing the group who were proud of having 'knowledge' and reminding them about another group at Corinth. This other group of Christians had previously been worshippers of idols, and they did not want to eat food which had been offered to idols. They still believed that the gods which the idols represented (Greek gods such as Zeus and Hermes) might really exist. Therefore, if they ate this food, they were not just eating, they were giving a sort of honour to another god and so being disloyal to the one true God.

In v. 7 Paul was saying to the group who had 'knowledge': 'Understand those Christians who have different problems from your own. This other group of Christians are not so strongly aware of God as the only true God as you are ('conscience' here means a consciousness or awareness of God: see note on 10.25, p. 138). If you love them, you will take the trouble to understand them, rather than despising them.'

This teaching is clearly important for any group of Christians today who are tempted to feel that they are the 'inner circle' or the well-educated members of the congregation, and fail to understand those who are not.

8.8. Food will not commend us to God: 'You are not better Christians,' said Paul to the group who had 'knowledge', 'than those who cannot eat the idol-food.' God does not approve of us because we are strong enough to eat the food without being disloyal to Him. Nor, on the other hand, does He approve of us because we refuse to eat the food, in our wish to be loyal to Him. He approves of us and accepts us for a quite different reason, namely, because He loves us with all our different weaknesses and strengths. See also note on 7.19, p. 90: 'Neither circumcision counts for anything nor uncircumcision.'

At a recent Revival Meeting in Eastern Uganda many thousands prayed and sang and talked together. Some of them showed their joy and gratitude to God by dancing. Others who were present did not join in, because in their minds dancing belonged to the traditional religion which they had left behind. The disagreement that followed seemed likely to spoil the meeting. But someone got up and said, 'Brethren, neither dancing nor not-dancing will commend us to God.' By saying this, he helped to bring back unity amongst the members.

8.9. Take care lest this liberty of yours somehow becomes a stumbling block to the weak: The 'strong' Christians need not only to understand their 'weaker' fellow-Christians, but also to realize that the 'strong' have the power either to build up the 'weak' or to destroy them (v. 11).

The 'strong' ones in Corinth, unlike the 'weak ones', were so certain that there were no gods except the one true God that they felt 'free' to eat the idol-food. But what is freedom or 'liberty' for Christians? Freedom is not 'doing what we please'. It is rejoicing in having been set free *from* the forces that once controlled us, and, therefore, being free *for* the service ('building up') of other Christians. Paul gave the same teaching to those who said 'Surely we can do anything that is lawful' (6.12; 10.23; see note on p. 69).

So the question that Christians ask is not simply 'What ought I to do?', but 'What ought I to do, knowing the result which my behaviour may have on other Christians?' (Paul said the same in 1 Cor. 10.23 and Rom. 14.7: 'None of us lives to himself'.)

This is not an easy question to answer. The example which Paul gave in vv. 10 and 11 refers to idol-food. If the 'strong' ones persuaded the 'weaker' ones to eat with them, they might be leading the weaker ones to do wrong, i.e. to do something which (they felt) showed disloyalty to the one God. (Paul was not here laying down a rule, e.g. 'Never eat idol-food', but saying 'Ask yourselves this question out of your love for your fellow-Christians'.)

Christians have to ask themselves this question very often indeed.

A headmaster used to have a number of children staying with him in term-time who came from villages far away where there were no schools. He and his wife often had to say to each other, 'If we read this book, we shall be more knowledgeable and more useful people. But if we read it, the children will read it. What effect will it have on them?'

Another example comes from a country where it is a tradition to give expensive meals at a wedding, so that hosts are sometimes in debt for the rest of their lives. One rich man (a Christian) said, 'I can afford to give the traditional meal, but if I do so others in our congregation, who are poorer, may think that they have to do the same and may be ruined.'

In the story on p. 105 we read of those who danced to show their joy in the Lord. They had to ask and answer this question: 'Are we, by dancing, tempting some other Christians to return to their old religion?'

8.12. Sinning against your brethren . . . you sin against Christ:

1. **Brethren:** The 'strong' in the congregation are brothers to the 'weak' and, therefore, they must take care not to cause them to do wrong. 'Strong' and 'weak' belong together as closely as a brother and sister of the same father and mother. (In addition to this, Paul had said in v. 11 that the 'weak' ones were precious and important people because Christ had died for them.)

2. **Sin against Christ:** Anyone who causes a 'weak' brother to do wrong has not only sinned against him but also against Christ. Perhaps we find it convenient to talk about our duty to our neighbour on the one hand and our duty to God on the other hand, but in practice the two cannot be separated. The two commandments become one commandment, i.e. 'love' (Mark 12.29–31). Paul discovered this when, on his way to persecute

Christians, he found that it was Jesus whom he was persecuting (Acts 9.4; see also Matt. 25.40).

During a Church service in South India, members were greeting each other, as is their custom, by taking the hands of their neighbour in their own, and saying 'The Peace of the Lord'. A visitor who had not been in India before whispered to her friend, 'I won't do it. I have come here to meet my God, not my neighbour.' The friend said, 'Do it, and you may discover that your neighbour is the nearest place on earth where you can offer your love to God.'

8.13. I will never eat meat: This is not a vow which Paul made, nor is it a law that Christians must not eat flesh. Paul was saying, 'If I discovered that by eating one sort of food I was causing a fellow-Christian to do wrong, I would give up eating that food. In other words, I intend to practise what I have preached to you in this chapter.'

STUDY SUGGESTIONS

WORDS

1. (a) By what word is 'God' translated in another language known to you?

    (b) What does that word mean in ordinary conversation?

2. What does 'conscience' mean in chapter 8?

CONTENT

3. (a) To what question or statement was Paul replying in chapter 8?

    (b) What was the most important part of his reply?

4. What or whom did Paul want his readers to 'build up'? (8.1).

5. 'The question arose because the Christians in Corinth . . . took part in the life of the city' (p. 99).

    (a) Why did 'taking part' create questions and problems for those Christians?

    (b) Why does it do so today? Give an example.

6. (a) What was the difference, according to Paul, between God and gods? (see 8.4–6.)

    (b) What is your own opinion?

BIBLE

7. (i) What did the writer say about idols in each of the following passages?

    (a) Exod. 20.3–5   (b) Ps. 115.4–7   (c) Isa. 46.1–7

    (ii) What did Paul say about idols in each of the following verses?

    (a) 1 Cor. 8.4   (b) 1 Cor. 10.14   (c) 1 Cor. 12.2.

8. Read Romans 14. In which four verses do you most clearly see the same teaching as we see in 1 Cor. 8.9–12?
9. What single truth do we find in all the following passages?
   Matt. 25.37–40   Acts 9.3–5   1 Cor. 8.12.

DISCUSSION AND RESEARCH

10. 'The gods which the idols represented are not real' (p. 102).
    (a) Find out what traditional idols, fetishes, and shrines there are in your country or neighbourhood.
    (b) Do the worshippers of these idols or shrines believe that their gods are real, or only names?
    (c) Do they believe that the god lives in the idol or gives it power?
11. 'Things to which people pay the same respect which is paid to an idol' (p. 102). What sort of 'things' do you think many people are tempted to treat in this way at the present time?
12. 'What ought I to do, knowing my behaviour will affect other Christians?' (p. 106).
    (a) If you are a Christian and were invited to the Hindu festival of Diwali, would you take the *prasad*? (p. 99). How would you reach your decision?
    (b) If you had been at the Revival meeting referred to on p. 105, would you have danced or not? How would you have reached your decision?
    (c) If you were the headmaster or his wife referred to on p. 106, in what ways, if any, do you think you would have changed the way you lived because of the children who lived with you?
13. 'Freedom, for Christians . . . is not "doing what you like"' (p. 106).
    (a) How free are Christians?
    (b) A Christian student said: 'We are only free to choose whose slave to be. We are not free in any other way.' What is your opinion?

9.1–18   Self-discipline

We give up our 'rights' for the Gospel's sake

OUTLINE

9.1–2: You can be sure that I am a real apostle, because I saw Jesus and because of my work among you.

9.3–7: We who are apostles have the right to be given support and hospitality by the Churches (vv. 3–6), just as workmen have the right to be paid for their work (v. 7).

9.8–12a: According to Moses's law even an ox should be allowed to eat some of the crop. So also should those who plough and thresh. We apostles

have an even greater right to be supported by those amongst whom we work.
9.12b: And yet, although I have this right, I have given it up. I have disciplined myself in this way in order that the Gospel may be preached effectively.
9.13–14: But I repeat, it is my right to be supported, just as it was the right of the Jewish priests. And Jesus Himself said that His workers should receive wages.
9.15–18: Yet I have given up my rights. The only thing I boast about (and the only reward I receive) is that I preach the Gospel without pay.

INTERPRETATION

In chapter 8 Paul had said, 'You have the right to eat food which has been offered to idols. But be willing to give up that right for the sake of other Christians.' Now, in 9.1–18, he said, 'In the same way, I, as an apostle, have the right to receive payment. But I have given up that right, so that no one should say that I am preaching in order to make money. I have given up that right, so that as many people as possible may accept the good news about Jesus.'

The word that Paul used to refer to himself in these verses was 'apostle' (see note on p. 5). He had already assured them that he was a real apostle and that Jesus Himself had commissioned him (see 1.1). But perhaps since he wrote that, he had received further news that some of the Christians at Corinth were saying that he could not be a real apostle because he did not receive payment or hospitality. So in chapter 9 he wrote once again about himself as an 'apostle'. See notes below on v. 1 and v. 16b.

Although Paul was answering questions about himself, some of the questions are important for leaders of Christian congregations today, e.g. 'Can they do their work best by being paid by the Church and by being full-time leaders, *or* by earning their wages by other work, like Paul?' See note on v. 12b.

NOTES

9.1a. Am I not free? Am I not an apostle? Paul was saying: 'You say that you are free (see 8.9), and I agree that you are. But I have even more right to be free, because I am an apostle. If you doubt that, remember I have seen Jesus and remember the work I did among you; that shows that I have the authority which an apostle has.'

1. **Apostle:** What was an apostle?

(a) The Greek word means someone who has been 'sent'. We could translate the word as 'missionary' or 'envoy' or 'representative'. (See also Phil. 2.25, where it is translated 'messenger'.) For Christians it usually means 'someone whom God sends'. But a Christian apostle is not only a person who has been 'sent'. He comes as God's representative or agent. He acts and speaks with God's authority. So in this sense all Christians can be called 'apostles', e.g. they serve their fellow human beings, believing that God has sent them to do so.

(b) But among early Christians the word usually meant 'the Twelve', or at least those who had been a 'witness to the resurrection of Jesus' (Acts 1.22,26).

(c) There were, however, others who were also called apostles, with the result that there was some doubt who was an 'apostle' and who was not. The author of Acts used the name only for the Twelve (1.21–26) and for Paul and Barnabas (14.14). But Paul wrote in 1 Cor. 15.1–11 about Jesus's 'appearing to the twelve' (v. 5) and then added 'then to all the apostles' (v. 7). In Romans 16.7 he gave the names of two other 'apostles'.

(d) Nowadays the English word 'apostle' usually means one of the Twelve or St Paul. It may also be used for whoever first carried the Gospel to a particular country, e.g. St Patrick is sometimes called the 'apostle' of Ireland.

2. Why did Paul have to tell the Corinthians he was a real apostle?

(a) Because some Christians at Corinth were saying that he was teaching only his own ideas, not God's, and he wanted to emphasize that this was not so. He had been 'sent' by God.

(b) Because there were people at Corinth who wanted to follow other leaders instead of Paul, saying that they would 'examine' him (v. 3).

(c) Because, as we have seen, there was doubt as to who was an apostle.

(d) Perhaps because being humiliated had always been more painful to Paul than it is for most people (see 2 Cor. 11.5). If this is so, then he probably felt that people were questioning his authority even when they were not doing so. Certainly in 2 Corinthians 10.8 he seemed to know that he talked too much about his own authority.

9.1b. Have I not seen Jesus our Lord? Paul said this to show that he was a real apostle. Of course not everyone who saw Jesus was an apostle. But according to Acts 1.22 no one could be an apostle unless they had seen Jesus.

What 'seeing' did Paul refer to? From Acts 9.1–7 and 1 Corinthians 15.8 it is clear that he was referring to the vision which he had of the risen Jesus on the road to Damascus. This vision, more than anything else, made Paul sure God had called him to be an apostle. But it did not make others sure. They had not seen his private vision.

Does this mean that Christians cannot usefully speak about their private experiences of God? No. But it does mean that the behaviour which results from those experiences is far more likely to convince someone else of the truth of the Gospel (see Matt. 5.16; 7.16).

9.2. You are the seal of my apostleship in the Lord: The second way in which Paul showed that he was a real apostle was by referring to the work which he had been able to do in Corinth. It was because of him that the Church existed in Corinth, members had received the gifts which God's Spirit gives, and they were living a new sort of life. He said that this was a 'sign' that he was an apostle.

The Greek word he used for 'sign' means 'seal'. When someone had written an important document and wanted to prove that he and no one else had written it, he dropped some soft wax on to it, and then pressed a metal or stone seal on the wax. The seal had on it a letter or a diagram to indicate the owner. So today someone in authority may put a 'seal' on a legal document to show that he regards it as a true statement, and that it is a document with authority.

The Church in Corinth was Paul's seal. It was a sign that he was one whom God had commissioned as an apostle. See 2 Corinthians 3.2 and 3 (where Paul called the Corinthians 'the letter which everyone could read') and 2 Cor. 12.12.

What does this mean for us? If we see that a leader of a Church has a large number of members in that congregation or that he is in charge of many congregations, does that prove that God has really called that person to that work? Or if people call that leader 'successful', does that show that God has chosen him for that work? No. Paul did not mean that. In Pakistan for example, a Christian leader may be a dedicated servant of God and yet for 20 years never see more than a handful of people in the congregation. Paul meant that his actions rather than his words would persuade the Corinthian Christians that God had commissioned him as an apostle.

9.4. Do we not have the right to our food . . . ? We shall see in vv. 12b–18 that Paul had given up his rights as an apostle. These 'rights' were to receive hospitality for himself and (if he were married) for his wife also.

Paul gave four reasons for saying that he had a right to this:
1. The other apostles receive this hospitality.
2. All workmen have a right to some reward (vv. 7–13).
3. The Old Testament said so (vv. 8–10).
4. Jesus said so (see note on v. 14).

Not all religious bodies follow this teaching. Not all give their leaders payment. But in Churches which do follow it, what reward have these leaders a right to receive? We cannot give a general answer, since the reward or payment depends on (a) the agreement which they make with their Church authorities when they are commissioned; (b) the amount of support which the congregation can give; (c) whether the leader works full-time for the Church or not.

But many full-time Church leaders today receive a house to live in, money to buy food and clothes for themselves and their families, and a pension when they retire.

9.5a. Do we not have the right to be accompanied by a wife? In chapter 7 Paul explained that, although he himself was not married, marriage was good. Now in 9.5 he added that:

(a) The apostles had the right to be married.

(b) Some of them were married.

(c) Their wives as well as themselves had the right to be given hospitality.

Today, more and more wives of Church leaders are helping their husbands in their ministry. Some of them take an active share in the work, e.g. leading a women's group or visiting members of the congregation. On the other hand, other wives regard it as their chief work to be a good wife to their husband and a good mother to their children, so that the home of the Church leader may be a sign that God is at work. (We have spoken here as if all Church leaders were men, as they were in Paul's time. But more and more women are becoming leaders in the Church, and their husbands are having to discover how to help them, e.g. by helping with the household work or spending time looking after their children.)

9.5b. The brothers of the Lord, and Cephas: The 'brothers' were either the sons of Mary and Joseph, born after Jesus's birth *or* the sons of Joseph by a former wife. Mark (6.3) referred to four of the brothers by name, and also to His sisters.

Paul probably mentioned Cephas (Peter) because Cephas (and perhaps his wife) had visited Corinth. We have seen (1.12) that some members of that Church had formed a special group and called themselves the 'followers of Cephas'.

9.9. Is it for oxen that God is concerned?

1. *The chief thought* in these verses is that 'all those who work have the right to receive a reward.' In order to support this teaching, Paul quoted a law (Deut. 25.4) by which all oxen must be allowed to eat the grain while they were threshing it. They must not be muzzled.

2. *Method of interpretation.* Paul interpreted that Old Testament passage as an 'allegory', i.e. he treated the language as picture-language rather than explaining what the words meant to those who wrote them. This is why he wrote in vv. 9 and 10: 'When God inspired Moses to make that law, He was not thinking of the needs of the oxen, He was thinking of the needs of Church leaders today to receive a reward.'

Paul often used this 'allegorical' method of interpretation. It was the way in which he had been trained to interpret the Scriptures by the Jewish Rabbis. Most Christians today, on the other hand, find that it is unwise to use this method, because it is too easy to make the passage mean what we want it to mean! In order to avoid this danger, we should find out what the words meant to the writer when he wrote them. After we have done that we are more likely to discover what message God wants to give us through that passage. (In the case of Deuteronomy 25.4 we see that Moses was saying that farmers must treat their oxen well.)

3. *The treatment of animals.* It may be that Paul was not interested in the treatment of animals, and that perhaps he thought that God was not interested in their treatment either. It may be that the Greek philosophers had influenced Paul, those philosophers who thought highly of creatures who could think and reason, but who were not concerned with other creatures.

Whether or not Paul held those views, we should note:

(a) According to Jesus, God is concerned about the welfare of the whole of His creation: 'Your heavenly Father feeds . . . the birds of the air' (Matt. 6.26).

(b) It is therefore important that we treat God's creation as one. Human beings and all other living creatures share God's earth and its atmosphere. 'These *all* look to thee to give them their food' (Ps. 104.27). Human beings are affected by other creatures. Other creatures are affected by human beings.

9.12b. We have not made use of this right: Paul was able to give up his 'right' to be rewarded because he earned enough money by making tents out of rough goat-hair cloth. When he first came to Corinth, he stayed with Aquila and Priscilla who were also tent-makers, and he and they worked together (Acts 18.1–3).

The results of this were: (a) that the members of the newly-founded congregations did not have to provide him with money; (b) that no one could say that he had invented a new religion in order to make a profit dishonestly ('We endure anything rather than put an obstacle in the way of the Gospel of Christ'). Another result was that many Christians regarded him as having less authority than those apostles who did accept a reward.

Since the time of Paul there have always been fully-authorized Church leaders who earned their money by doing other work as well. Leaders of 'house-churches' (see p. 150) are usually unpaid and earn their money in the same way as the other members earn it.

A visitor to Hong Kong found recently that out of sixty authorized ('ordained') Church leaders in the Chung Hwa Sheng Kung Hui (Anglican Church), fifteen were earning their living from other work and were not paid by the Church. Most of them were teachers. There were also a public health inspector, a radiographer, and a marine engineer. In the diocese of Nyanza, Tanzania, recently, fifteen men were ordained to be leaders ('shepherds') of congregations. Six of them are earning their living by doing other work as well, e.g. as taxi-drivers, teachers, government employees. In each of these cases the bishop of the diocese had encouraged this sort of leadership for two reasons. First, because some of the congregations were very poor and could not have paid their own 'minister'. Secondly, because the 'tent-making leaders' were usually in closer touch than the 'full-time leaders' with the people of the city, especially the traders and public officials. (We may think of Paul learning much, both about the good and about the evil in human beings, as he bargained for his goat's-hair in the market at Corinth.)

9.14. The Lord commanded that those who proclaim the Gospel should get their living by the Gospel: This is the fourth reason Paul gave for saying that he had a 'right' to payment for preaching the Gospel, i.e. 'Jesus said so' (e.g. in Luke 10.7).

It is one of the few passages where we can see that Paul had been told some of Jesus's sayings. (Other passages are 1 Cor. 4.13; 7.10,11; and Gal. 6.6.) It may be that he made only a few references to Jesus because he had been told very little about Jesus's teaching, or (more likely) because it was the presence of the risen Jesus Christ (rather than His teaching) which had changed his life.

9.15. My ground for boasting: The sentence means 'No one shall make my boast an empty thing, i.e. my boast that I preach without payment.'

In Paul's letters 'boasting' is used in two different ways. Sometimes it means 'thinking that we can live uprightly without God's grace'. In 1.29; 1.31; and 3.21 Paul criticized such boasting. But in other passages it means 'being glad about my achievements'. This is its meaning here (see also 2 Cor. 7.4; 7.14; 8.24; 11.18; 11.21).

Some readers think that in 9.15 Paul showed us one of his weaknesses, and that he had given into the sin of pride (pride that he was better than those apostles who did accept payment). This may be so. Of course Paul had weaknesses.

But others say that although he used the word 'boast' he only meant 'I rejoice that with God's grace I have been able to do this work without payment'.

9.16b. Necessity is laid upon me. Woe to me if I do not preach the Gospel: For notes on 'preaching' see 1.17 and 2.1. Paul's chief thought in this part of the chapter (vv. 15–18) was: 'Being able to preach without receiving payment is the only reward I want.' He explained this in the following way:

'I am not asking you to give me money or hospitality. I would rather die than allow anyone to take away my boast that I preach without payment (v. 15).

It is not preaching that makes me want to boast. Preaching is something which I cannot help doing. I should be a lost person ('woe to me') if I did not do it (v. 16).

Perhaps if I had chosen to do this work, I should deserve a reward. But I did not choose it. Christ chose and commissioned me (v. 17). But I do have a reward. The reward is preaching without payment' (v. 18).

We see here Paul's chief motive or reason for preaching. There are many good reasons why Christians do the work of preaching; e.g. (1) they believe they have been commissioned by God; (2) they have been authorized by the Church; (3) by doing so they have the joy of using gifts which

God has given them; (4) they are paid to do it. There are of course other reasons why people preach. Not all of them are good reasons.

Paul's chief reason was the first of those mentioned above: he had been commissioned by Christ. He said this also in Galatians 1.15,16, and in his speech to King Agrippa (Acts 26.15). He had not chosen to be a preacher. In this matter he was Christ's slave (Rom. 1.1). Therefore he did not expect payment.

Some of the great prophets had a similar experience, e.g. Amos 3.8; Jeremiah 1.7; Ezekiel 3.16,17. People who have had an experience like this have a special strength in themselves when they meet opposition and persecution.

9.18. What then is my reward? Paul did not accept financial rewards. But there was a different sort of reward which he certainly had. This reward, as we have seen, was being able to preach without payment.

Jesus often spoke about rewards. Some rewards come to Christians in this life, other rewards come after this life (see p. 34, note on 3.8). Therefore Church leaders are right to enjoy the rewards of their work. In most countries these rewards do not usually include a lot of money. When a group of Church leaders in Nairobi were studying this passage, they made a list of rewards (other than money) which had come to them from their work. The list was:

A position (sometimes a position of honour) in the community;

A deeper understanding of the Bible;

A greater freedom than most workers have to plan the day's work;

Time to see members of one's family, because Church leaders' work is often based on their home;

The joy which comes from seeing the difference which one has been able to make to people's lives;

The friends which one makes while doing one's work.

When the list had been made, one member of the group asked the others, 'Would you rather have rewards like this or go without them and receive more money?'

STUDY SUGGESTIONS

WORDS

1. (a) Which *four* of the following phrases have the same or nearly the same meaning as 'having rights'?
being entitled   having the strength   having the authority
being free   being forced   having the right   being pleased.
(b) In which *six* verses of 1 Cor. 9.1–18 do we read about 'having rights'?

CONTENT

2. What is the thought which Paul expressed both in chapter 8 and chapter 9?
3. What people are called 'apostles' in the New Testament?
4. What did Paul mean when he called his readers the 'seal' of his apostleship?
5. (a) For what *four* reasons did Paul say that 'all workmen have the right to a reward' (p. 111)?
   (b) To what sort of payment did he say that he had that right?

BIBLE

6. 'I have the authority which an apostle has' (p. 109).
   (a) In which verse of 2 Cor. 10 did Paul refer to his authority as an apostle?
   (b) Why did he do so?
7. What is the connection between:
   (a) 1 Cor. 9.1 and Acts 9.17 and 1 Cor. 15.8?
   (b) 1 Cor. 9.14 and Matt. 10.10 and Luke 10.7?
8. 'The brothers of the Lord' (9.5).
   What do we learn about Jesus's brothers and sisters from the following verses?
   (a) Mark 6.3; (b) John 7.5; (c) Acts 1.14; (d) 1 Cor. 9.5; (e) Gal. 1.19
9. (i) Whose work and (ii) what sort of work does each of the following passages refer to?
   (a) Acts 20.34 (b) 1 Cor. 4.12 (c) 1 Thess. 2.9 (d) 2 Thess. 3.8.

DISCUSSION AND RESEARCH

10. 'If people call that leader "successful". . .' (p. 111). What is a truly successful leader of a Church?
11. 'Do we not have the right to our food and drink?' (9.4). Many workmen belong to a trade union in order to obtain their rights. Should full-time Church leaders form their own trade union? Give reasons for your answer.
12. 'Do we not have the right to be accompanied by a wife?' (9.5).
    (a) What are the advantages and disadvantages of a Church leader's wife sharing his work with him?
    (b) When a man is being interviewed for the position of leader of a congregation, is his wife also interviewed, in your experience? What are the advantages of doing this?
    (c) If the leader's wife was present at the interview and you were conducting the interview, what questions would you want to ask her?
13. 'Treat God's creation as one . . . Human beings are affected by other creatures . . . Other creatures are affected by human beings' (p. 113). Give examples to show: (a) How human beings are affected by other

creatures; (b) How other creatures are affected for good by human beings; (c) How other creatures are affected for evil by human beings.

14. 'Paul earned enough money by making tents' (p. 113).

(a) How many authorized Church leaders are there in your neighbourhood who are paid from doing other work and not by the Church?

(b) From what work are they paid?

(c) What do their congregations think are the advantages and disadvantages of having a leader of that sort?

(d) What is your own opinion?

15. 'Woe to me if I do not preach the gospel' (9.16). Ask one or two Church leaders (or yourself if you are one):

(a) What were their chief reasons for preaching when they first began to do so?

(b) What are their chief reasons now?

16. 'What then is my reward?' (9.18).

Apart from receiving wages, what do you think are the rewards of being a Church leader?

9.19–27 Freedom to Serve

I am free to serve all groups equally

OUTLINE

PART 1

9.19a: Since I do not accept payment from any one group of people, I am free to serve all groups equally.

9.19b: My goal is to lead them all to believe in Jesus Christ.

9.20–22: Because that is my goal, I do not keep myself apart from any group, but I put myself in their shoes, whether they are Jews (v. 20a), Christians who still keep Moses's law (v. 20b), Gentiles (v. 21), or immature Christians (v. 22).

9.23: I do this, not only so that they may believe the Gospel, but so that I myself may have the benefits which the Gospel brings.

PART 2

9.24a: Runners in athletic sports have a clear aim, namely, to win.

9.25a: We Christians also need to have a clear aim.

9.25: Athletes give up many things in order to win. We Christians also must give up our rights to many things in order to obtain our prize.

9.26: I have a clear aim, like a boxer.

9.27: And, like a boxer, I give up many things. If I did not, I should lose the benefits which I have proclaimed to others.

INTERPRETATION

In chapters 8 and 9.1–18 Paul had written about 'giving up rights', e.g. the right of Christians to eat food which had been offered to idols (chapter 8), his own right to receive payment (9.1–18). Now in 9.19–27 he referred again to what he gave up.

First of all he had given up the right to keep himself apart from those who held different ideas from his own. The people of Corinth were divided into groups. If you were a Jew, no one ever told you to make friends with a non-Jew (a Gentile). You had a right to be apart from them. It was the same in the Christian congregation. Christians who still kept the Jewish law felt that they had a right to keep themselves apart from Christians who did not keep the Jewish law.

But Paul had to serve the members of all groups. So he gave up his right or freedom (v. 19) to belong to one group and to be separate from the other groups. As a result he was free to be 'all things to all men' (v. 22b).

These words sum up the most important thought in this section of the letter. They show us how Paul behaved (or tried to behave) towards those who held different views from his own. They tell us how he did his evangelism, and are thus of special interest to present day evangelists.

What was this way? Paul placed himself *alongside* and not against them. He *respected* them instead of judging them. He *loved* them instead of fearing them (see note on v. 22b, pp. 121–123).

In vv. 20–22 Paul gave examples of groups and people with whom he behaved in this way.

In the second part of this section (vv. 24–27) he wrote again about 'giving up his rights'. This time he compared himself to athletes and boxers who give up freedom in order to be successful.

NOTES

9.19b. I have made myself a slave to all, that I might win the more:

1. **Slave:** Paul was a 'slave' or 'servant' to the people whom he wanted to help. He wanted to serve them, not to rule them.

He had already explained that apostles and indeed all Christians were 'slaves' or 'servants', not lords and masters. Sometimes he said that they served Christ (4.1 and 7.22). Sometimes he said that they served their fellow human beings (9.19 and 16.15). (See note on p. 91. We note that in 7.21 and 12.13 he used the word 'slave' with a different meaning.)

2. **All:** Paul served everyone. He was able to do this only because he

Paul 'compared himself to athletes and boxers who give up freedom in order to be successful' (p. 118), like these Olympic athletes who have just received their medals for success in the 800 metres race.

What are some of the 'freedoms' which Christians must give up if they are to serve God effectively?

was 'free from all men' (v. 19a), i.e. he did not depend on any one group to support him or to approve of him.

This is one of the reasons why Church leaders are sometimes lonely. In order to serve all groups of people, they must avoid forming a small group of 'favourites'. They must avoid taking the side of one group only. It is not easy to do what Paul did. One Church leader believed that he ought to support one political party publicly and naturally those who supported the same party came to his house more often than the other Church members. This made it difficult for him to serve everyone equally. Another leader took no interest at all in politics. He too found it difficult to serve everyone equally, because some of his members regarded politics as very important.

3. **Win:** Paul was the servant of everyone in order to 'win the more', i.e. 'win over as many as possible' (NEB) to love and obey Jesus Christ.

In v. 22 he said that he was 'all things to all men' (see note on p. 121), i.e. he placed himself alongside those who held different ideas from his own. But he did so in order to 'win' them, not because the differences were unimportant.

9.20. To the Jews, I became as a Jew: The first example which Paul gave of people whom he was serving was the Jews. He said that he served them by 'becoming like a Jew'. On several occasions he kept the Jewish law of Moses although he believed that, since Jesus had come, it was no longer necessary to do so. He circumcised Timothy in Lystra only because that was the Jewish custom (Acts 16.1–3). In Jerusalem there were four men who had made a vow to be 'purified' according to Jewish law, and Paul went with them and was purified along with them (Acts 21.23–26).

We notice the word 'as'. When Paul circumcised Timothy, he was behaving 'as' or 'like' a Jew. He did not, even for a short time, cease to be a Christian and become a Jew again.

9.21a. To those outside the law, I became as one outside the law: The second group to whom Paul referred was the Gentiles, those who were 'outside' Moses's law because they were not Jews. Paul served them as he served the Jews, i.e. by valuing and enjoying the things which they valued and enjoyed, e.g. in Lystra he showed that he, like them, believed in a 'living God' who took care of all races (Acts 14.15–17). In Athens he accepted an invitation to speak in the Areopagus where Greeks were accustomed to discuss religion and while he was there spoke of God 'who is not far from each one of us' (Acts 17.27), and quoted the words of one of the Greek poets (Acts 17.28).

9.21b. Not being without law toward God, but under the law of Christ: In v. 20 Paul had said that, although he sometimes kept the old law of Moses for the sake of the Jews, he was not any longer under it, i.e. he did not need to obey it any longer. But his readers might think that Paul was 'without law towards God', i.e. that he had given up obeying God at all. So in this verse he referred to the law which he did try to keep, namely the 'law of Christ'.

He did not mean that he had exchanged one law for another law. That is a mistake which some people make when they have experienced renewal in their lives, or have just become Christians. They think that the most important things that have changed are the rules. One man said that before he joined a small prayer group he felt that he had to go to church every Sunday, but that now the rule he kept was to attend his group and confess his sins to the other members. Another man had been a Muslim and had been baptized as a Christian. The neighbours said that the only difference they could see in him was that he stopped work on Sundays instead of stopping work on Fridays. Such people have not understood that the change should take place in themselves.

But Paul did not make that mistake. 'If you are led by the Spirit,' he said in Galatians 5.18, 'you are not under the law', i.e. you no longer see God only as a law-giver, you now see Him also as a 'forgiver'.

Then what did Paul mean by the 'law of Christ'? He meant that Christ was now his master, and that it was Christ's spirit of loving which now guided him. This is how he used the word 'law' in Galatians 5.14: 'The whole law is fulfilled in one word, "you shall love . . .".' There are some lorry-drivers who drive at a moderate speed only because there is a law against fast driving and because they will be punished if they break it. But there are drivers of another sort who drive at a moderate speed mainly because they are concerned about the safety of their passengers and of other people on the road. Drivers of this sort do not need the law (as Paul said he did not need the law of Moses). They do not need it because they have concern or *love* for other people. As Paul said, 'Bear one another's burdens and so fulfil the law of Christ' (Gal. 6.2).

9.22a. To the weak I became weak: Everything that Paul was saying in these words he had already said in 8.7–12 (see note on p. 105). The 'weak' were those Christians whose faith in Jesus Christ was not yet strong. They felt that if they ate food which had been offered to idols they would be tempted to return to the worship of idols.

'I became weak' means 'When I was in their company I behaved as if I were tempted as they were tempted.' So when he was with them he did not eat the 'idol meat', even though he himself would not have been tempted if he had eaten it. In other words he put himself *alongside* them. He did not judge or despise them. We see this also in Romans 14.1; 15.1; and 2 Corinthians 11.29.

9.22b. I have become all things to all men:

1. What does this mean? We have seen part of its meaning in the Interpretation (p. 118). In the NEB it is translated, 'I have become everything in turn to men of every sort.' He put himself in the place of people whose religion was different from his own. He 'stood in their shoes',

so to speak. He tried to understand why they believed what they believed. He learnt the value of the things which they valued.

Clearly neither Paul nor any other Christians have really become 'all things' to others. Men cannot fully know what it feels like to be a woman. Christians cannot fully know what it feels like to be a dedicated Muslim. But they can do their best to know.

2. How do Christians put it into practice? We have seen some of the ways in which Paul did. See notes above on vv. 20, 21 and 22a. Here are some other examples:

The principal of a theological school was troubled about one of the students, who had lost interest in his studies since his mother died. How could the principal help him? One thing in which the student was very interested in was the local cinema, so the principal went to the cinema with him whenever possible, even though he had to do much of his work late at night as a result. The student said afterwards that what the principal did had 'saved' him.

A Christian in India made friends with a group of Hindus, and used to sit down with them every week to talk and drink tea together. He said, 'We asked each other many questions, and I discovered from them truths about God which we both believe. I took off my shoes when I visited them because that was their custom, but by doing this I was also acknowledging the presence of God among them.'

Another Christian, in Iran, meets regularly with a Muslim and says, 'I do not argue with him. I worship God with him and thank God for the kindness which He has given to my friend.'

Another has neighbours who have rejected all religions. He listens to them as they make their criticisms, e.g. as they say that traditional religions have often been on the side of the rich against the poor. There is much with which he does not agree, but he hears many truths which the Old Testament prophets and Jesus Himself used to declare. On one occasion, instead of attending his own church, he joined them on a Sunday morning march to protest against the imprisonment of a local magistrate. (This man was in prison because he had found a Government servant guilty of fraud.)

For many years a group of Roman Catholic priests in France worked in the factories of big towns. They were not chaplains. They were employed in the same way in which other workers were employed. In these factories many of the workers were Communists, and for this and other reasons were against the Church. These 'worker-priests' believed that they could serve the workers better by doing the same work as they did and wearing the same clothes, than by paying visits to the factories as chaplains. This sort of work is still being done in various parts of the world. But it came to an end in France because several of the priests ceased to be priests and some became Communists. This does not mean that Paul was wrong in trying to be 'all things to all men'. It means that it is a very difficult task.

3. What makes it possible? Christians can only be all things to all men if:

(a) They keep in mind the object (see below).

(b) They believe that God's Spirit is at work in those who are outside the Church as well as in Christians.

(c) They are willing to endure criticism from other Christians who may accuse them of being disloyal to Jesus Christ. (Paul must have been severely criticized for having Timothy circumcised.)

(d) They love people enough to treat them as human beings rather than as rivals.

4. What is the object? Paul said it was 'in order to serve some' (v. 22b), 'for the sake of the Gospel' (v. 23).

(a) Christians try to be 'all things to all men' in order to 'win' some of them for Christ, not in order to increase the size of the local church congregation.

(b) They need to say openly that this is their aim. A Christian in Sri Lanka, writing about a Buddhist friend, said 'I do not think (and I do not tell him) that God's mercy is only for Christians. But I do tell him that a human being is most fully human when he walks in the steps of Jesus, and that this is my prayer for him.'

9.23. That I may share in its blessings: Some of the Corinthians to whom Paul wrote were far too confident that they would receive God's blessings (see 10.12). Paul himself was not at all confident. He knew that at every stage of his life he was in need of the Gospel which he preached. He always felt that it was only because of the extraordinary grace of God that God was blessing him at all (1 Tim. 1.12–14).

The most effective evangelists and preachers are those who are most aware that they themselves need the good news which they proclaim.

9.24b. Run that you may obtain it: In vv. 24–27 Paul used the illustrations of running and boxing because these athletic sports were part of the Isthmian games which took place near Corinth. Except for the Olympic games, they were the most important 'games' in Greece at that time. The Gentile members of the congregation at Corinth (but probably not the Jewish members, see p. 21), must have watched or taken part in these games. In them the winner received a crown or wreath made from a branch of a pine tree.

In v. 24 Paul was again saying that Christians need to have a clear aim (see note on p. 120 above). Although in a race only one receives the prize, all the runners are trying to get it. They know what they are aiming at. He repeated this idea in v. 26 which means, 'A boxer knows what he is aiming at, it is his opponent's body!' The West African proverb is true, 'If you chase two rats, you don't catch either!'

Paul's teaching about 'aims' is true, (a) for all Christians, (b) for Church leaders and evangelists, (c) for every congregation.

(a) In this letter Paul referred to the goal of all Christians in various phrases, e.g. to be saints (1.2), to glorify God (10.31), make love your aim (14.1), inherit the kingdom of God (15.50). But these are not different goals, they are the same one.

It is important that all Christians ask themselves the question 'what is my aim?' i.e. what do I really want to achieve more than anything else in the world? Sometimes a person may not realise what his real aim is, although other people know what it is because they have watched his behaviour. As one girl said to her friend, 'I think your main object in life is to avoid discomfort'.

(b) Church leaders and evangelists, when they meet together, do not usually speak of their aims in the same way. One may say, 'To build up a congregation of ministers and evangelists'. Another, 'To preach Jesus Christ and him crucified' (1 Cor. 2.2). Another, 'To wait on God at each moment for his guidance'. What matters is that each one should know what he is trying to do, even if he often fails to do it.

(c) The same is true of a whole congregation. In one church members used to meet from time to time and decide what they were trying to do, how far they were doing it and whether it was the best thing to be trying to do. At one such meeting a member said, 'Our chief aim at present is to maintain the church building, and we are doing this successfully. But we should have a better aim.' Paul referred several times in this letter to what aim the congregation at Corinth should have, e.g. in 12.25.

9.25. Every athlete exercises self-control: Athletes give up their right to freedom (they 'exercise self-control') in many ways in order to win races in the games, e.g. they give up time in order to train. They may give up eating food which they enjoy so that their bodies may be the right weight. They may eat food which they dislike in order to strengthen their muscles. In the same way Paul had given up his freedom in order to be of service to as many people as possible (as we saw in chapter 8 and 9.1–18).

All Christians need to 'exercise self-control', and to find out what ways are right for them. One (a student) may give up his freedom to talk with friends, in order to study. Another (a hard-working owner of a shop) may stop work at a fixed time each evening, so as to keep healthy and fresh in mind. Another may give up his freedom to sleep in bed and get up early in order to 'put the day into God's hands in prayer'.

The reason for self-control is important. According to Paul, Christians (like athletes) do it for the sake of the goal which they are trying to reach. It is not because controlling is itself a good deed. Christians do not fast because fasting itself is good, but in order to reach a goal, e.g. because by fasting they find they can pray better, or they can give away food to those who are desperately in need. When Paul wrote in v. 27, 'I pommel my body and subdue it', he did not make the mistake of the 'Manichean Christians', i.e. by regarding the body as something evil which had to be punished. In

v. 27 his thought was 'Boxers have to give up comfort in order to win their fights. In the same way I have to give up many things in order to be what God has called me to be.'

9.27. Lest after preaching to others I myself should be disqualified:

1. The first thought is that a preacher must *do* what he preaches. Paul preached that the Corinthians must give up some of their freedom for the sake of 'weaker' members, therefore he himself must give up some of his own freedom. If he did not, he would be disqualified.

In one country where there are far too many people and there is far too little food, the Government has appointed Family Planning Officers. Their job is to encourage parents not to have more than two children. There is at this moment one of these officers who has thirteen children who are all girls. He is hoping for more so that one of them may be a boy. Should he be dismissed? Should Christian preachers be dismissed if they fail to do what they tell others to do?

2. Although Paul had truly experienced conversion on the road to Damascus, he never believed that 'of course' God would give him the 'prize' of eternal life. He thought that it was always possible that he might lose it (see note on v. 23). Paul was not like a spectator at the athletic games, watching other people trying to win prizes. He, like every Christian preacher, was one of the runners.

STUDY SUGGESTIONS

WORDS

1. 'Apostles, and indeed all Christians, were *"slaves" or "servants"'* (p. 118).

    Read the following passages in 1 Corinthians and say in each case:
    (i) Who did Paul refer to? (ii) What word did he use, 'slave' or 'servant' (or 'service')? (iii) What word is used in another language translation known to you? (iv) Did they serve other people or God?
    (a) 4.1   (b) 7.22b   (c) 9.19   (d) 12.5   (e) 16.15.

2. It was said (p. 118) that the phrase 'become all things to all men' meant 'placed himself alongside others', and on (p. 121) 'stood in their shoes'. What two phrases in another language known to you would you use to interpret that phrase of Paul's?

CONTENT

3. What did Paul mean by saying that he was 'free from all men' (9.19)?
4. In 9.19–27 Paul referred many times to his 'aim' or 'goal'. What *eight* phrases did he use?
5. Give *one* example in each case, from the Book of Acts, of what Paul did in order:

(a) to 'become as a Jew' (9.20);

(b) to 'be as one outside the law' (9.21).

6. (a) What were the Isthmian Games?

(b) What sort of prize did runners receive?

(c) What, according to Paul in vv. 24–27, did (i) runners, (ii) boxers, aim to do?

BIBLE

7. In 1 Cor. 9.20–23 and 2.1–5 Paul wrote about the way he behaved towards those whom he wanted to lead to the truth.

(a) In what way is his thinking in one passage different from his thinking in the other?

(b) In what way is it similar?

(c) Should an evangelist today follow both passages or follow one rather than the other? Give reasons for your answer.

8. (i) What single truth about the Christian life do we find in all the following passages?

(a) 1 Cor. 9.24–27   (b) Phil. 3.12–16   (c) Heb. 12.1 and 2.

(ii) What *two* words in each passage point most clearly to that truth?

DISCUSSION AND RESEARCH

9. (a) What group of people are there in your neighbourhood who hold different opinions from your own, e.g. people of a different religion?

(b) After reading on p. 121 of Christians being 'all things to all men', give examples to show how you and your fellow-Christians (i) *are* 'being all things' to members of those groups, or (ii) *could* 'be all things' to them?

10. (a) What is the chief difficulty of 'being all things to all men'?

(b) What is the chief danger?

(c) What is the chief aim?

Illustrate your answer from your experience, if possible.

11. 'What do I really want to achieve more than anything else in the world?' (p. 124).

What would be:

(a) Your own answer?

(b) The answer of the council of a Christian congregation which you know?

10.1–13 Testing

Even regular worshippers will not withstand temptation unless they are relying on God

OUTLINE

10.1–5: I have just said that I could be 'disqualified' in the race of living. This could happen to you, too. It happened to some of the Israelites in the desert. God gave them all the help they needed, but they did not use it properly. As a result they failed to reach the promised land.

10.6–11: This story is a warning to us all, because we have serious temptations, e.g. to be disloyal to God (v. 7), to misuse our sexuality (v. 8), to lose confidence in God (vv. 9–10).

10.12–13: Therefore keep on putting your confidence in God who is completely trustworthy. In saying this I am both warning you and encouraging you. I am warning those of you who think that because you have been baptized, and receive the bread and wine at the Lord's Supper, you are strong enough to do anything. But I also want to encourage those who feel they are too weak to resist temptation.

INTERPRETATION

Paul wanted to warn the Corinthians that they were in danger of losing the blessings which God meant them to enjoy. When they ate food which had been offered to idols, they were in danger of slipping back into their old religion. They seemed to think that they were magically protected against this danger because they had been baptized and attended the Lord's Supper. The whole of 1 Corinthians 10 is a warning against idolatry.

In vv. 1–5 Paul told the story of the Israelites who had been saved from Egypt, in order to illustrate the danger the Corinthians were in. He called the experience of the Israelites 'baptism', because they escaped from Pharaoh and then followed Moses, just as Christians escape from the power of sin and now follow Christ (vv. 1, 2). The Israelites received special food and drink from God just as Christians receive bread and wine in the Lord's Supper (vv. 3, 4). It was Christ who led the Israelites into freedom, just as He led the Corinthians (v. 4). In spite of this the Israelites were disloyal to God, and were destroyed. (We can read the events to which Paul referred in verses 1–10 in Exodus chapters 13, 14, 16, 17, 32 and Numbers 14, 21, 25, 26.)

Earlier in this letter Paul had warned the Corinthians against relying too much on their own knowledge and not enough on God. They were so pleased with the new knowledge which they had gained since they became

Christians, that they could not see their own weaknesses. They forgot how much they needed God's power at each moment of the day (see note on p. 125).

NOTES

10.4. They drank from the supernatural Rock which followed them and the Rock was Christ: In this verse Paul added two things to the story as we find it in the Book of Exodus:

1. The Jewish legend that the rock followed the Israelites. By this Paul meant that God kept on giving the Israelites His help wherever they went. (We do not know why Paul used a Jewish story in writing to the Christians at Corinth, most of whom were not Jewish.)

2. That it was Christ who gave them this help. This means that Christ existed before He was born in Bethlehem. Paul was not the only writer who taught that. See John 1.1: 'In the beginning was the Word . . .' This teaching was a way of saying to non-Jews that Christ is God and that Christ was not limited by time.

Some Christians find that this teaching is important to them because it supports their belief that Christ is God. Others find that it is not so helpful because it makes it difficult for them to understand that Christ was also really and fully human.

10.5. God was not pleased . . . they were overthrown: Although Paul did not write 'God overthrew them', this is what he actually meant. See also vv. 8, 9, 10.

Does God really send suffering as a punishment to destroy sinners? See 3.17; 5.5; 11.29; and 16.22a, and the notes on those verses.

1. Some Christians say 'Yes, He does. If we do not believe this, we shall not take Him seriously. He is a consuming fire (Heb. 12.29). Also we shall forget that God is personal and acts personally. Jesus spoke of someone who was 'liable to the hell of fire' (Matt. 5.22c), and of others 'going away into eternal punishment' (Matt. 25.45,46).

2. Others agree that God is personal and that He is a stern God. But they believe that, because God loves us, He does not send suffering to punish us. They say that, because God loves us, He has made a world in which things happen in a regular and orderly way, e.g. when we drop heavy things they fall, they do not fly up into the sky. So if we drop a heavy stone on our toes we should not blame God. We blame ourselves (because we have been careless). But when we think about it, we can also thank God, because He has given us a world in which things happen in an orderly way.

10.6. These things are warnings for us: The NEB translation is 'These events happened as symbols to warn us.' The Greek is simply 'These things became "types" for us', i.e. these events are 'typical' of the way God treats us, and 'typical' of the disaster which comes when we disobey Him. See also vv. 11 and 12, in which Paul said, 'As you read these stories, see that you do not make the same mistakes'.

There are two other ways of interpreting this verse and verse 11 which Paul probably did *not* have in mind:

(a) That God caused those events in order to warn us Christians;

(b) That those who wrote the stories down intended to warn us today.

10.7. Do not be idolaters: See note on 8.4.

10.8. We must not indulge in immorality as some of them did, and 23,000 fell: See note on 'immorality' pp. 71–73. We cannot discover from the Book of Numbers why the immoral Israelites 'fell' (i.e. died). Perhaps they caught tick-typhus or some other infectious disease from the bodies of the Midianite women. But as in 5.1, Paul's chief message was 'Avoid unfaithfulness and disloyalty.' In Numbers 25.9 we read that 24,000 died. So it seems that Paul, writing from memory, made a mistake. Some readers, like Tom Paine in his book *The Age of Reason*, written in 1790, have said that since Paul made a mistake like this his whole message to us is of no value. But we do not read Paul's letters because he never made a mistake. We read them because we have found in our experience that the teaching which he gave about living as Christians helps us to live as Christians today.

10.9. We must not put the Lord to the test: i.e. do not eat food offered to idols, thinking that you have already been saved from ever committing idolatry again.

Someone who had once been a slave to alcohol said, 'If I drank just one glass of beer now, I should be testing God. I should run the risk of being enslaved again, and expecting God to rescue me again magically.'

10.10. Nor grumble: 'Grumbling' means thinking, 'If I were God, I would organize the world better than this.' All grumbling is blaming God. This is different from asking God questions, e.g. asking why He has allowed so much suffering. Christians are right to put such a question to God. See Psalm 22.1 and Mark 15.34.

10.11. Upon whom the end of the ages has come: The Corinthians were living in the time when God's promises were being fulfilled, i.e. the promises which we read in the Old Testament about a Messiah who would come.

10.12. Let anyone who thinks that he stands take heed lest he fall: This sums up the whole message of vv. 1–13 (see Interpretation, p. 127). Even regular worshippers will 'fall', i.e. they will not withstand temptation, unless they rely on God at every moment of their lives.

Nearly every Christian congregation that ever existed knows members who have 'fallen' or 'lapsed' or 'ceased to meet' as the Methodists say. Such congregations need to go on loving their lapsed members, and trying to understand why they did 'fall'. There are many different reasons. Perhaps they married a non-Christian wife or husband. Or they have made

'Even regular worshippers will "fall" . . . unless they rely on God at every moment of their lives' (p. 129).

The people who built these houses in Chile thought they were safe enough, until unusually heavy rains caused a land subsidence.

What can prevent baptized Christians from believing that they are protected for ever against sinning?

a god of their possessions and have no room for God. One common reason is that when they became Christians they did not know that they would have to suffer. So when suffering came, e.g. when their work for Christ was not successful, or when their political party broke its promises, or when their fellow-Christians failed to support them, they felt that God had 'let them down'. So they fell. In truth, when we become Christians we begin to share the sufferings of Christ (2 Cor. 1.5). And Paul said in these verses that we cannot do that unless we depend on God.

Readers may perhaps point to 1 John 3.6–9, which seems to say something different. They may think that 'no one born of God commits sin' (v. 9) means that a man cannot 'fall' if he is a real Christian. But John did not think that. According to 1 John 1.8–10 he said clearly that no one at all is sinless. What John meant in v. 9 was that someone who had become God's son could not be habitually sinful.

10.13a. No temptation has overtaken you that is not common: The word which is translated 'temptation' should be here translated 'test'. Paul was saying, 'So far you have been tested in ordinary ways, you may have to stand up to more severe tests. So be prepared!'

God allows us to be tested so that we can learn to rely on Him and discover how He can help us. We have a great many decisions to take every day, which make us either stronger or weaker, either help or hinder other people, and bring either honour or dishonour to God's name. But in all this we can be sure that:

1. God never wants us to do wrong, i.e. He never tempts us. See James 1.12, 13, 'Blessed is the man who endures trial . . . (but) let no one say when he is tempted, I am tempted by God.'

2. God will not allow the tests to be too severe.

10.13b. God is faithful and He will not let you be tempted beyond your strength:

1. Paul's aim was to point to God, saying, 'You will have more serious tests before long. You will be tempted to follow pagan customs. But God has promised to support you and He keeps His promises.'

These words have encouraged very many Christians in times of difficulty. Here is one example. A Muslim in Iran became a Christian. Muslims kept on visiting him and trying to persuade him to become a Muslim again. They offered him a well-paid job, knowing that his wife was an invalid and that he needed more money. They even offered him a new house. They told him that his children would not get jobs on leaving school if he remained a Christian. They even went after him when he travelled 600 miles to live with friends. Throughout a period of two years the words of this verse were very important to him. They helped him to stand firm as a Christian.

2. But some Christians seem to have been tested beyond their strength. A woman had five young children and her husband left her to go with

another woman. The time came when there was no more food for the two babies. A chance came to steal food, and she did so. We may think that she was tested 'beyond her strength'. In that case we shall say that Paul's words were not exactly true for everyone all the time. Or we may say it was the husband, not the woman who did wrong, or perhaps there was something else that the woman could have done. But, whatever we think, this verse is true for most Christians most of the time.

10.13c. He will provide the way of escape: NEB, 'way out', is a better translation. God does not encourage Christians to run away from times of testing; He gives them help to get through them without being overcome. A man in Brazil has told how he reached a sick friend by paddling his canoe 100 miles up a river. When he came to very rough water and dangerous rocks it was possible for him to turn back and escape the danger. But the only way to save his friend was by discovering a way out through the rocks and to go forward. And this he did.

STUDY SUGGESTIONS

WORDS

1. The Greek word *peirasmos* is translated in the RSV as 'temptation' in v. 13, and *tupos* is translated 'warnings' in v. 6. In each case compare these words with the translations given in:
   (a) another English version,
   (b) another language version that you know.
2. What is meant by saying that God is 'faithful'?

CONTENT

3. Why did Paul write this paragraph?
4. 'The whole of chapter 10 is a warning against idolatry' (p. 127).
   (a) In which earlier part of 1 Corinthians did Paul write about idolatry?
   (b) What is idolatry? Give examples from everyday life to support your answer.
5. What did Paul mean by 'putting the Lord to the test'?

BIBLE

6. What is the connection between James 1.12,13 and 1 Cor. 10.1–13?
7. There are four different events referred to in 1 Cor. 10.1–4.
   (a) What are they?
   (b) In what chapter and verses of the Old Testament do we find each of them recorded?
8. Paul taught that Christ was with the Israelites in the desert (v. 4).

(i) What do the following verses tell us about Christ existing before He became man?
(a) Rom. 8.3 (b) 2 Cor. 8.9 (c) Gal. 4.4 (d) Col. 1.16.
(ii) What is your opinion of this teaching? What difference does it make to a man's life if he believes it?

DISCUSSION AND RESEARCH

9. 'Our fathers . . . all passed through the sea . . . they were overthrown in the wilderness' (1 Cor. 10.1–5).
(a) According to Paul, why were those Israelites 'overthrown'?
(b) In your experience, what are the chief reasons why Church members 'lapse'?

10. 'Does God . . . send suffering as a punishment?' (p. 128).
What is your opinion? Give your reasons.

11. Do Paul's letters become less valuable to us if it seems that he has given an incorrect figure in 1 Cor. 10.8?
Explain your answer.

12. Is it true that no Christian is tested 'beyond his strength' (v. 13)? Illustrate your answer from your own experience and from the lives of other people as you have observed them.

13. If you were a Christian preacher and wanted to explain to your listeners that being baptized and attending Holy Communion was not enough to save them from committing sin;
(a) What would you tell them that they needed?
(b) Would you use the stories from Exodus and Numbers which Paul used in 1 Cor. 10.1–10? Give reasons for your answer. If not, what example would you use?

10.14—11.1 Idolatry

Run away from idolatry for your own sakes and for the sake of others

OUTLINE

10.14: Have nothing to do with the worship of a false God.

10.15—18: We know from our sharing in the Lord's Supper that worshippers have fellowship with the Lord whom they worship, and with each other. The Jews also, who share the food left over from sacrifices, have fellowship with each other.

10.19—22: I agree that idols are not real gods. But when anyone eats a meal in a building where there is an idol he has fellowship with the demons of that place. You cannot be loyal to Christ if you have fellowship with demons.

10.23,24: You say that 'everything is lawful'. But there is another truth: if you love your neighbour you will not want your behaviour to harm him.

10.25–27: You may eat what you buy and what your hosts give you without asking where it came from.

10.28—11.1: But if you know that the food has been offered in a sacrifice, do not eat it. What you do influences other people.

INTERPRETATION

1. *Why did Paul write these verses?* Chiefly in order to warn the Corinthians against idolatry. He was adding to what he had already said in v. 7: 'Do not be idolators', and in v. 12: 'Let anyone who thinks that he stands take heed lest he fall.' See the note on 'idols' on p. 102 (8.4b). Secondly, Paul wrote to repeat what he had said in chapter 8, that someone who really loves God will also love people. See notes on vv. 17 and 23 below.

2. *A Contradiction:* In chapter 8 Paul had said that there was no reason why a Christian should not eat the meat from an animal which had been sacrificed in a building where there was an idol. It would only be wrong to eat it if, as a result, a fellow Christian acted against his own conscience. He said something like this in 10.23–11.1. In vv. 14–22, however, we read that Christians ought not to eat this sort of food at all. If they did so, they would come under the influence of the demons. Scholars have tried to explain why there is this contradiction. Some think that Paul wrote 10.14–22 at a later date, after he had heard that idolatry among Christians at Corinth had increased. Others say that in chapter 8 and 10.23—11.1 Paul was thinking of a meal to which Christians had been invited privately (so that it was not harmful to eat the food), but that in vv. 14–22 he was writing about meals which form a part of religious worship. (This explanation is probably the better of the two, but there is no proof that it is correct.)

If we regarded Paul's writings as a book of laws for all Christians, this contradiction might trouble us. We might ask, 'Which of the two is the law which we must follow?' But, as we have seen, Paul's writings were not laws. We read them today in order to find great truths which are true for every generation. See paragraph 1 of this Interpretation, above, for the two great truths to which Paul pointed in these verses.

NOTES

10.16a. The cup of blessing which we bless: i.e. the cup of wine which we drink at the Lord's Supper. Paul referred to the Lord's Supper because it was the worship which all his readers knew. He was saying, 'At any sort of worship, including the Lord's Supper, those who are present have fellowship with, and come under the influence of, the God who is being worshipped. Therefore keep away from pagan sacrifices.' He wrote 'the cup of blessing' because as the Christians drank the wine they probably followed the Jewish custom of 'blessing' God, i.e. thanking God. The prayer was, 'Blessed are you, O Lord our God, who gives us the fruit of the vine.' Although in this verse Paul referred to the wine before he referred to the bread, worshippers at the Lord's Supper usually shared the bread before the wine.

10.16b: Is it not a participation in the blood of Christ? Paul did not, of course, mean that Christians drank the blood which had been in Jesus's body in the days before he was crucified. In this verse Paul was expressing many things in very few words. He meant, 'As we drink the wine, we have our share of the blessings which can be ours because Jesus shed His blood for us.' (This 'blessing' is, for instance, the forgiveness which God offers.) The Greek word which is here translated 'participation' is *koinonia*. Elsewhere it is also translated as 'communion', 'sharing', 'fellowship', etc. Writers in the New Testament used it in three ways, showing that:

1. Christians have a share in the Spirit of God Himself. See Philippians 1.7: 'You are all partakers with me of grace.' From such a verse we see that there are two thoughts, not one: (a) Christians have fellowship with God; (b) they are together in having this fellowship. This is the way in which Paul used the word in this verse (10.16): 'We all share in God and in the benefits which result from the death of Jesus.'

2. Christians and Christ together share such things as human life and human suffering. See Philippians 3.10.

3. Christians have fellowship with other Christians. See Acts 2.42: 'the apostles' fellowship'; Acts 2.44: 'had all things in common'; and Galatians 2.9 'gave to me the right hand of fellowship'. Since Christians expressed their fellowship in a practical way, Paul could use the word *koinonia* in Romans 15.26 and 2 Corinthians 9.13 for the money (the 'collection') which one group of Christians sent to another group.

We have noted above three ways in which writers used the word in the New Testament. But these are only three ways of looking at one thing. In practice a Christian cannot choose which of the three he will have. Paul showed this in 1 Corinthians 10.16,17: 'Anyone who has real fellowship with Christ will of course have fellowship with other Christians. You cannot have one without the other.' In the same way, we do not find lasting fellowship among Christians unless these Christians are together in fellowship with God. 'Have fellowship with us; and our fellowship is with the Father . . .' (1 John 1.3). When Christians have fellowship with God the fellowship they have with each other is strong and deep.

10.17. We who are many are one body: In v. 16 Paul had written of the fellowship which worshippers had with Jesus. In this v. 17 he looked at *koinonia* from the other side, as the fellowship which worshippers have with each other. But in order to describe the worshippers he used the same word 'body' which he had used in v. 16. In v. 16 it meant Jesus, and in v. 17 it meant the congregation. So Paul was saying, 'Because worshippers have fellowship with the same Lord, they have fellowship with each other.' If we really love God, we shall also love each other. See note on 'body' on p. 157 (1 Cor. 11.29).

10.18. Consider the people of Israel: Jewish priests ate parts of the animals which they had sacrificed, and others could share in this food (see Lev. 10.12,13). Also, of course, both priests and people believed that they received God's blessings as the result of a sacrifice. Paul was repeating his teaching, 'Worshippers are joined in fellowship and in loyalty to the One whom they worship.'

10.19,20. Do I imply . . . that an idol is anything? No: An idol of wood or metal is not a God, and has no power in itself. See note on 8.4b. Nevertheless, Paul said that those who had a meal in a building where there was an idol were uniting themselves with whatever powers or demons existed there. Christians could not give complete loyalty to God if they were under the influence of demons.

10.20. I do not want you to be partners with demons: What did Paul mean by 'demons'?

1. They were unseen spirits which could exist apart from human beings.

2. They had power to harm people. Therefore it was important to distinguish between being filled with a demon and being filled with the Holy Spirit (1 Cor. 12.10).

3. Each one was separate (as each person is separate from others).

4. They existed in special places, e.g. in those buildings to which Paul referred in this chapter.

5. Their leader was Satan (or 'the Devil').

This is also what many other Jewish writers believed. We read in Deuteronomy 32.17 (which Paul referred to in v. 20) of people who forsook God and sacrificed to demons. It seems that this is what followers of many traditional religions have always done all over the world, to persuade the spirits, e.g. of a stream or a tree, not to hurt them.

Jesus spoke of 'casting out demons' (Mark 9.25) and said that His followers would be able to do the same (Luke 9.1).

Some readers are doubtful if demons such as Paul believed in, really exist. They say that:

(a) In the past, people spoke of a demon whenever something happened for which they could give no reason at that time, e.g. a whirlwind or disease.

(b) We now know the real reason for many of these happenings, e.g. we know why whirlwinds take place, and we know the real reason for many diseases.

(c) Jesus and Paul believed in demons only because all people of their race living at that time believed in demons, i.e. Jesus would not have been fully human if He had held a different belief.

(d) There is only one God, not two gods one of whom is good (God) and the other of whom is evil ('Satan').

What is the truth? Christians do not all give the same answer. But most of them agree on the following:

1. Evil is not just the absence of goodness: it is an active force which comes at us.

2. A Christian's task is to fight against it at all times. See Ephesians 6.12.

3. God's power is greater than the power of any evil. This is the message to give to those who are afraid of demons. Jesus 'cast them out'.

10.21. You cannot drink the cup of the Lord and the cup of demons: This is the main teaching of the whole paragraph: 'If you are loyal to Jesus Christ you cannot serve any other power. You must make a choice.' (See Matt. 6.24.) In the same way, a Christian who promises to love and marry a woman promises to be faithful 'only to her'.

Paul said that the Corinthian Christians owed loyalty to the Lord and to each other because they had all drunk from His cup. Readers may know of secret societies whose members are loyal to each other because they have drunk the same drink or taken part in the same ceremony or sacrifice.

As we see in v. 27, Paul did not mean that Christians must isolate themselves from non-Christians. He meant that wherever Christians go they must know that they owe complete loyalty to Christ.

10.22. Shall we provoke the Lord? i.e. 'Surely we do not want to do something for which God will punish us.' If they ate a meal in a building where idols were kept, they might come under the influence of evil spirits. In that way they ran the risk of rejecting Christ, and of coming under God's judgement (see note on p. 44). If we reject Christ, we suffer.

10.23. Not all things build up: This is the beginning of a new paragraph. In it Paul was mainly saying (as he said in chapter 8): 'Support other Christians in what you do. When you buy food in the public market or are invited to a meal with a non-Christian, do not just say, "Is this right?" Say, "If I do this, will it help to build up the Christian congregation?" Paul gave the same teaching to those who were speaking in tongues (see note on 1 Cor. 14.3–5). It is an important question for Christians to ask themselves, as we saw in the notes on 8.7 and 8.9. In one Church the council had to discuss the case of a man who had left that Church to join another religion, and who was now asking to return. As they discussed his request, they had also to answer a second question: 'If we receive him back, what will be the effect on the congregation?'

10.25,26. Eat whatever is sold . . . for 'the earth is the Lord's': This shows that Paul, when he wrote this, had ceased to keep the Jewish religious laws. A religious Jew could not eat food unless he had made sure that it had not been offered in a pagan sacrifice. Paul's reason for eating 'whatever is sold' was that the Lord is in control of all the earth (the words came from Psalm 24.1). So God is in control of whatever demons there may be in the idol-house. (This is rather different from what Paul said in v. 20. See note on p. 136.)

'The earth is the Lord's' also reminds us that we are answerable to God for the way in which we use the earth, with its soil and water and air. We are not free to use it wastefully. It is His, not ours. He has lent it to us.

10.27. If one of the unbelievers invites you . . . eat: From these words it is clear that the Christians in Corinth had friends among the non-Christians of the city. They had to remain loyal to Christ while mixing with those who served other gods. It was a difficult task. Some Christians, e.g. in countries where most of the people are Muslims, find it too difficult. They build walls round the district where they live, and meet non-Christians as little as possible. In this way they hope that they will not be tempted to become Muslims. Yet it is not possible in this way for them to show their non-Christian neighbours how great is their Master Jesus. Bishop Deqani-Tafti of Iran, thinking of John 13.1–10, has said that when there are only a few Christians in a place their task is 'feet-washing rather than wall-building'.

10.31. Do all to the glory of God: Here the words mean: 'You will honour and glorify God, (a) if you give your loyalty to Him rather than to the demons, and (b) if you think of the well-being of the whole congregation rather than of your own conscience alone.'

But Paul added 'or whatever you do'. So in everything that we do we can honour Him. One college used a form of prayer in their chapel in which the leader referred to all the activities of the students, and after each sentence the others made the response, 'Hallowed be your Name' (i.e. 'May You, Lord, be honoured above all'). The first three sentences were:

When we are alone in your presence ('Hallowed . . .');

As we live and work together ('Hallowed . . .');

When we rest and sleep ('Hallowed . . .').

10.32. Give no offence to Jews or to Greeks or to the church: Again Paul was saying that a Christian must consider the needs of everyone he meets.

1. When he eats and drinks with Jews or Gentiles he must not lead them to break the rules of their own religion;

2. He must not make it more difficult for them to become Christians (we see from v. 33 that Paul wanted to lead people 'to be saved');

3. When he meets another member of the Church he must consider the other person's conscience.

11.1. Be imitators of me, as I am of Christ: This verse is closely connected with 10.32 and 33, and therefore means, 'In your actions, consider the needs of the people you are with, as I do, and as Jesus Christ did'. There are other verses in which Paul told his readers to 'imitate' him, e.g. 1 Corinthians 4.16.

In what ways should we imitate other Christians or imitate Christ?

1. We should imitate the *way* in which they behaved, if that way was good, i.e. we should let the same Holy Spirit work in us who worked in them and in Christ.

2. We cannot always imitate *what* they do, not even what Christ did. First, this is because their circumstances may have been different from ours. A doctor today has to take many decisions which Christ and Paul never had to take. Most of the medicines which he uses or decides not to use did not exist when Christ was healing people in Galilee. So it is not very helpful for the doctor to say, 'What did Christ do? What would Christ have done?' Secondly, God has made each person different from all other people. He has not intended that anyone should become a copy of another person. But He offers the same Holy Spirit to each of us.

STUDY SUGGESTIONS

WORDS

1. What *five* words in the following list have the same or nearly the same meaning as 'participation' (1 Cor. 10.16 and 17)?
   partnership   offering   fellowship   sharing   sacrifice   service   communion   partaking

CONTENT

2. In chapter 8 (and in 10.23—11.1) Paul said that it was not always wrong to eat food which had been offered to idols. 'In vv. 14–22, however, we read that Christians ought not to eat this sort of food at all' (p. 134). What explanations do scholars give of the difference between the two passages?

3. What two great truths did Paul refer to in 1 Cor. 10.14—11.1?

4. (a) What cup did Paul refer to?
   (b) What did he mean by 'participating in the blood of Christ' (1 Cor. 10.16b)?

BIBLE

5. 'Is it not a participation . . .?' (1 Cor. 10.16b).
   (i) Who were the participants, or sharers, according to the following passages? and
   (ii) What did they share?
   (a) Acts 2.44   (b) 1 Cor. 10.16b   (c) 1 Cor. 10.18
   (d) Phil. 1.7   (e) 1 John 1.3

6. 'You must make a choice' (p. 137).
   (i) What choice do the following passages refer to in each case?
   (a) Josh. 24.14–21   (b) Matt. 6.24   (c) 1 Cor. 10.21
   (ii) Describe a situation in which you (or someone else) had to make a choice of this sort.
7. 'Be imitators of me' (1 Cor. 11.1)
   (i) What is the difference between copying another Christian and imitating him in the way that Paul meant here?
   (ii) The following passages refer to imitating or following someone's example. Say in each case (if possible) who the readers were told to imitate and in what way.
   (a) Rom. 15.13   (b) 1 Cor. 11.1   (c) Eph. 5.1 and 2
   (d) Phil. 2.4–8   (e) Phil. 3.17   (f) 1 Thess. 1.6   (g) 1 Pet. 2.21

DISCUSSION AND RESEARCH

8. (a) By what word is 'demon' translated in another language known to you?
   (b) What is the usual meaning of this word?
   (c) What do you believe about demons? (See note on p. 136.)
9. 'All things are lawful, but not all things build up' (10.23). Give an example of a time when it seemed right to you to do something, but when you did not do it because you believed it would have harmed someone else's conscience.
10. 'The Christians in Corinth had friends among the non-Christians' (p. 138).
    (a) What verse in 1 Cor. 10 shows us that this is so?
    (b) Do you have only a few friends among non-Christians, or many?
    (c) If you have only a few or none, explain why. If you have many, which of you has most influence on the other, and why?
11. 'Whatever you do, do all to the glory of God' (1 Cor. 10.31). See the note on p. 138, and add to the form of prayers which is referred to there. Do it in such a way that you include many sorts of activity.

11.2–16 Women in the Congregation

It is important to keep the customs of the day

OUTLINE

11.2–10: Women should wear veils at public worship. This is a sign, according to the custom of the city, that men are the leaders in the congregation.

11.11–12: I am not saying that women are less important than men. A man needs a woman just as much as a woman needs a man.

11.13–15: But it is surely natural for a woman to cover her head.

11.16: And this is the custom in other Christian congregations.

INTERPRETATION

It is likely that Paul wrote these verses in reply to a letter from Corinth. Probably someone had written to say 'Some women are coming to the Lord's Supper without wearing a veil. What is your opinion?' In his reply Paul not only gave his opinion about women's veils, but also other thoughts about women. His thoughts were:

(a) That women should treat the leaders in the congregation with respect (see vv. 5 and 6). Here, as in most of these verses, Paul was referring to women's behaviour in the congregation rather than at home.

(b) That they should keep the customs of their city, unless there was a strong reason for breaking them. It was the custom in Corinth for women to wear a veil.

(c) They should be allowed to pray aloud or preach in public worship: 'Prays or prophesies' (v. 5).

(d) They should treat their husbands as 'head' (see vv. 3a, 8 and 9 and note below on v. 3a).

(e) They should behave like women and not pretend to be men (see vv. 5, 6, 13 and 15 and note on v. 5).

(f) They are as important as men (see note below on vv. 11 and 12).

WHAT DID PAUL TEACH ABOUT WOMEN IN OTHER PASSAGES?

(a) He repeated that men and women are equally valuable in God's eyes. (See Gal. 3.28: 'There is neither male or female: for you are all one in Christ Jesus.')

(b) He added that a man owes loyalty to his wife just as much as a woman owes loyalty to her husband (see 1 Cor. 7.3 and 4; and note p. 79; and Eph. 5.21–31, especially note v. 25).

(c) See also note below on 1 Cor. 14.34 – where Paul told women not to interrupt public worship.

Note: In the above verses Paul was writing about those who live 'in Christ', not to women in general.

HOW SHOULD WE REGARD PAUL'S TEACHING TODAY?

(a) There are some verses in which we see that Paul broke away in a surprising way from the customary Jewish thinking about women – see especially 1 Cor. 7.3 and 4; Eph. 5.21–31; Gal. 3.28. In these verses Paul was saying something very different from the prayer which Jewish men said every morning: 'Lord, I thank you that you did not make me a woman.'

(b) There are other verses where Paul was *not* able to depart from the traditional Jewish ways of thinking, e.g. in his teaching about women serving their husbands because God created the woman after the man (see note on v. 3b).

(c) But in his teaching Paul never said that he was providing rules for all generations. (It is true that some Christians do treat his words as rules, e.g. they forbid women to go inside a church without putting a hat or handkerchief on their heads because Paul wrote 1 Cor. 11.5.) What Paul was doing was writing down guidance on marriage in the light of the Old Testament and of the new teaching of Jesus. No one had ever done this before! In these verses Paul was just beginning to think out this guidance. Therefore what we find in Paul's teaching about women is that he was being led by God's Holy Spirit to give guidance:

1. So far as he was able to understand God's will.
2. To Christians living in AD 54 in Corinth.

(d) We, who read Paul's words, therefore, need to remember that God has given us the same Spirit, and that He expects us to discover His will for our own generation.

NOTES

11.3a. The head of every man is Christ: Paul wanted to say that in public worship women should treat a man as the 'head'. In order to explain this he referred to the various 'heads' in God's creation: God was the head of Christ, Christ was the head of man, man was the head of woman.

What did Paul mean by 'head'? We can see his meaning by discovering in what ways Christ is the head of man:

1. Christ came first. He was 'ahead' of man, the first-born of all creation (Col. 1.15–18).
2. Therefore a man exists to serve Christ (John 21.19c).
3. He depends on Christ (1 Cor. 8.6c).
4. Christ is different from men (Heb. 1.2–4).

11.3b. The head of a woman is her husband: We have seen that Paul wanted women to veil themselves when they spoke in the congregation,

'Paul broke away from the customary Jewish thinking about women' (p. 142).

In West Africa today, many police jobs are done by women, and in Bulgaria a woman rose to be a Major-General in the armed forces. But the Indian doctor's family below still keep the tradition by which father and sons sit down first to meals, while mother and daughters serve them, even though the girls have university degrees like their brothers.

What are your own ideas about the position of women today?

because that would suit the customs of Corinth. If people thought that Christians disregarded the customs of the time, it would hinder them from accepting the Gospel. But in vv. 3–9 Paul gave another reason why women should wear veils: 'because God created man to be head of a woman'. When a woman wore a veil it was a sign that she accepted a man as head.

There are questions that readers may ask here, e.g.:

(a) *What did Paul mean by calling the man 'the head'?* He meant that man is head of woman in the same way as Christ is the head of man (see note above on v. 3a): i.e. (1) a man was made before a woman; (2) therefore women exist to serve men; they were made for men (v. 9); (3) Women depend on men; (4) Women are different from men. But Paul did not say that women were 'inferior' to men.

(b) *Why did Paul call the man the 'head'?* Because he was quoting Genesis 2.18–23. According to this Creation story God made woman after He had made man, and He made her for the sake of man. But there is another Creation story, in Genesis chapter 1, and according to this story God made man and woman at the same time, and made each one equally in His image. Probably some of those who read this letter pointed this out and asked why Paul had only quoted one passage.

(c) *How have Christians interpreted those words?*

1. Most Christians in the past have interpreted them to mean that women should be the servants and men be the masters, both in marriage and in the congregation. They have probably made this interpretation for two reasons: (a) because they treated Paul's words as rules for all generations; (b) because in most generations and in most places it has been the custom of the country that women should behave in that way.

2. In recent times many Christians have believed that it is God's will that women should be partners with men, both in marriage and in the Church congregation. They think that women should be the partners rather than the servants of men, for reasons such as the following: (a) this seems to be God's will if we read Genesis 1.27; (b) customs concerning women have changed in very many parts of the world, or are changing.

Many women have received the same school education as men, and some women have become Presidents or Prime Ministers of their countries. The result is that in very many Churches today members are asking, 'Should women be leaders in a congregation?' Some Churches have already appointed women as leaders of a congregation. At the same time, the relationship between husbands and wives is changing, as in more and more marriages the man and his wife are partners. (This is so great a change that many difficulties arise from it.)

These changes have not taken place everywhere. God's will for the people of one part of the world and at one time may not be the same as His will for those in another part and at another time.

11.3c. The head of Christ is God: In addition to this verse, there are two

144

other verses in this letter where Paul seems to say that Christ is 'less than God the Father'; 'Christ is God's' (3.23); 'The Son Himself will also be subjected to him', i.e. to God (15.28).

Did Paul really believe that Christ was 'less than' God?

Some readers have said: 'No. In these verses Paul was pointing to two truths only: (1) that God the Father came before Christ in time (this seems to be the chief thought in v. 3c); (2) that Christ was the obedient agent of His Father (see especially 3.23 and 15.28). Someone who obeys is not 'less' than the person whom he obeys. See also verses in John's Gospel where the theme seems to be Jesus's obedience, e.g. 6.44; 6.57; 8.28.

But it is more likely that Paul did think of Christ as being in some way 'less than' God, because he had not completed his own thinking on the subject. Later on he saw clearly that 'in Christ all the fulness of God was pleased to dwell' (Col. 1.19). See John 10.30: 'I and the Father are one'.

Since that time, Christians have continued to search for the truth about the relationship between God and Christ. Those who drew up the Nicene Creed (AD 325) described this relationship in the words: 'Christ is one in being with the Father'. This is an important matter, since Christ could not have completely reconciled us to God unless He had been fully God as well as fully man. We see how important this is when we meet one of the 'Jehovah's Witnesses' who quote such verses as John 6.44 (see above) to 'prove' (as they say) that Jesus is *not* fully God.

11.5. Any woman who prays or prophesies with her head unveiled dishonours her head:

1. By saying this, Paul was giving his approval to women who prayed aloud or preached in public worship. (For a note on 'prophesies', see p. 178.) His instruction was that they should cover their heads. When he wrote 'Women should keep silence' (1 Cor. 14.34) he was probably not saying anything different, but telling women not to interrupt in the congregation (see p. 183).

2. As we have seen, Paul wrote this chiefly because in Corinth it was the custom for women to cover their heads, both in the congregation and in the wider community of the city. It was also the custom for men not to do so. The Gospel was already difficult for people to accept. Christians should not make it more difficult by breaking the customs of the city. This is perhaps why Christian women in Iran wear veils over the lower part of their faces. If they do not, people would regard them as immoral women. In North India Christian women wear a dot or *gopi* on their forehead and pull their sari up over their heads when they leave the house. Those are the customs of the people who live around them, who are mostly Hindus.

3. We have already seen some of the reasons why Paul told the women to wear veils. We may note here a further reason: in order to show that they were women and not men. There were ways in which women could work for the Church in Corinth, *because* they were women and not men. So

today it is very important that women should be free to serve the community in those ways in which men cannot serve it.

Is it important nowadays that women should wear special clothes to show that they are women? In some countries it is important. In others, e.g. where women do the same jobs as men, it is probably not important.

11.10. A woman ought to have a veil on her head because of the angels: The Greek word for which in this verse the translators of the RSV used 'veil' really means 'authority'. No one knows why Paul called a woman's hair her 'authority', nor what angels have to do with it.

11.11. Woman is not independent of man nor man of woman: We have seen that in previous verses in this chapter Paul kept very close to the Jewish traditional ways of regarding a woman, e.g. that she should treat a man as her 'head' (v. 3). But in these verses, 11 and 12, and also in 7.3 and 4, Paul broke away from the old Jewish ways of thinking, and taught that a man and a woman depend on each other.

Although Paul was chiefly thinking about men and women in the congregation, we can see his meaning most clearly by thinking of the ways in which a husband and a wife need each other. There are ways in which he can help her because he is a man, and ways in which she can help him because she is a woman. There are times when he is strong, in good health and good spirits, and she is the one who is in need of support. There are other times when she is strong and he is the one who is in need of support. In a marriage which is healthy, each is learning more and more how to strengthen the other and how to be strengthened by the other. 'All things are from God' means that both men and women have equally been made by God, and that both are equally answerable to Him for the way they live.

11.13. Judge for yourselves: How could Christians in Corinth judge 'for themselves' what was right and what was wrong in public worship? In these verses Paul referred to four different ways of judging. These were:

1. By the custom of the city (vv. 5, 6 and 13). Although Christians serve a different Master from the gods whom others worship, they cannot serve Him well if they needlessly break the customs of the time.

2. By the Old Testament (vv. 7 and 8). It is not easy to find guidance in the Old Testament, because there are different interpretations (see note p. 44). But God certainly helps us to make right judgements by means of it.

3. By what is 'natural', our 'common-sense' (see v. 14). Again, it is not easy to know what is natural, since each civilization and each generation has its own ideas about what is 'natural'. We may say that women 'naturally' have less physical strength than men, but this is not true of all women. Or again in some countries people think that it is 'natural' for women to be the leaders of their families and for the eldest daughter to be the heir. But in most other countries this seems to be 'unnatural'.

4. What the leaders of the various other Churches teach (see note below on v. 16). In the next part of the letter we see that Paul referred to a fifth

way by which his readers could 'judge' for themselves, namely by remembering what Jesus did. That is the reason why he referred to the Last Supper (see p. 150).

Paul showed here that it is important to use the many and different ways which God has provided so that we may make right judgements. Christians often make wrong decisions because they have chosen one way only, e.g. saying that 'The Bible is the only guide I read', or 'Common sense is good enough for me'.

11.16. We recognize no other practice, nor do the churches of God: By the 'churches', Paul meant the many different congregations of Christians in Asia Minor (see note on 1.2). Paul's teaching was, 'One way for your congregation to find out what is right and wrong is to discover what other congregations do. God has not intended you to live apart from other groups of Christians (see also 7.17 and 14.33, and note on 14.36, p. 183). So a modern congregation needs to know what Christians have believed and done in the past, and also what other Christians are doing in other places at the present time.

A group of Church members from Western Europe once visited Russia, where a group of Russian Christians entertained them. When they were leaving they asked the Russians: 'In what way can we repay you?' The Russians said that what they needed more than anything else was a magazine in which they could read what other Churches in Russia were doing and thinking. At that time there was no way of knowing.

STUDY SUGGESTIONS

WORDS

1. (a) If you were describing the teaching of 1 Cor. 11.2–16 concerning *Christ* in relation to God and a *woman* in relation to a man, which *five* of the following words would you use?

   helper   subject   property   slave   dependent   obedient   subordinate.

   (b) Which of those words, if any, would you use to describe the proper position of women in relation to:

   (i) their Christian congregation today?

   (ii) their husbands?

CONTENTS

2. For what *two* reasons did Paul tell women to wear veils?

3. Which two verses in this section seem to contradict the teaching of the other verses?

4. From which words in this passage do we discover that Paul was willing for women to speak during public worship?

BIBLE

5. In what way is Christ 'the head of every man' (11.3a), according to each of the following passages?
   (a) Mark 1.16,17   (b) 1 Cor. 8.6   (c) Col. 1.16

6. Concerning the relationship between men and women:
   (a) What is the chief difference between 1 Cor. 11.3–9 and 11.11,12?
   (b) What is the chief difference between Gen. 1.27 and Gen. 2.18–23?
   (c) In what way is the teaching of the following passages alike: 1 Cor. 7.3,4; Eph. 5.21–31?

7. By 'the churches' (11.16) Paul meant the many different congregations of Christians in Asia Minor (p. 147).
   (i) What congregations are referred to in each of the following passages?
   (a) 1 Cor. 16.1   (b) 1 Cor. 16.19   (c) 2 Cor. 8.1   (d) Gal. 1.22
   (ii) How far from Corinth was each of those places, approximately?

DISCUSSION AND RESEARCH

8. He meant that . . . 'women exist to serve men' (p. 144). What would you reply to someone who said that God made women to be servants of men?

9. 'Customs concerning women have changed in very many parts of the world' (p. 144).
   (a) In your experience, what have been the two biggest changes of this sort?
   (b) What are the benefits of such changes?
   (c) What, if any, are the difficulties?
   (d) In many countries the government has plans to encourage women to share more actively in the life of the community, e.g. in Papua, New Guinea.
   (i) How wise is it for a government to make this official government policy?
   (ii) How necessary is it?

10. 'Should women be leaders in a congregation?' (p. 144).
    (a) In what matters do the women already take a lead in your congregation?
    (b) Should they be ordained as leaders? Give reasons for your answer.

11. 'Women should be free to serve the community in those ways in which men cannot serve it' (p. 146).
    What are those 'ways'?

12. 'A husband and a wife need each other' is a comment in 1 Cor. 11.11 and 12. Give two examples from present-day life to show that this is true.

13. 'Use the many and different ways which God has provided so that we may make right judgements' (p. 147).

Consider a decision on an important matter which your local Church Council or School Council took recently.

(a) What ways did the members use to reach their decision?

(b) Which, if any, of the ways referred to in the note on 11.13 did they use?

14. 'God has not intended your congregation to live apart from other groups of Christians' (p. 147).

(a) In what ways do members of your congregation work or meet with other congregations?

(b) What is the last occasion on which this took place?

11.17–34 Fellowship at the Lord's Supper

You cannot honour God in worship unless you are also honouring one another

OUTLINE

11.17–22: When you meet together you are going wrong in three ways:

(a) There are divisions among you (vv. 18 and 19);

(b) Your rich members refuse to wait for the poor members (v. 21a);

(c) Some of the rich get drunk (v. 21b).

11.23–26: I will remind you of Jesus's Last Supper in order to show how far you have fallen away from true worship.

11.27–32: Unless you change your behaviour, God will judge you rather than bless you.

11.33,34: So consider each other's needs when you meet.

INTERPRETATION

1. *Why did Paul write these verses?* Because Christians at Corinth had sent a message to say that when the congregation met to have a meal together and to worship God, the members were disorderly and divided. They were so disorderly that some members got drunk. They were so divided that the richer members forgot the needs of the poorer members, and thought that in spite of this they could worship God quite satisfactorily. Paul had already referred to other reasons why they were divided (see notes on 1.12 and 1.17). We consider further reasons in the note on 11.18 below.

2. *The main teaching* concerns ways in which this divided congregation could be united. Paul referred here to three ways:

(a) By remembering Jesus: As Christians meet together, they need to

149

remember the way in which Jesus 'gave Himself'. See 'my body which is for you' (v. 24).

(b) By understanding that 'loving God' and 'loving each other' go together. It is nonsense for a member to say 'I love God' while he is failing to show respect and love for a fellow-member (see note on v. 20).

(c) By each member examining himself. Everyone who joins in the public worship of God needs to stop and ask himself, 'How far am I building up the fellowship of this congregation by my behaviour?' These were not, of course, the only ways in which the Corinthians at that time or members of a modern congregation could be united. See notes on p. 12 and p. 162.

3. *The Last Supper.* Although Paul wrote vv. 17–34 mainly to restore order and fellowship in the congregation of Corinth, vv. 23–26 are of special importance for Christians. These four verses contain the earliest reference which we have to Jesus's Last Supper.

NOTES

11.17. When you come together . . .:

1. In the whole of chapter 11 Paul urged the Corinthians to cleanse their public worship of its evils. In this section (vv. 17–34) he referred to the evil of division (see v. 18), and emphasized the importance of fellowship and unity. The phrase 'come together' occurs three times in the RSV translation of vv. 17–34, and there are other words and phrases which refer to fellowship, or to the lack of it, in the congregation.

2. What sort of 'coming together' was it? From 10.14–22 and 11.17–34 we can picture the scene as it was in many congregations at that time:

It is evening, and the Christians have finished their day's work. They have met to eat a meal together, perhaps in the house of one of the members. It is a meal which they have regularly. Members have brought their own food and drink, and are expected to wait for the others to come before starting to eat. Someone lights the oil lamps. Then the meal begins, as the leader takes a loaf of bread, says a prayer of thanksgiving, and then breaks the bread so that everyone can share it. After that the rest of the meal follows. Finally the leader takes a cup of wine and everyone drinks from it.

3. In what way was this meal different from other meals?

(a) The chief purpose in having it was not to satisfy their hunger and thirst, but to honour Jesus Christ as Lord. It was 'the Lord's' Supper.

(b) It was based on the Last Supper which Jesus had with His disciples as He prepared to give His life on the cross.

(c) Those who took part did so in order to share the benefits which God offered them as a result of Jesus's obedience and death.

(d) How is this supper different from the Lord's Supper as later Christians celebrated it? Later Christians separated the meal from the worship. They called the meal *Agape* or 'Love-Meal', and used the name 'Lord's Supper' for the worship. Later still, Christians no longer had any meal. They met simply for the service of the Lord's Supper. They have given this service many other and different names: e.g. Holy Communion, Mass, Eucharist, the Liturgy, the Breaking of Bread. Today some Christians are once again combining the service of Holy Communion with a fellowship-meal.

11.18. When you assemble as a Church, there are divisions among you:

1. The word 'church' (Greek: *ecclesia*) means the People of God meeting together (see note on 1.2, p. 5). If they were not united they were harming the worship. It was necessary for them to heal their divisions, as it is necessary for present-day Christians of a congregation to heal theirs.

2. What caused divisions? From vv. 21 and 22 it seems that rich members separated from the poor members. Perhaps also those who spoke in tongues sat apart from those who did not. And perhaps the Jewish members refused to eat with the Gentiles. Since those days other and perhaps even worse divisions have arisen, e.g. one group in a congregation has separated from the rest and has gone away to become a separate body. Why have these divisions occurred? Sometimes because of 'doctrine' or 'theology', i.e. because Christians interpret the Gospel in different ways. One group says that its members have true doctrine but that other groups have not. Sometimes divisions occur for personal reasons. In some parts of India, those who are descended from Brahmin (high-caste Hindu) families worship apart from those who used to be 'low-caste'. In other places the more educated people sit apart from the less educated, or those with darker skins worship apart from those with paler skins.

3. But in spite of divisions in the congregation in Corinth the members did continue to meet together for the Lord's Supper, and Paul encouraged them to do so, in order that they should become more united. In contrast to this, many Christians today believe that they should not share the bread and wine at Holy Communion *until* they are fully united. The question is an important one: 'Does the Holy Communion exist chiefly to *express* a unity which the worshippers have already, or to *create* unity among them?'

11.19. There must be factions among you: Perhaps Paul was here just stating a fact: 'Some of you are so puffed up that you think you are superior to the rest, and so long as you think this there will be divisions'. Or perhaps he was giving them a warning, by referring to the separation which God makes and will make between human beings, as he did in 2 Corinthians 5.10: 'We must all appear before the judgement seat.' Whatever he meant, Paul did *not* mean, 'Ah well, people will always quarrel. It can't be helped!' In this chapter and in 1.10–31 he was urging them to heal their divisions. If present-day Christians follow that teaching, they will do everything to help members of the congregation to know and respect each other. They will also live in fellowship with neighbouring congregations as far as others will allow.

11.20. It is not the Lord's Supper that you eat: This is the first time in this letter that Paul used the phrase 'Lord's Supper'. What did he mean by saying that the supper was 'the Lord's'? Mainly that it was held in 'honour of Jesus' or 'in honour of what He did for us' or 'in remembrance of Jesus'. But the Christians at Corinth were not eating the supper in 'honour of the Lord', because each person was concerned about *getting* things for himself (see v. 21).

The Lord's Supper was based on Jesus's Last Supper in which Jesus said that He was *giving* Himself, 'My body . . . for you' (v. 24). No Christians can honour Jesus and what He did if they are dishonouring each other. See v. 22: 'Humiliate those who have nothing'. Paul had first discovered this truth when he was going to Damascus to persecute the Christians. He heard the voice, 'I am Jesus, whom you are persecuting' (Acts 9.5), i.e. 'It is Jesus, not just Christians, whom you are attacking.' If, in our own worship, we are in any way failing to honour individuals or groups in the congregation, we are failing to honour God.

11.23a. I received from the Lord what I also delivered to you:
1. **'I received'.** What Paul had 'received' was the account of the Last Supper. As he had received it, so he had passed it on to the Corinthian Christians. Now he reminded them of it in vv. 23–25. He said 'I received' to show that neither he nor other Church leaders of that time had invented the story.

2. **'From the Lord'.** This might mean that Paul had received it from God in a vision. More likely it means that he received it from fellow-Christians who had been told about the Last Supper by those who were present. In this way it was originally 'from the Lord'. If Paul 'received' it in a vision, would it be a more reliable account than if he had received it from other Christians? Not necessarily. Not everyone who has a vision about God receives the whole truth from God.

11.23b. That the Lord Jesus on the night when he was betrayed . . . : This is the beginning of Paul's account of the Last Supper in vv. 23–25. He told it to his readers in order to correct their unloving behaviour. He was saying, 'Let the Spirit of Jesus at the Last Supper come into you when you meet together.' This message is of course important for all Christians as they meet in the name of Christ.

This passage concerns present-day Christians for another reason also: it shows how the Holy Communion service began. Verses 23–25 are the earliest reference to the Last Supper which exists. Paul wrote in AD 54; Mark probably wrote ten years later; Luke and Matthew later still. The four passages are not the same, but they all show that as Jesus gave His disciples bread and wine, these things were a sign that He was giving His

'What did Paul mean by saying that the supper was "the Lord's"?' (p. 152).

This family in the Philippines are having their supper.

Do you think that this sort of meal could be called 'the Lord's'? If so, for what reasons?

life for them and for all mankind. This is 'the Spirit of Jesus' at His Last Supper.

11.24a. When he had given thanks, he broke it: Jesus gave thanks to God for the bread, i.e. He 'said grace', or said a 'blessing' for it. The Greek word is *eucharist-esas*. It is because of this word that many Churches have called the Holy Communion service a 'eucharist'. Jesus probably said words which were often spoken by the head of any Jewish household: 'Blessed are you, O Lord our God, King eternal, who brings forth bread out of the earth.'

'In the same way' (v. 25) means that He also 'gave thanks' for the wine. From 10.16 we see that those who spoke at the Lord's Supper in Corinth also 'gave thanks' for the bread and wine.

11.24b. This is my body which is for you: People often ask 'How could the bread be Jesus's body? Did Jesus mean that He was changing the bread into His body? In considering such questions, we need to remember:

1. The disciples could see Jesus, and they could see the bread. They could see that the two were not the same.

2. It was the custom of Jesus and of other Jewish teachers to speak in picture-language (see note on p. 32). In the Jewish Passover service (which is still used today) someone asks the question, 'What do you mean by this?' (pointing to the bread and other food). When the leader replies, 'This is the bread of affliction which our fathers ate . . .' no one thinks that the bread has been changed. We also note on p. 65 that the word 'body' means something different from 'flesh'. We may interpret it as meaning 'self' or 'personality'.

3. Jesus spoke these words on the very day on which He was crucified (the Jewish day began at sunset. See v. 23b). So 'body' meant 'the body which I am this day giving or sacrificing'. 'Blood' meant 'my life which I am today giving away by dying'.

4. Jesus held the Last Supper at the time of the Passover Festival. See 1 Corinthians 5.7: 'Christ our paschal (i.e. Passover) lamb'. At Passover time the Jews ate the bread in thanksgiving that God had delivered them from Egypt. They called it 'the body of the Passover'. So when Jesus gave His disciples bread He was showing them that He was delivering them and setting them free. So the words in 11.24b mean, 'I am giving myself to set you free'. It seems that Jesus was wanting to show the reason *why* He was sacrificing Himself rather than to show *what* the bread was.

11.24c. Do this in remembrance of me:

1. What did Jesus want them to do in remembrance of Him? He wanted them to take the bread, to say a prayer of thanksgiving, to break the bread, and to share it, as He had done. So the first Christians did these things at the 'Lord's Supper'. But as they did these things Jesus also wanted them to give themselves in love and service to other people (as He was giving Himself). The Corinthians were not good at doing this. So for Christians,

'doing this' is not only worshipping at a Holy Communion service. It is worshipping in such a way that they are set free to give themselves away in love.

2. What did they remember? They remembered what God had done for them through Jesus Christ, just as the Jews at the Passover remembered what God had done for them in Egypt. But for Christians 'remembering' is more than thinking about something that happened in the past. It is thinking about the past in such a way that it makes a difference to the present. A woman who looks at her wedding ring may remember her wedding some years ago. But as she does so, it is an opportunity to rededicate herself to love her husband in the present. So Christians who 'remember' the death of Jesus by eating bread and drinking wine share in the benefits of His death; e.g. they are set free to love one another and to serve Christ in the world today.

Some people ask further questions, such as these:

(a) Did Jesus say these words? They are not in Mark's or Matthew's Gospels, nor in most versions of Luke's Gospel. All that we can say with certainty is: (1) Paul's account is the earliest account, and it is likely to be accurate; (2) the Christians of Paul's day had the Lord's Supper because they believed that Jesus had said these words.

(b) What is meant by 'bread'? Is it necessary to use barley or wheat bread as Jesus did, in order to obey these words? Most Christians have said 'Yes'. But in some places it is not possible to obtain this sort of bread. In other places it is so expensive that Church members do not believe that it is right to spend money in buying it. So they use something else, e.g. rice bread and tea, instead of wheat bread and wine. In other places, e.g. in parts of Melanesia, many Christians use coconut juice and sweet potato, which are their ordinary food. They do this because Jesus used the ordinary food of His time (bread and wine). The Church authorities in every area have to decide what is right.

11.25. This cup is the new covenant in my blood . . . do this as often as you drink it in remembrance of me:

1. The words are different in the various accounts in the Gospels, but the meaning is not very different. By dying, Jesus was making possible a new 'covenant' or agreement between God and man. This is what He was showing His disciples when He gave them the cup.

2. There was an old covenant which existed between God and the Israelites since the time of Moses. According to Exodus 24.8 it was made by the shedding of blood. Now through the obedience of Jesus and through His willingness to shed His blood there was a new covenant. There was a new relationship. Those who joined in the Lord's Supper could enter into this new relationship with God as they drank the wine.

3. In what way was this covenant 'new'? It was 'new':

(a) Because it had only existed since the death of Jesus;

(b) Because it now existed for everyone who was committed to the service of God in Jesus Christ, and not only for Jews;

(c) Because those who live under it realize that it exists through the grace, generosity, and forgiveness of God. In the past it was known that God was a God who forgives people, but there was a belief that His covenant with His People partly depended on His People keeping the law.

4. What does 'Do this as often as you drink it' mean? It seems to mean, 'Whenever you drink wine at a Lord's Supper remember this new relationship (which is possible through my life and death)'. Some Christians, e.g. the Society of Friends (Quakers), believe that it means, 'Whenever you drink anything in fellowship with others, remember this new relationship', i.e. 'Let every meal at which you drink be a meal at which you remember my life and death.' It is certainly good if Christians use meals in this way. 'Saying grace' helps them to do it.

11.26. You proclaim the Lord's death until he comes: How did they proclaim it? We do not know whether Paul meant: 'You show by your actions (breaking and sharing a loaf and pouring and sharing wine) that Jesus gave His life for us,' *or* 'You proclaim this in words'. But since Paul's time it has been the custom at Holy Communion to proclaim Jesus's death both by actions and by words. In this verse the two important truths are:

1. It is Jesus's death, i.e. His obedience and self-giving, that they must proclaim. Paul meant, 'Compare this with the way that some of you are only concerned with what you can get for yourselves at the Lord's Supper.'

2. The Lord's Supper is a time of looking forward (see 'until he comes'). The life and death of Jesus were part of the whole work of God, which He will one day complete (see note p. 201). Then all evil will be overcome. So the Lord's Supper was a time of hope and joy. In many modern Holy Communion services the people declare: 'Christ has died! Christ is risen! Christ will come again!'

11.28. Let a man examine himself, and so eat . . .: From vv. 17–22 and vv. 33, 34 of this chapter it is clear that this means, 'Someone who is going to eat and drink at the Lord's Supper should test himself about his attitude to other worshippers' (see v. 31, 'If we judged ourselves'). So a worshipper asks himself, 'What are the needs of the other people present? Who is in trouble today? Who is a stranger? What can I do to build up the fellowship among us? How have I failed in this respect?'

As a worshipper tests himself concerning his attitude to other members, he will need also to test himself concerning his whole attitude to God and to himself. The words do *not* mean that this worshipper should make sure that he is without sin before he 'eats and drinks'. The Lord's Supper was (and Holy Communion is) for sinners. It is for sinners who rejoice that God forgives them under the new covenant. See note on v. 25 above.

11.29. Anyone who eats and drinks without discerning the body . . . eats and drinks judgement upon himself:

1. 'Not discerning (i.e. not seriously concerning oneself about) the body' may mean: (a) eating the broken bread and drinking the poured out wine without realizing that they represent the death of Christ, or (b) eating and drinking without noticing the other worshippers or caring about them. As in chapter 12, 'body' refers to the whole congregation (see 12:12,13,25,26). But in practice the two interpretations are the same. Anyone who really remembers the self-giving of Christ will want to give himself for other people. Anyone who tries to give himself for other people will need to be filled with the spirit of Jesus.

2. 'Not discerning the body' is the same as 'eating the bread . . . in an unworthy manner' (v. 27). The result is judgement which the person concerned brings upon himself.

11.30. That is why many of you are weak: This does not mean that whenever someone behaves badly God sends sickness to him. But God has made the world in such a way that when Christians do not love each other they become more open to the forces of evil and sickness that are always at work in the world. We see this, for instance, among those people who refuse to forgive others. There are certain illnesses which, according to many doctors, come to such people. Note that the word 'weak' has not the same meaning as it had in 8.7 and 9.22.

11.32. When we are judged by the Lord we are chastened: ('chastened' means 'disciplined' or 'corrected'). When we have brought judgement (and suffering) on ourselves, it can become a way of our being corrected and renewed, so that 'we may not be condemned'. A man who continually lost his temper with other people discovered one day that he had no friends left. He was overwhelmed by a feeling of loneliness. He saw what he must do in order to start a useful life again. God was 'chastening' him. God who is stern is also merciful. So while we suffer, we have hope.

11.33. Wait for one other: Here Paul summed up what he had said in vv. 17–34: 'Consider the needs of your fellow-members when you have the Lord's Supper'.

In some Churches the members have done exactly what the words say. Most of the congregation of the Dominican (Roman Catholic) church in Amsterdam in Holland arrive more than half an hour before the Sunday 'Mass' begins at 11 a.m. During this time they talk and sing together (often learning a new hymn) while others are arriving.

On Sunday evening in the church in Yezd, in Iran, the members meet at 6.30 p.m. and drink tea together. If it is warm they meet outside, if not they meet inside. When the service begins at 7 p.m. they sit together.

In both these churches they find that they can pray together and pray for each other with understanding because they have already sung and spoken together.

STUDY SUGGESTIONS

WORDS

1. The phrase 'come together' occurs three times in the RSV translation of vv. 17–34 (p. 150).
   What *three* other words or phrases are there in these verses which refer to fellowship among the worshippers?
2. (a) What does the word 'church' mean in 11.18?
   (b) What two other meanings can this word also have?
3. (a) What does the word 'covenant' (11.25) mean?
   (b) With what word is it translated in another language known to you?
   (c) What does that word mean when used in ordinary conversation?

CONTENT

4. (a) What sort of things did some of the Christians at Corinth do which showed Paul that there were 'divisions' among them?
   (b) Paul's aim in vv. 17–34 was to heal these divisions. Why did he refer to Jesus's Last Supper?
5. How did Paul know what happened at the Last Supper?
6. What did Jesus mean by saying, 'This is my body', when He took the bread into His hands?
7. 'This cup is the new covenant in my blood' (11.25). In what *two* ways was that covenant 'new'?

BIBLE

8. What is the single piece of teaching which we find in all the following passages? Matt. 25.45; Acts 9.5; 1 Cor. 11.20–22.
9. The accounts of the Last Supper in the New Testament are not the same (see note on 11.23b). Compare 1 Cor. 11.23–25; Luke 22.17–20; and Mark 14.22–24.
   (a) What words of Jesus are the *same* in all three accounts?
   (b) What word of Jesus do we find in Mark and 1 Corinthians, but not in Luke?

DISCUSSION AND RESEARCH

10. 'He emphasized the importance of fellowship and unity' (p. 150). Why is it important for a congregation to be united?
11. What do you think are the *two* biggest differences between
    (a) The Lord's Supper which Christians celebrated in Paul's time, and
    (b) The service of Holy Communion which you celebrate in your congregation?
12. 'Does the Holy Communion exist chiefly to *express* a unity which the

worshippers have already, or to *create* unity among them?' (p. 151). Give reasons for your reply.

13. 'If, in our own worship, we are in any way failing to honour individuals or groups . . . we are failing to honour God' (p. 152).
    (a) In what *two* ways can Christians show honour to one another when they meet as a Church?
    (b) How far are these ways proving effective in creating unity in your local congregation?
14. 'Jesus gave thanks to God for the bread', i.e. He 'said grace' (p. 154).
    (a) Does your family 'say grace' before meals? (b) What is the value of doing so?
15. For Christians, 'remembering' is more than thinking about something that happened in the past (p. 155).
    (a) Give an example from everyday life to show the truth of this quotation (similar to the example of the woman remembering her wedding).
    (b) What did Jesus want His disciples to 'remember'?
16. 'In some areas they use . . . rice-bread and tea instead of wheat-bread and wine (at Holy Communion)' (p. 155). (a) What are the advantages and disadvantages of doing that? (b) What is your own opinion?
17. Christians meet together for the 'Lord's Supper' or 'Holy Communion'. They also take other meals together. What is the chief difference between the two?
18. 'Let a man examine himself' (11.28).
    (a) What sort of examination or test did Paul want his readers to give themselves before they met with other worshippers?
    (b) What ways do Christians of your own congregation use to examine themselves?
    (c) How far do they ask others to help them?
    If possible, ask questions (b) and (c) from members of other Churches and record the answers.

12.1–31 Ministry

You need each other

OUTLINE

Again Paul had to write about a number of problems which the Corinthians put to him. In this outline we (a) suggest what each problem was, and (b) give a summary of Paul's reply.

1 Cor. 12.1–3: *Their problem:* 'Some people are cursing Jesus in worship, and saying that the Spirit of God is leading them to do so.'

Paul's answer: 'The Spirit of God leads people to call Jesus "Lord". No one who curses Jesus is being led by the Spirit.'

1 Cor. 12.4–11: *Their problem:* 'Different Christians have different gifts, and people are saying that each gift comes from a different God.'

Paul's answer: 'There is only one true God, who is the giver of all gifts.'

1 Cor. 12.12–13: *Their problem:* 'There are many different sorts of people in our congregation. Should each kind form their own group?'

Paul's answer: 'No! Different Christians need each other as much as parts of the human body need each other.'

1 Cor. 12.14–27: *Their problem:* 'Some members are saying that they have the important gifts and are despising those who do not have the same gifts.'

Paul's answer: 'You all need each other.'

1 Cor. 12.28–31: *Their problem:* 'Some members who have special gifts are saying that those who do not have the same gifts as themselves are not truly Christian.'

Paul's answer: 'It is God's intention to give us Christians different gifts, so that we can support each other.'

INTERPRETATION

The Corinthians who had become Christians had received new power in their lives, which Paul called the power 'of the Spirit'. They could do things which they had not been able to do before. This was wonderful, and Paul thanked God for it (1.4). But some of them began to say that only those who had special gifts, e.g. the power to do miracles or to speak in tongues (v. 10), had really received the Spirit. They said that the others were not truly Christians. As a result, the congregation was divided. Those with special gifts despised those without them; those without gifts envied those who had them.

Paul's reply is in chapters 12, 13 and 14. In chapter 12 he compared the Christian congregation to a 'body'. He chose this word for two special reasons:

1. A body has unity, i.e. each part of it depends on the other parts for its health (see note on p. 162).

2. Its parts are different from each other. It has 'variety'. Paul's message was that the Corinthian Church would be healthy if its members behaved like a human body in those two ways; i.e.:

1. *By being united.* Corinthian Christians needed to be united, first, in order to avoid confusion in worship; secondly, to do their special work in the world, e.g. to declare the Gospel clearly; thirdly, in order to survive in a non-Christian world.

No doubt their Church was united when Paul founded it. But how could

'You all need each other' (p. 160).

These fishermen in the Solomon Islands need each other when they load their heavy nets into the canoe before setting out for the evening's catch.

What are some of the ways in which the members of your congregation 'need each other'?

it keep its unity? How does any congregation keep its unity? Paul's answer in chapter 12 was:

(a) By members being loyal to the same Lord. See v. 27a: the body is Christ's.

(b) By all recognizing that some of them should be given the authority to be leaders. See v. 28 'God has appointed . . . apostles . . . prophets . . . teachers'.

(c) By learning to depend on each other.

There was an underground prison in Bucharest (it is probably still there) where there were no windows and no light. Water dripped from the roof and all through the year it was cold. On one occasion eighteen elderly members of the National Peasants Party were put in it. They survived only because they made themselves into a human chain and walked round and round in the dark. Although they were all soaked by the icy water, by clinging together each man got warmth from the ones behind and in front of him. They survived because they knew that they needed each other. The same is true of any Christian congregation today.

2. *By having variety* among the members. This was important in order that each member might live as God's Holy Spirit moved him to live: 'Do not quench the Spirit' (1 Thess. 5.19). In this way members would be open to new ideas, and would be free to make changes when changes were needed. It was important because each member, if he was allowed to be different from others, could make his own special contribution (v. 21).

These two ways in which a human body keeps healthy – by having 'unity' and by allowing 'variety' – are the two main subjects of this chapter. And they are two ways in which every congregation keeps healthy. Every congregation needs to work for 'unity' and for 'variety' at the same time. If it places too much importance on 'unity', it is likely to be too much controlled by its leader or its traditions. If it places too much importance on 'variety', members become separated from each other and become insecure and disorderly.

NOTES

12.3. Jesus is Lord: Paul wrote this verse because the Corinthians were puzzled. They had said, 'If someone speaks in an extraordinary way ("in tongues"), our members are greatly impressed (just as people are impressed by magic). But is it always the Spirit who has inspired such a person?' Here Paul said 'No! If someone curses Jesus, you cannot say that it is the Spirit who has inspired him! You can tell if a man is led by the Spirit by what he says about Jesus – e.g. if he acknowledges the authority of Jesus ("Jesus is Lord").' We note:

1. The fact that a person speaks in an extraordinary way does not prove that he is speaking the truth. In a district of Uganda the leader of a small

162

religious sect used to preach with extraordinary power. But in his preaching he often abused other Church leaders. One of them asked him why he did so. 'When I speak with you now,' he replied, 'I accept you as a brother, but when I preach I am filled with the Spirit, and what I say is what the Spirit is saying.' It was this kind of mistake which Paul was referring to here.

2. By using the words 'Jesus is Lord', Christians were saying something very important about Jesus Christ. 'Jesus' was the name of the man who grew up in Nazareth. 'Lord' was the name given to God Himself. See note on 'Lord', p. 7. A Christian should use both names: (a) 'Jesus', the Person who became flesh according to the Gospels, (b) the 'Lord', the eternal God who sends us His Holy Spirit.

3. Later on, Christians used these words, 'Jesus is Lord', as the creed which candidates must say before they were baptized (see Phil. 2.11). Why are the creeds we use today longer and more complicated? Partly because people at different times have asked a great many questions which had to receive an answer in the creeds, e.g. 'Is Jesus fully God?'; partly because false answers were often given.

12.4. There are varieties of gifts, but the same Spirit: God had given the Corinthians different 'gifts'. It is important to notice that the list in vv. 8–11 is a list of 'gifts' (or 'powers' or 'talents') and not a list of titles or positions which members held in a congregation.

Some members had the power to express in words what they believed (v. 8). Others were able to heal the sick because of their faith in Him (vv. 9 and 10a). Some could 'prophesy' (see note on p. 178); others knew when a speaker was being inspired by the Holy Spirit and when he was not ('distinguish between spirits', v. 10). Others could speak in 'tongues'; and others could interpret such speech. See v. 10, and Special Note C, p. 185. We see that Paul put the gift of 'tongues' last in the list, whereas the Corinthians were putting it first.

The Greek word *charisma*, here translated 'gift', is connected with the word *charis* ('grace'). Perhaps the best translation is 'grace-gift'. So Paul meant: (1) if you have a gift, remember that God gave it to you because He loves you, not because you earned it; (2) look at God the giver, rather than at those who have not got your gift. In this way you will avoid feeling 'superior', and others will not feel envious.

Most of the gifts referred to in vv. 8–10 are rather unusual ones. But Paul's words are equally true for all gifts which members of a congregation have. Some are good at listening, some at talking; some are naturally adventurous, some are cautious; some tend to emphasize the tenderness of God, some see more clearly His severity. A Christian is happy that there are 'varieties', i.e. that other members are different from himself, have had different experiences of God, express themselves differently. Verse 4 shows how absurd it is for anyone to say 'I became a Christian when I was 12 years old or at a prayer-meeting, so this is how it should happen to you.' It is as absurd as saying, 'Everyone ought to be like me,' or 'Everyone ought to have a face like mine'!

12.5. There are varieties of service, but the same Lord: The word which is here translated in the RSV as 'service' is *diakonia* (usually translated 'ministry', see note on 3.5b, p. 33. So Paul was saying in this verse that there are many sorts of 'ministry' in a congregation, and that the members must together share 'ministry', i.e. share in serving the congregation.

Although the practice of sharing ministry was common in the first two hundred years of the Church's history, very many congregations since that time have departed from this practice as seriously as the congregation in Corinth departed from it. For example, they have thought that there were two classes of people in the Church, those who minister and those who are ministered to. They have mistakenly given the title of 'minister' to one person, and as a result other members have forgotten that each of them also had a ministry. (It is because of this that we have used the name 'Church leader' in this guide instead of 'minister'.)

In order to correct such mistakes, congregations today need to return to Paul's teaching about sharing ministry under 'the same Lord'. Indeed more and more Churches are doing so. In the services of worship, more members are being trained to take an active part, and are not leaving this sort of ministry to one person. Members and leader together visit people and care for them and make the Gospel known among them. A group of members share the work of administration. In order to thank God for the 'varieties of ministry' at a recent Diocesan Synod in Nigeria, the Bishop made a presentation both to a woman who had been a cleaner in a village church for 45 years and to an ordained Church leader who was retiring. See v. 22.

This does not mean that because ministry is shared, a leader is not needed, or that the leader should not have 'authority'. Paul taught in v. 28 that leaders were 'appointed by God'. Indeed, the more that members share in ministry, the more they need a leader to train them and keep them working in unity.

Nevertheless, there is a difficulty concerning the leader which every Church has to solve: How can the congregation respect the authority of their leader and yet give equal honour to all those who share ministry with him?

12.12. As the body is one . . . so it is with Christ: Paul wrote this verse in a very much shortened form. If he had written it out fully, we should have read something like this: 'As the human body is one, so is the congregation, and the congregation is the body of those who have been baptized and are "in Christ"' (see note, p. 7). The words do not mean that the Church congregation *is* Christ. It is not true to say that when the Church leaders speak, then it is certain that Christ is saying what they are saying.

12.13a. By one Spirit we were all baptized . . . : In order to show that the various members were one body, Paul here reminded them that they had all been baptized with water. The Greek is '*In* one Spirit' (not 'by'), i.e. when they first became Christians and were baptized, they had all shared in the same Holy Spirit of God. Therefore they were one body.

Members of many Pentecostal Churches, however, interpret this verse quite differently. They say:

That 'baptism by one Spirit' in this verse does not refer to water-baptism at conversion;

That Paul was referring to a different event which all Christians need to experience;

That this 'event' usually happens after conversion, and is often accompanied by speaking in tongues;

That it is the event referred to in Matthew 3.11, where John the Baptist says 'He will baptize you with the Holy Spirit', and in Acts 1.5, where we read 'You shall be baptized with the Holy Spirit' (these words are quoted in Acts 11.16).

We can certainly agree that Christians need to 'grow' after they have been converted and baptized with water. See Special Note on p. 187. *But*:

1. This is just what the Christians in Corinth were failing to do. Paul was certainly not referring here to an event which came after water-baptism, or congratulating them on it. He was reminding them that, having been baptized with water, they all belonged to the one Church.

2. It is not likely that Paul knew about an event called 'baptism-in-the-Spirit' which was different from water-baptism. In the whole of the New Testament there is no reference to baptism in the 'Spirit', except the two passages mentioned above. But there are fifteen references to the water-baptism of Christians in the Book of Acts alone.

We can see how important it is to interpret these words correctly, from a letter which a Christian in Melanesia sent to the leader of his Church:

'I have been a baptized member of the Church for ten years. Although I never did anything very wicked, my faith was very weak. Recently some friends asked me to attend a meeting, and when I went they prayed for me and put their hands on me. Immediately I felt new and clean and close to God. My friends say that I have been baptized by the Holy Spirit, that I am now a 'real Christian', and that soon I shall speak in tongues. I do not understand what has taken place. Can you explain what did happen?'

12.13b. Into one body: We have seen some reasons (p. 160 above) why Paul used the word 'body'. We may note that it is a 'picture-word' (see note on p. 32). Paul found it a useful word. But it was not the only suitable picture-word to use when referring to a congregation. Paul had already called them a 'field' (3.6–9), a 'building (3.9–15), a 'temple' (3.16). People today use many other words, e.g. 'family', 'team', 'tree'. General Booth called his followers an 'army' – the Salvation Army. In one district of

South India the usual word is *jumaat*, the same word which is used for a class taught by a teacher.

Church leaders cannot do without these picture-words. But there are dangers in using them especially if the leader chooses only one word and, like General Booth, bases his teaching on that word. There may be special dangers also in comparing Christians to something which is not living, like 'building'. We may note here that when Paul used the word 'body' in chapter 12, he was referring to the congregation in Corinth. In other letters he used it to refer to the whole Church of God (see Eph. 4.4; Col. 2.19).

12.23. Those parts of the body which we think less honourable we invest with the greater honour: The teaching was: 'Therefore show special respect to Church members who seem to be less important.' Was Paul really saying here that some parts of the body are less honourable than others? If he was, he was contradicting what he wrote in 6.19, that a person's body is God's temple, i.e. that all parts are honourable. We do not cover up some parts with clothes because they are 'less honourable'. We do so chiefly for the sake of comfort, to protect the body from heat or cold. But it may be that Paul, in writing these words, was using the language of people in Corinth, and that it was not his own belief that there are parts of the body which are less honourable than other parts.

12.26. If one member suffers, all suffer together: If one member of the congregation at Corinth was suffering because others despised him, then the whole congregation was weakened. Why? Because all the members needed the special contribution of that member, and they were not receiving it. In the same way, the others will be strengthened if the despised member is treated with honour.

We see this easily in a small congregation. It is less easy to notice that it is happening in a large congregation, where the suffering of one member may affect the other members much less. Does this mean that all congregations should be small? Should a very big congregation split up into separate smaller groups so that members can know each other, and can therefore be more aware of each other's sufferings?

12.27. You are the body of Christ: The members of a Church congregation are not simply a body. They are the 'body of Christ'. See note on 12.12 (p. 164). The important truths in this phrase are:

1. The members did not create the Church in Corinth (as people might form a debating society or a sports club). Christ created it, and it is His. So members look to Him as the owner. They acknowledge His authority and headship, and are answerable to Him for the way they use His Church.

2. The more that each member acknowledges Christ's authority, the more united all the members become.

3. In a human being, the body is the means by which a person expresses his will. So in each place the Church is the body by means of which Christ expresses His will there and does His work. As St Teresa said, 'Christ has

no body now on earth but yours, no hands but yours . . .'. Paul expressed this more fully in Ephesians (4.1–16) than in 1 Corinthians.

12.28. God has appointed in the church, first apostles, second prophets . . . : All kinds of 'service' or 'ministries' which members give are equally necessary and equally important. See v. 5. This is the message of vv. 28–30. For this reason, 'First apostles, second prophets . . .' cannot mean 'first in importance, second in importance . . .'. These three 'ministries' come before the others in the list simply because they existed before the others. The Church in Corinth would not have existed unless an 'apostle' had first come to Corinth, and 'prophets' and 'teachers' had built up the congregation by teaching and preaching. The other 'ministries' came later.

It is not clear what all the other words in the list mean. 'Helpers' may mean social workers, those who cared for people in special need. 'Administrators' translated the Greek word *kuberneseis*, from which the English word 'government' comes. It is not possible to say which (if any) of the forms of 'ministry' in our modern Churches are the same as the 'ministries' in this list. But it is useful to compare them: see Study Suggestion 6, p. 168. Note that in vv. 29 and 30 the form of each question in Greek shows that Paul expected his readers to answer, 'No'. The translation should be: 'Is everyone an apostle? Of course not!' and so on.

12.31. Earnestly desire the higher gifts: If this is a correct translation, then the words contradict what Paul had said above. He had been explaining that one gift is not 'higher' than another. But these words are probably a statement, not a command. So the meaning is: 'You are earnestly desiring to have gifts which are more important than other people's. Well, I will show you a gift which everyone needs equally, a gift which is more important than any gifts which you have been discussing.' Then he wrote chapter 13 about *agape* or 'love'.

STUDY SUGGESTIONS

WORDS

1. (a) What is the full meaning of the word which is translated 'gifts' in this chapter (vv. 4, 9, 30, 31)?
   (b) How is it translated in another language known to you?

REVIEW OF CONTENT

2. What mistakes had the Corinthian Christians made, to which Paul referred in 1 Cor. 12?
3. Why is it important for a congregation: (a) to have unity? (b) to have 'diversity' or variety?
4. Why did Paul write about feet, hands, eyes, and ears in vv. 14–21?

BIBLE STUDY

5. Compare 12.7 with 10.23, 10.33, 14.12, and 14.26. What single truth did Paul declare in these verses?

6. Paul referred to different 'ministries', i.e. ways in which Church members can give service, in the following four passages: 1 Cor. 12.8–10; 1 Cor. 12.28; Rom. 12.6–8; Eph. 4.11
(a) Which *five* ways of ministering appear in more than one of those passages?
(b) In which of the ways mentioned by Paul are members giving service in your own congregation? (If possible give the names of the members in each case.)

7. (i) To what did the writers of the following passages compare the Church?
(a) Rom. 12.5 (b) 1 Cor. 12.12,13 (c) Eph. 2.20–22 (d) 1 Pet. 2.4–8 (e) 1 Pet. 5.2
(ii) What other picture-words have you heard used for the Church?
(iii) What is (a) the value (b) the danger of using each of the picture-words which you used in replying to (ii) above?

DISCUSSION AND RESEARCH

8. 'Jesus is Lord' (12.3).
(a) What does your Church ask adult candidates to say before they are baptized?
(b) If they have to say more than 'Jesus is Lord', explain why more is needed.

9. 'There are varieties of gifts' (12.4).
Consider the members of a school or college class you belong to, or of a small congregation you know.
(a) What gifts has God given to each of them?
(b) How far is the Church using these gifts for the 'common good' (12.7)?

10. Every congregation needs to work for 'unity' and for 'variety' (or 'diversity') at the same time (p. 162).
(a) How can anyone tell that a congregation is (i) working for unity? (ii) working for variety?
(b) In a congregation which you know well, to what extent do you think the members are working for both unity and variety?

11. Paul was saying . . . 'The members (of a congregation) must together share "ministry"' (p. 164).
(a) What did Paul mean by 'ministry' ('service' in RSV)?
(b) How can a congregation respect the authority of their leader and yet give equal honour to all those who share 'ministry' with him?
(c) What are the best ways of helping each member to use his special gifts in the life of the congregation?

12. 'If one member suffers, all suffer together' (12.26).
    (a) Give an example from your experience.
    (b) 'It is less easy to notice that it is happening in a large congregation' (p. 166). What is your opinion?
    (c) If this statement is true, does it mean that a big congregation should 'split up into separate smaller groups' (p. 166)?
13. 'Baptism-in-the-Spirit' (p. 165).
    Part of a letter written in Melanesia is given on p. 165. The writer asked: 'Can you explain what did happen?' If you had been the leader of that Church, how would you have replied?

13.1–13 Love

'Loving' means whole-heartedly wanting the best for other people

OUTLINE

13.1–3: We Christians may fulfil all sorts of religious duties, but what we do is useless unless we love each other.
13.4–7: A person is 'loving' if he wholeheartedly wants the best things for other people.
13.8–13: The day will come when human beings no longer need gifts from God. But there will never be a time when we do not need to love people.

INTERPRETATION

1. Paul wrote this chapter for the same reason that he wrote chapter 12. It was because the Corinthian Christians were divided amongst themselves. He had to show them a way of becoming a stronger fellowship. In chapter 12 he had said, 'You are like the different limbs of a human body. God has given you different gifts. You need each other.' In chapter 13 he said:

(a) You do excellent things because of the gifts God has given you. But everything you do is useless unless you are loving each other.

(b) This is true of everyone, whatever the gifts are that he has received.

2. In this chapter, then, Paul was making a comparison – between the gift of love and other gifts. He was not giving a description of love. (See, for example, vv. 4–7 in which he was chiefly showing what love is *not*.)

In order to find out what 'loving' means we need to study the way in which Jesus lived, according to the Gospels.

3. But Christians do not learn the meaning of 'loving' unless they meet

each other and work with one another. Studying the word in a dictionary is of some help but not very much. We learn to love by loving. Some years ago the Archbishop of Canterbury was lecturing on 1 Corinthians 13 to a group of clergy. When it was time for them to eat, there was not enough food. Some of the clergy rushed forward to get some before it was all taken. The Archbishop said to someone near him, 'It is at times like this that we can really learn what loving is!'

4. This chapter 13 is mainly about Christians and the way in which Christians need to treat each other; i.e. it is about the behaviour of the Christian congregation as a whole. But what Paul has written here is important also for the ways in which, (a) an individual Christian should behave, (b) Christians should treat everyone, whether they are Christian or not.

NOTES

13.1–2. If I speak in the tongues of men . . . if I have prophetic powers: In verses 1–3 Paul made a list of some of the 'excellent things' that members of a Christian congregation might do, because of the gifts that God had given them. He then explained that if they did these things without loving, what they did was useless. He did not say that they 'ought' to love each other. He said, 'You are wasting your activity unless you love.'

The list of 'excellent things' is:

(a) Speaking in tongues (v. 1) (see Special Note, p. 185).

(b) Prophesying or preaching (v. 2a). (See chapter 14, Interpretation, p. 178.)

(c) Using their minds in understanding religion (v. 2b).

(d) Having great confidence in God (v. 2c, 'all faith').

(e) Sharing their possessions (v. 3a, 'give away all').

(f) Sacrificing their own comfort and safety on behalf of other people (v. 3b, 'give my body . . .').

When a group of Church leaders met recently for a conference, the chairman asked each of them this question: 'What good things is your congregation sometimes tempted to value above loving each other?' One replied, 'Good preaching'. Another, 'A desire to increase in numbers'. Another, 'Activity'. Another, 'Efficiency'. Another, 'Good music' (his congregation had just paid many thousands of dollars for a huge organ). Another, 'Surviving'. What was true of the congregation at Corinth and in many present day congregations is also true of individual Christians.

It is not uncommon to find a Christian who is working hard and giving up his time to help people and yet doing so without love for the people whom he is serving. An ordained Church leader in Sri Lanka wrote his life-story, and referred to verses 1–3 in the following way: 'As a pastor I refused to appeal for funds and relied entirely on prayer. I gave a tenth of my small income to the Church. I had left work which I enjoyed and taken myself and my family to a part of the country that nobody had ever heard of. I never had a holiday. Yet a time came when I felt that something very important was missing in my work.'

13.1: Love:

1. *God's love:* Writers in the New Testament used this word 'love' (the Greek word is *agape*) to mean the way in which we treat each other when we have realized how God, in Jesus Christ, has treated us. Zacchaeus began to care about other people only after Jesus had taken the trouble to visit him (Luke 19.8).

Thus, when we love, it is the result of having been loved. 'We love because He first loved us' (1 John 4.19). Only a strong person is able to love. But none of us has enough strength in himself. We realize this when we read 1 Corinthians 13, especially vv. 4–7. It is impossible for us to love like that unless we are allowing God to work in us.

However, we do not lie down and wait for this to happen to us. Paul told his readers to make it their aim to be loving (14.1).

2. *What 'love' means:* Although Paul did not mention Jesus in chapter 13, it was Jesus who, in His living and dying, has shown us what 'loving' means. He wholeheartedly wanted the best for everyone. He wanted them to have all that was good. Because He wanted this so much, He gave Himself for them.

It is clear, then, that 'loving' (*agape*) is not the same as some other good ways of treating one another which people also call 'loving', e.g.:

(a) It is not the same as the good and strong sexual desire which God has given to a man and his wife for each other's bodies, or the pleasure which God wants them to have from sexual intercourse.

(b) It is not the same as the good and natural feelings which a mother has for a baby whom she has borne, or which a villager has for the village to which he belongs.

(c) It is not the same as liking another person because he or she is attractive and likes the same things that we like. It is far more than friendliness.

13.4: Love is patient and kind . . . not jealous: In vv. 4–7 Paul gives his readers some examples of a 'loving' person:

Patient (v. 4): See also 'bears all things', 'endures all things' (v. 7). They are 'loving' if they are willing to suffer and to go on suffering if that is necessary in order to help someone else. They are like someone who has a wound which is never quite closed.

An old man walked six miles every day for a year, after he had done his day's work, in order to sit with a lonely man in hospital.

A woman is at present living with her sister. The sister is mentally ill, bad tempered, refuses to wash herself, and never shows gratitude or affection. But the woman goes on looking after her with care.

'People are "loving" if they are willing to suffer . . . in order to help someone else' (p. 171).

The crew of inshore lifeboat *Atlantic 21* have volunteered for service in which they often risk their lives to help ships in danger in heavy seas.

Do you think that loving is more valuable when it involves possible suffering? If so, valuable to whom?

Archbishop Luwum of Uganda showed, in a very costly way, his love for his fellow Christians and fellow-countrymen. After very many of them had been killed by the government soldiers, he and the other bishops wrote to the authorities to protest vigorously. When he had written the letter he said to a friend, 'We had to do this for the sake of the Church, but the authorities will not forgive me for it.' A few days later he was arrested and killed.

Kind (v. 4): A person is 'loving' if he looks out for ways of giving practical help to other people. After a burial service a group of mourners were walking towards the widow. One man said, 'I am so sorry for her.' Another man said, 'How sorry are you? I am sorry £5.'

'Loving' is wanting to serve people or serving them in a practical way. Jesus put the emphasis in His teaching on our positively and actively loving one another, rather than telling us 'not to be selfish'.

'Not jealous or boastful' (v. 4b): A person is 'loving' if he so strongly wants other people to be good and happy that he is content when they (rather than he himself) are successful. He is satisfied when someone else's wife (not his own) is chosen to be an 'elder' in the Church. He is just as happy to talk about the large eggs which his neighbour's hens have laid as he is to talk about his own remarkable vegetables.

Not arrogant or rude . . . does not insist on its own way (v. 5a): In a study group a person is 'loving' if he lets the other members talk. He listens carefully to what they say. He expresses his own opinion, but leaves the other members free to accept or reject what he has said.

The headmaster of a Christian school in South Africa has recently written about his staff: 'Some of them are in favour of violent resistance to the existing government. The others believe that resistance must be non-violent. The two groups find it very difficult indeed to listen to each other. But they are able to do so and to do so in love.'

Not irritable (v. 5): A person is 'loving' if, when others criticize him, he believes that their words can help him. For example, a preacher is grateful to a Church member who says that she cannot understand his sermons; a husband is grateful to two fellow-Christians who say that they think he has been speaking harshly to his wife; a teacher thanks students who said they could not hear a question, and repeats the question.

Not resentful (v. 5): A person is 'loving' if he forgives people who have injured him. He receives the hatred which someone has shown to him, instead of throwing it back at the other person.

Towards the end of the second world war a small group of soldiers who were prisoners of war, watched by enemy guards, were waiting in a railway station in Thailand, about to be taken to a new camp. They were the only survivors of their original regiment. All their friends had died as a result of the cruelty of their captors, the enemy who had taken them prisoner three years before. Then a train-load of passengers came into the station and the prisoners saw that they were soldiers from the enemy army. But these soldiers had just come out of a battle and were ragged, starving, dirty, and badly wounded. The prisoners who watched them arrive walked over to them, cleaned their wounds, and shared with them their own tiny stores of rice. The guards who saw this asked, 'Why are you treating your enemies in this way?'

Not rejoice at wrong, but rejoices in the right (v. 6): A lawyer and his wife who lived in a small town had great difficulty in bringing up their children as Christians or as honest citizens. They wished they were as successful as their next-door neighbours whose children were well-behaved, as everyone knew. One day they heard a rumour that their neighbours had been accused of theft. The lawyer confessed to his wife that he was tempted to be glad when he heard this. But what he actually did was to offer the neighbours his help as a lawyer. Later he discovered that they were innocent, and successfully defended them in court. They had a joyful party together to celebrate the result of the case.

Believes all things, hopes all things (v. 7): A school-teacher who loves his pupils believes ('has faith') and hopes that they can make progress. He refuses to despair even when they behave badly or show no interest in learning. He does so because he believes and hopes in God, who lives in them and loves them all.

Endures all things (v. 7): See note on 'patient' (v. 4).

13.8. Love never ends: In verses 8–13 Paul compared 'loving' with the gifts which God had given to Christians in Corinth. The gifts referred to in v. 8 are the gifts which the Corinthian Christians valued so highly: prophesying and preaching (see note, p. 178), speaking in tongues (see p. 185), and 'knowledge' (see p. 101). They are all gifts which God has given to the Church because they are necessary to us on earth 'now', i.e. so long as this world exists.

But loving is necessary and valuable for ever. It is the *only* thing which we can have now in this world and which will continue to be precious after the world has come to an end. Why did Paul say that it is for ever? Because when we love each other we are also loving God through the other person, so to speak. And this relationship with God continues for ever.

If we believe this, then of course we shall regard loving as more important than possessing 'gifts'. We shall not think we are wasting our time if we go on loving. A mother went on writing letters to her absent son year after year, but he never replied. She was not wasting her time or her money. She was sharing in God's activity, His activity of loving.

13.11. When I became a man, I gave up childish ways: In verse 8 Paul showed the difference between the 'gifts' which will one day become unnecessary, and 'loving' which will never disappear. In verses 11 and 12 he used two illustrations of things that become unnecessary. His first illustration in this verse 11 is: We give up many of our childish habits, because we no longer need them, e.g. sucking our mother's milk or holding on to her hand in order to walk.

13.12. Now we see in a mirror dimly, but then face to face: This is Paul's second illustration. The people of Corinth used to make metal mirrors. We can imagine someone looking into one of these mirrors and seeing in it the face of another person who has just arrived and is standing behind him. But he can't see who it is because the mirror is not very clear (it is 'dim'). Then he turns round and sees that it is his own father.

So Paul compared the difference between life on this earth ('now') and life in the world to come ('then'). On earth we need God's gifts because we only know Him 'dimly' (the Greek word means 'in a riddle'). In the world to come we shall know Him clearly, i.e. in the way in which He has always known us.

Christians know God 'dimly' even though He has given Jesus Christ to the world. We know Him in part and not completely. We know Him through signs and symbols. When we realize this we are more likely to have fellowship with other Christians. Each one can share with the others the truth that everyone's understanding of God is incomplete and 'dim'. One cause of disunity is Christians claiming to have greater knowledge of God than is actually possible in this world.

13.13. Faith, hope, love abide . . . the greatest of these is love: This verse surprises many readers. They expect to read 'When other gifts pass away, only love remains.' But they see that 'faith, hope and love' remain. Why do we need 'hope' in the world to come?

Perhaps Paul meant that life in the world to come will, like this life on earth, be like a journey. Therefore as we progress along the journey we shall still need to approach God with faith in Him and hope in Him. But above everything else we shall need to love.

STUDY SUGGESTIONS

WORDS

1. In which *two* of the following sentences does the word 'love' mean the same as it does in 1 Corinthians 13?
   (a) 'Love your neighbour as yourself.'
   (b) He was making love to his wife when the roof fell in.
   (c) He loves his friends because they are always ready to talk to him.
   (d) That cat loves her kittens.
   (e) I hate fish but I love meat.
   (f) It is difficult to love those who have hurt us.
   (g) She has a book called 'The Love-life of the Bower-Bird'.
2. (a) By what word is *agape* translated in another language which you know?

(b) What is the full meaning of this word?

(c) How far does it bring to readers the meaning of 'whole-heartedly wanting the best things for other people' (p. 169)?

CONTENT

3. Why did Paul write chapter 13?
4. Describe a 'loving' Christian, in 30 to 40 words.
5. How is Christian love for someone different from (a) being friends with him, (b) wanting to marry him?
6. What did Paul want to teach when he wrote about the mirror?

BIBLE

7. What do we discover about the meaning of Christian love from each of the following pairs of passages?
   (a) John 13.34 and 1 John 4.19
   (b) John 13.1b and Eph. 4.2
   (c) 1 John 3.18 and 2 Cor. 8.24
   (d) Luke 6.32–35 and Matt. 5.46
8. Which verse (or verses) from each of the following passages most clearly shows Jesus as 'loving'?
   (a) Matt. 26.18–29   (b) Mark 1.21–28   (c) Mark 10.17–22
   (d) Luke 7.36–50   (e) Luke 19.1–7   (f) Luke 23.32–38

DISCUSSION AND RESEARCH

9. What would you say to a reader of 1 Cor. 13 who said, 'But there are people whom I *can't* love!'
10. Notes are given on p. 171 on the words or phrases with which Paul referred to 'loving' in 1 Cor. 13.4–7
    Give examples from everyday life of *four* of them. (Take *one* word or phrase from each verse.)
11. (a) In 1 Cor. 13.1–3 Paul referred to six things which it is very good to do, but which are useless if they are done without love. What were those six things?
    (b) What is your own answer to the question which the Conference Chairman asked (p. 170): 'What good things is your congregation sometimes tempted to value above loving?'
    (c) If you went to live in a new place and joined the Christian congregation there, how could you tell if the members valued 'loving' above everything else?
12. (a) Do 'loving' parents punish their children? Give reasons for your answer.
    (b) What words in chapter 13 help us to answer this question?
13. Some boys were talking about two women in their village. One said,

'Mrs David is so kind to anyone in trouble that the whole village loves her.' Another said, 'But Mrs Samuel is a better Christian, because she nurses very old people who have no way of thanking her.'

What is your opinion? Is it *more* loving to serve others without receiving love in return?

14.1–40 Order in the Congregation

Preaching rather than 'speaking-in-tongues' will strengthen the congregation in its worship

OUTLINE

14.1–12: Preaching which people can understand is more helpful than speaking in tongues. If someone does not understand what you say, he cannot respond to your message.

14.13–25: When you speak, make sure that all the people who attend the service can understand what you say. Remember the untrained members and those who are not Christian.

14.26–33a: Therefore, people should not speak in tongues unless someone acts as interpreter. Those who preach must not all speak at once.

14.33b–36: Women must not interrupt the service.

14.37–40: Your first task is preaching and teaching. But this does not mean that you should stop people from speaking in tongues.

INTERPRETATION

We have seen that Paul wrote chapters 12 and 13 mainly because of the divisions in the congregation at Corinth. He wrote chapter 14 because these divisions were seriously spoiling their worship together. He had already criticized this worship in chapter 11, e.g. vv. 20 and 21: 'When you meet together, one is hungry and another is drunk.' In chapter 14 we read of other ways in which their worship was being spoiled. Some members were speaking in a way that no one could understand (v. 2), several of them were preaching at the same time (v. 27), and women were interrupting the speakers (v. 35). There must have been great disorder.

Those who lead congregations today may find comfort from reading this chapter, and say: 'So Paul faced many of the difficulties which I am facing, and the same Spirit which God gave to Paul, He offers to me.' Probably Paul wrote chapter 14 because someone had written to him, telling him of the disorder in the worship and asking the question, 'How can we make better use of the gifts which God has given us?' Paul's reply was twofold: (1) Take special care about the arrangement of the worship; (2) Treat preaching ('prophesying') as more important than speaking in tongues.

1. *Arranging public worship.* Paul gave the Corinthians his instructions under six headings:

(a) Consider the needs of the whole congregation (vv. 4, 5, 12, 26);

(b) Use your minds (vv. 15, 20);

(c) Try to help those who do not yet trust in God through Christ (vv. 16, 23);

(d) Allow different people to share in leading the worship (vv. 26, 27);

(e) See that there is order (vv. 31, 33, 40);

(f) See that women do not interrupt the service (vv. 34, 35).

2. *Prophesying.* Paul compared two ways of speaking: 'speaking in tongues' and 'prophesying'. For speaking in tongues, see Special Note C, p. 185. The following note shows who 'prophets' were at that time.

(a) 'Prophets' were a group of Christians within a congregation, who taught the people, mainly by preaching. It seems from 1 Corinthians 14.31 that anyone could join this group who believed that God had given them this gift. We read about one group, at Antioch, in Acts 13.1 and 15.30–32.

(b) We learn about the work of 'prophets' from the following phrases in this chapter: 'upbuilding', i.e. of the congregation (v. 3); 'encouragement and consolation' (v. 3); 'convict' and 'call to account' (v. 24); to lead 'unbelievers' to worship God (v. 25). See notes below on the above verses.

(c) The main work of a prophet was not to foretell the future. It was to become aware, first, of the will of God, and secondly, of the situation in which he and his people were living. Because he was 'aware' in these ways he had a message or 'prophecy' from God. This is true of the prophets of the Old Testament, the New Testament, and of the present day. People called Jesus a prophet, but it was not because He foretold the future (see Matt. 21.11; Luke 24.19; John 4.19).

(d) However, God does give us guidance concerning the future, and 'prophets' can declare what that guidance is. For example, a Christian may meet a young person and see that he has the ability to be a musician when he grows up, and God may use that Christian to guide him. Or someone may notice the great gap between the rich and the poor in his country, and foretell the disaster that will occur if that gap is not closed.

In the New Testament we read of a prophet, Agabus, who predicted a famine (Acts 11.27,28). Paul was acting as a 'prophet' when he gave teaching about the 'end' (e.g. in 1 Thess. 5.1–5; 2 Thess. 2.1–12).

But such 'prophets' were not concerned with predicting such matters as the time and date of the 'end' (as some modern preachers are). Jesus Himself said that no one can do this (Mark 13.32).

(e) Like all Christians, the prophets at Corinth sometimes made mistakes and fell into bad habits. This is why Paul wrote vv. 26–33a of chapter 14.

NOTES

14.3. He who prophesies speaks to men for their upbuilding and encouragement and consolation:
Upbuilding: This word is translated as 'edify' in other verses in the RSV. It does not mean that the prophets increased the size of the congregation. Their work was to instruct the members and to help them to become more mature and more united (see 8.1; 10.23).
Encouragement and consolation: Both words mean 'helping someone by being alongside them'. Prophets did not strengthen people in need only by talking *to* them. They listened to them and talked *with* them. See also note on v. 24. This is how Jesus gave encouragement. It is the way in which His followers today can best give help to neighbours who are ill or lonely or bereaved.

14.4. He who speaks in a tongue edifies himself, he who prophesies edifies the Church:
1. Paul allowed people to speak in tongues, because the speaker himself could be helped by doing it. He did it himself (v. 18).
2. But some of those who spoke in tongues were thinking mainly of themselves. They received great joy from this sort of speaking, but they forgot the needs of other worshippers. Finding new life and speaking in tongues does not prevent a person from doing wrong. And he is doing wrong if he forgets the rest of the congregation and thinks chiefly of his own joys and his own needs. When anyone does this, God's gift (e.g. of 'tongues') no longer builds up the congregation. It has begun to break it down. The congregation becomes divided. People begin to leave it.
3. Thus the 'prophets' were more useful to the congregation than those who spoke in tongues.

14.5. Unless someone interprets:
1. If someone interprets the words which are spoken 'in tongues', then the congregation can be helped. Interpretation is a gift of God (12.10). The person who speaks in tongues may himself interpret (v. 13). More often someone else does it. Sometimes it is like a simple translation from one language into another. More often the interpreter gives an outline of what he believes the speaker has said.
2. What Paul said about interpreting 'tongues' is true about other sorts of speaking in Church. If a preacher loves his congregation enough he will use words which the people can understand. When he chooses a word or an illustration he will ask, 'What will this mean to the hearers?' For example, he may himself know the meaning of the great Bible words (e.g. 'grace', 'heaven', 'kingdom of God'). But do his hearers know it? How can

'If someone inteprets . . . then the congregation can be helped' (p. 179).

When these two leaders from different countries consulted together they needed an interpreter (the dark-haired younger man in the picture) to enable them to understand each other.

What gifts does God offer to someone who prays 'for the power to interpret'?

the preacher find out? Some preachers never do find out: it is just as difficult for an ordinary Christian to understand their language as it is to understand a speaker in tongues.

14.15. I will pray with the spirit and I will pray with the mind also: The teaching is: Worship God with the whole of yourself, 'with the spirit and with the mind'. Most of us already know the difference between these two, e.g. when we praise footballers. If our side has won, we probably shout and sing 'with the spirit', i.e. in order to express our deepest feelings. But a little later we may praise them 'with the mind', as we explain to our friends exactly how the winning goal was scored.

With the spirit: In vv. 14–16 Paul used the word 'spirit' four times, and meant by it 'a person when he feels in the depths of himself rather than thinks'. We shall see (Special Note C, p. 185) that a speaker in tongues is expressing what he"feels'. And there are other ways in which worshippers express their feelings rather than their thoughts, e.g. by the way they greet each other or sing or show their sorrow for sin.

Some people interpret 'spirit' in vv. 14–16 in a different way. They use a capital letter for the word because they believe it means 'The Holy Spirit of God which moves me to express my feelings rather than my thoughts'. But this interpretation seems to go against what Paul said elsewhere in chapters 12–14. Paul taught that God the Holy Spirit works in and through the whole of a person. This includes the person's mind. It was a group of Corinthian Christians who limited the power of the Holy Spirit. They were so eager to say that the Holy Spirit was in them when they spoke in tongues, that they forgot that He could equally well be in them when they were using their minds.

With the mind: Christians need also to use their minds in worship. 'Praying with the mind' means praying in a way that the speaker can understand and which others can understand. 'In thinking be mature' (14.20); e.g.: in reading a Bible passage one of the leaders of the congregation should discover who wrote the passage and what it meant to those who first heard it or read it, and should also compare it with other parts of the Bible. In singing hymns the leader should choose words which are true, and not only choose tunes which are enjoyable. When preachers are preparing sermons they need to find out how other Christians have interpreted the passage chosen. (This Guide to 1 Corinthians has been written to help them to do that.)

In listening to a sermon the worshippers should use their judgement. And they should ask 'What effect will this have on outsiders and visitors?' (As Paul said in v. 16, 'the "outsiders" cannot even say "Amen" if they have not understood what you are saying.')

So the leaders of worship must endeavour to give the congregation opportunities to worship God with the *whole* of themselves: i.e. (a) to express what they feel, and (b) to think.

14.24. If an unbeliever enters, he is convicted by all . . .: In vv. 24 and 25 Paul showed what could happen if an 'outsider' understood what the preachers were saying:

1. He could discover what kind of person he himself was, and in what ways God wanted him to change his ways of living ('convicted' . . . 'called to account' . . . 'secrets disclosed').

2. He could prostrate himself and reverence God ('falling on his face . . . worship').

3. He could see that it was God who was inspiring the preachers ('God . . . among you').

14.26. When you come together, each one has a hymn, a lesson . . . : This is one of the verses which show that in Paul's time there was considerable freedom in the ways in which people worshipped in public. No one prepared an exact order of service beforehand. If someone believed that God was moving him to lead a hymn, or to share with the congregation some truth which he had seen clearly, or to speak in tongues, he did so.

Paul's teaching was:

1. It is good that many different people should take part in a service. If the leader prevents someone from speaking or singing, he may be preventing God from reaching him.

2. But the congregation must be orderly. See v. 27: 'each in turn'.

It is easy to obtain order by preventing members from speaking. It is easy to obtain freedom by allowing everyone to do what they please. But a congregation has to find ways of obtaining both order and freedom for all its members.

14.29. Let two or three prophets speak, and let the others weigh what is said: Who are the 'others' who should 'weigh' (i.e. judge or test) what the 'prophets' said?

(a) They are other members of the congregation. They are not to swallow the prophets' words as babies swallow milk, but to 'test' them, e.g. to ask 'Does his sermon agree with the teaching of the New Testament as a whole?' or 'Could people understand what was said?' A famous preacher received a letter one day from a member of his congregation: 'I enjoy your sermons every Sunday, but please don't use so many words which none of us understand.' The preacher wrote back: 'Thanks for your letter. Here is a plan. If I send you notes of my sermon every Tuesday, will you underline the words which you don't understand and send them back.' So that is what they did, and the preacher found better words to express his message.

(b) 'Others' also means 'other prophets'. Every Church leader needs to receive the criticism of other leaders. Some leaders are isolated and cannot meet others. When this happens their work suffers. (See also note on v. 36.)

14.34. The women . . . are not permitted to speak, but should be subordinate: Compare 11.5, where Paul gave his approval to women to

182

pray aloud, on condition that they wore a veil. How can we explain this 'contradiction'?

Some readers think that since he wrote 11.5 Paul had received information from Corinth which made him change his mind (see note, p. 145).

Others say that Paul only meant in this verse that women should not interrupt those who were already speaking. There were many ways in which the congregation was being disturbed. Some people spoke in tongues and were not interpreted (v. 5). Several members were preaching at the same time (vv. 29, 30). So it was important that women should not make things worse by interrupting. Why did he say this about women and not about everyone? Perhaps because among non-Christians at that time women were not educated and not accustomed to speaking in public. When they became Christians they were tempted to talk too much because it was something they had never done before.

This is what Paul said about women to that Church at that time. Do his words give us any guidance today? Certainly we can learn from them. But we have much more to guide us than those words. God has given His Holy Spirit to Christians so that they can together discover how women can most fully lead and share in public worship today. For a note on 'they should be subordinate', see p. 144.

14.36. Are you the only ones the word of God has reached? After giving them instructions about women in church Paul said, 'You Corinthians are not the only Christians. Find out what Christians in other places do, and learn from them.' (See note on 11.16, p. 147.) At that time it was difficult for one congregation to find out what other congregations were doing, because there were not many of them and they were separated from each other. But it was important to do so. Today there are many small congregations in the world who find it almost impossible to get in touch with other Christians. But most Christians are able to meet other Christians, and they need to do this in order to work with them and to learn from them.

Why do some congregations keep themselves to themselves? It is partly because they believe that the only way in which God guides them is by coming directly to them. But He often guides one congregation through another group of Christians, just as He often guides a husband through his wife.

We note that Paul gave the same teaching to congregations as that which he gave to individuals: 'God has given each one different gifts. Each one sees a different side of the one truth. You need each other.' (See chapter 12, especially vv. 14–26.)

STUDY SUGGESTIONS

(See also the suggestions following the Special Note on
Speaking in Tongues.)

WORDS

1. A Greek word which occurs several times in chapter 14 is translated 'edify' in v. 4.
   (a) What does 'edify the Church' mean?
   (b) How is this word translated in another language which you know?

CONTENT

2. What *two* reasons did Paul give in 14.14–19 for saying that prophesying in public worship was more helpful than speaking in tongues?
3. (a) According to chapter 14, what did Paul hope that unbelievers would do when they came to a Church service?
   (b) What did he say would help them to do it?
4. For what two reasons did Paul write chapter 14?
5. (a) What did Paul say in chapter 14 about the part which women should take in public worship?
   (b) Why did he say that?
6. Why do some congregations keep themselves apart from other congregations?

BIBLE

7. To what single truth do the following passages all point? 1 Cor. 14.24,25; Acts 2.37,38; John 4.29.
8. What does each of the following passages show us about the work of a Christian 'prophet'?
   (a) Acts 11.27,28 (b) Acts 15.32–35 (c) 1 Cor. 14.3.

DISCUSSION AND RESEARCH

9. In chapter 14 'Paul gave his instructions (about public worship) under six headings' (p. 178).
   (a) Which *four* do you think are the most important in the congregation to which you at present belong?
   (b) How could you in each case follow them in practical ways?
10. 'If a preacher loves his congregation enough, he will use words which the people can understand' (p. 179).
    (a) Why do some preachers use words which the people cannot understand?
    (b) How could such a preacher be helped to preach better?
11. Suggest another title for this chapter of the Study Guide.

12. Some examples are given on p. 181 of people praying, (a) 'with the spirit', (b) 'with the mind'. Give an example of each from your own experience.

13. Do you think that women should be full-time leaders in the Church today? Give reasons for your answer. (Compare this with chapter 8.)

14. 'There was considerable freedom in the ways in which people worshipped' (p. 182).

(a) In what verses of chapter 14 do we find evidence of this?

(b) Why is it important to 'have freedom' in worship?

(c) Which of the Churches that you know have the most freedom?

(d) Which does your own congregation chiefly emphasize, freedom or order?

(e) How far do you think your congregation is right in this respect?

Special Note C
Speaking in 'tongues'

1. WHAT IS SPEAKING IN TONGUES?

Paul showed that there were different sorts of speaking in tongues. See 1 Corinthians 12.28: 'various kinds of tongues'. Here is one sort, an account (very much shortened) which one Christian has given of her experience: 'I asked the Lord to give me the gift of tongues and I opened my mouth. After giving a little cough, I heard myself speaking in a language that was not my own. My mind was clear and was in control of what was happening. And God seemed closer than I had ever known Him. I felt free and full of joy. It was as if the whole of me was rising up in worship as I spoke.'

We note that this sort of speaking is not like the confused speech of someone who is mentally ill. It is more like another language. But there is no word which describes or translates it properly. The Greek word which Paul used is translated in the RSV 'speaking in a tongue' (14.2) or 'in tongues' (14.5). In the NEB it is translated 'using the language of ecstasy'; in GNB 'speaking with strange sounds'.

2. WHAT CAUSES SPEAKING IN TONGUES?

According to Paul, it comes from God the Holy Spirit. 'To one is given through the Spirit various kinds of tongues' (12.8–10), though it does not usually happen unless the Christian is wanting it to happen. But not all speech in tongues is given by God. For example, some readers will know about people of other religions who speak in tongues while taking part in wrongdoing. In 1 Corinthians 12.3 we read of a test by which we can judge if the speaking comes from God or not: 'If it leads the speaker to treat Jesus as his "Lord", then it is God who has given it.'

3. WHO SPEAKS IN TONGUES?

According to Acts 2, Christians spoke in tongues on the day of Pentecost, though it is not clear whether it was the 120 brethren (Acts 1.15) or only the Twelve (Acts 2.14 – see note below). After that there are two accounts in Acts 10.44–48 and 19.1–7. And in 1 Corinthians Paul referred to the Corinthians and himself doing so. Apart from those passages there are no other references in the New Testament. We do not read that Jesus spoke in tongues.

In the first and second centuries AD speaking in tongues was quite common. Probably there have always been some Christians who have spoken in tongues. The practice seems to appear when the regular worship of the Church has become formal and stiff. Indeed it often happens at times of revival.

Today there are Christians speaking in tongues both in the Churches called 'Pentecostal' and in the main Churches of the world, especially in the Roman Catholic Church.

Note on Acts 2: Luke believed that the Christians at Pentecost did something different from 'speaking in tongues', something which has not been repeated. According to him, they talked in all the languages of the neighbouring countries without having learnt them, and were understood by 'outsiders' (Acts 2.8–11). If Luke was right, then their speaking at Pentecost was different from the tongues to which Paul referred. According to 1 Corinthians 14.16, 'outsiders' did *not* understand the 'tongues' in which the Christians spoke.

4. WHAT EFFECT DOES SPEAKING IN TONGUES HAVE ON THE SPEAKER?

The main effect can be to give him new joy and new strength. Paul said that he built himself up (14.4). He is stronger, because, as he speaks in tongues, he is somehow set free to be aware of himself as a person who feels deeply. Every person expresses himself in a number of ways. He expresses himself by thinking, and he is aware of his thoughts. He expresses himself by feeling, and he is aware of some of his feelings. But some of his feelings have become so strong that he is afraid that they may overcome him, and so he has pushed them away. Then he is not aware of what he really feels. What happens when people speak in tongues is that they become aware of themselves feeling very deeply, and use those feelings in prayer to God.

Unfortunately the effect of speaking in tongues on the speaker is not always a good one. The speaker may feel that he is superior to those who do not speak in this way. This is a temptation to which Paul referred in 13.1. There are many places in the world where a group of Christians have begun to speak in tongues and have broken away from their fellow-Christians. They have done this believing that the other Christians were somehow less Christian because they did not speak in tongues.

5. WHAT EFFECT DOES SPEAKING IN TONGUES HAVE ON THE SPEAKER'S OWN WORSHIP?

As we have seen, the speaker may find that he can praise God more joyfully and that he feels at one with other worshippers. But he cannot put the prayer into ordinary words. See Romans 8.26, 'sighs too deep for words'. Then, when he has finished speaking in tongues, he can begin again to do his thinking and his understanding: 'I will pray with the spirit, and I will pray with the mind' (14.15).

6. WHAT DOES IT DO FOR THOSE WHO LISTEN?

It does nothing for them unless someone interprets the 'tongues'. Paul said that the speaker himself was the best person to do the interpreting (1 Cor. 14.13), but that others also could do it (1 Cor. 14.6–12,27,28). The speaker in tongues has therefore to have enough love to remember the needs of the listeners. They need to join intelligently in the worship (1 Cor. 14.16,17). Enquirers and visitors need a clear explanation of what is happening (1 Cor. 14.23).

7. IS SPEAKING WITH TONGUES FOR ALL CHRISTIANS?

In 1 Corinthians 12.29 and 30 Paul said, 'God has not given everyone the gift of being an "apostle", nor has He given everyone the gift of speaking in tongues.' We cannot say that it is for all Christians.

8. WHAT DO WE LEARN FROM SPEAKING IN TONGUES?

We chiefly learn that it is God's will that a Christian should be increasingly controlled or occupied by His Holy Spirit. It is not enough for a Christian to look back to the time when he was baptized (see 10.12). Those who speak in tongues are experiencing this in one way.

But it is not the only way! Nor is it the most important way. Paul said in 1 Corinthians 7.19: 'neither circumcision counts for anything nor uncircumcision.' It is also true that neither speaking in tongues counts for anything nor does failing to speak in tongues. What matters is that we keep ourselves ready and open to receive new life in whatever way God gives it to us.

God uses many different ways of doing this. Sometimes He gives us new life suddenly. Sometimes it is over a long period that a Christian is gradually 'filled'. A lake can be filled either in a single day from rainfall and flooding, or gradually from a spring inside it.

STUDY SUGGESTIONS

WORDS

1. 'There is no word which describes or translates "speaking in tongues" properly' (p. 185).
(a) What translation is given in another language which you know?
(b) How far is it a satisfactory translation? Give reasons for your answer.

CONTENT

2. What is the chief difference between the apostles 'speaking in other tongues' as described in Acts 2.1–11, and the Christians 'speaking in tongues' which Paul referred to in 1 Cor. 12—14?

BIBLE

3. What did Paul say about speaking in tongues in each of the following passages in 1 Corinthians?
(a) 12.8–11 (b) 12.29,30 (c) 13.1 (d) 14.2 (e) 14.4 (f) 14.5 (g) 14.18 (h) 14.39
4. There are two accounts of people speaking in tongues in (a) Acts 10.44–48 and (b) 19.1–7.
(i) Who were the people in each case?
(ii) Compare the experiences of the two groups.

DISCUSSION AND RESEARCH

5. If you have met any of the following, say what effect speaking in tongues seems to have had on them:
(a) Members of Pentecostal Churches;
(b) Members of other Churches.
6. Find out what you can about non-Christians who speak in tongues.
7. If you speak in tongues yourself, in what ways is your experience (a) like, and (b) unlike the account given on p. 185.
8. Why do you think Jesus did not speak in tongues?
9. 'It is God's will that a Christian should be increasingly controlled or occupied by His Spirit' (p. 187).
(a) In your experience, does God usually give this opportunity at one time and at one event, or over a long period?
(b) Give an example to show what 'being more fully controlled by His Spirit' means.

15.1–11 The Gospel

Remember the Good News which we all share

OUTLINE

15.1–2: Remember the good news about God which I brought to you. It is through that good news that you are able to stand firm as Christians.

15.3–7: It is news about events which really happened, namely: that Jesus died, was buried, was raised up, and appeared to many people.

15.8–10: He appeared to me, and changed me from a person who tried to destroy the Church into someone who worked hard to help others to become Christians.

15.11: All the apostles preach the same message which I preach and which you believed.

INTERPRETATION

1. CHAPTER 15

Some Christians in Corinth were saying that God does not raise believers to life after death, as we see from 15.12. In order to correct this mistake Paul wrote chapter 15. The chapter is in seven parts:

   1. (vv. 1–11) Our message is that God raised Jesus from death.

   2. (vv. 12–19) If this were not so, and if Christians were not raised to life after death, then people ought to be very sorry for Christians.

   3. (vv. 20–28) But it is true. In Jesus, people can find new life.

   4. (vv. 29–34) I shall use illustrations to show you that it is true.

   5. (vv. 35–49) God will give a new sort of body to Christians who die.

   6. (vv. 50–57) At the last day God will complete His work of raising the dead to life.

   7. (v. 58) Therefore stand firm!

2. CHAPTER 15.1–11

These verses are a sort of summary of the Christian 'good news'. In this summary Paul drew attention to two truths:

   1. The 'good news' is not simply an idea or good advice; it is about things that actually happened. This is one reason why Christians need to take seriously what Jesus did. If we have had a marvellous experience of Jesus as alive and present with us now, we may be tempted to say that what He did on earth is not important. (Some of the Corinthians made that mistake.) But it is very important. Jesus could not be alive for us now in Spirit unless He had been alive in body, as the Gospels show. It is harmful when Christians separate what He is now from what He once did.

189

2. All the apostles agreed in the message which they preached about God raising Jesus. Jesus had appeared to them all. We note that Paul never tried to 'prove' that Jesus rose. He simply said, 'We all agree in declaring in faith that God raised Him and that we have experienced His appearing.'

NOTES

15.1. I preached to you the gospel: The first two verses of this chapter are confusing to us who read them today. Perhaps it was clear to the Corinthians, and perhaps Paul would have written more carefully if he had known that people were going to read it so many centuries later! This is what he was saying:

(a) I preached the Gospel to you (v. 1).

(b) You received it and stand firm in it (v. 1);

(c) And through it you are being saved as you hold it fast (v. 2);

(d) I hope that you really do hold it fast and that you have not fallen away after believing (v. 2). See NEB.

Some of the Corinthian Christians were saying that people do not have life after death (see v. 12). So Paul had to remind them of the message they had once believed.

1. **I preached:** We have seen that preaching is much more than speaking (see note on p. 178). But it certainly does include speaking about the events that took place when God became man.

2. **The gospel** or 'good news about Jesus'. See note on 1.17 (p. 14). From 15.1,2 we see two truths about it:

(a) It needs to be 'received' (i.e. studied and understood and accepted), not swallowed like medicine or a magic spell. When we 'receive' it, we make our own personal response to it. We not only hear the words, but we are grateful to God because He has come to us and given us new life.

(b) 'Receiving the gospel' is a beginning. As a result of it Christians are committed to Christ ('holding the Gospel fast', v. 2) and are on their way to being saved (v. 2).

15.2. By which you are saved:

1. *From what* does God save people? First, from the pain of being separated from Him as the result of their sin. Secondly, from being overwhelmed by the evil which can so easily control them.

We should note that God has not promised to save us from sinning in the future, or from feeling guilty when we sin, or from all pain, or from all suffering.

2. *For what* does God save people? For fellowship with Him and in order that they should serve other people.

3. *When* does God save people?

(a) Sometimes Paul described Christians as having 'been saved', i.e. he used a past tense (see 2 Tim. 1.9; Titus 3.5). When he said this he meant

'The gospel by which . . . you are saved' (1 Cor. 15.1,2).

The gospel which Paul outlined in 15.1–11 is like a lighthouse, which both guides sailors to their destination, and saves them from being destroyed on the rocks.

From what special 'rocks' does your congregation need to be saved by the gospel?

that there was a time when they had begun to know that God loved them, and when they had gratefully accepted His life and His plans for them. Similarly, he taught that God had, by sending Jesus (at a time in the past), done what was needed for our salvation.

(b) But usually Paul taught that Christians were 'being saved'. This is the meaning of 15.2. When a volcano was destroying an island in the Pacific the people who lived there had to escape in boats to another country. Although they were leaving their homes and feeling sea-sick in the boats they could say, 'We are being saved'. They were glad that they were going to a place where they could live safely. But they had not yet got there. According to Paul, Christians are like those people who were 'being saved'.

(c) But sometimes Paul thought of Christians as people who would be saved in the future. See 1 Cor. 3.15: 'will be saved', and Rom. 5.9: 'shall be saved', i.e. at the last day when God will judge the secrets of men (Rom. 2.16).

Note: We cannot translate v. 2 'You are saved if you hold it fast' (see note on v. 1). Paul never said that we would be saved *if* we were faithful. God saves us because He is generous and in spite of our failure to obey Him.

15.3a. I delivered . . . what I also received: In some countries the Post Office has messengers who deliver letters to houses and farms which are far from the towns. Paul was like one of those messengers. He handed on the message that he had been given. He said this in order to make clear that the 'good news' was not a message which he had invented himself. Messengers do not write the letters which they deliver.

In every age Christians have a double task.

1. To hand on the good news which we have received from those who lived before us. This good news remains the same.

2. To interpret this good news with the help of God's Spirit in whatever ways are suitable. The ways of interpreting are different according to the place and time and custom of the people among whom we live. There are two dangers here for Christians:

(a) We may pay so much attention to what God did in the past that we behave as if God were not alive to guide us today.

(b) On the other hand we may neglect 'the faith which was once for all delivered' (Jude 3). We may then believe that the only important truth is the truth which we think God has given to us personally.

This verse is also important because of a question which people often ask today, 'Did Paul change the simple teaching of Jesus?' Paul's answer, according to v. 3a, is 'No. I preach what others taught me.'

15.3b. Christ died for our sins: The two truths which Paul declared are: that Christ really died, and that by dying He did something for us.

1. **Christ died:** It is clear from v. 12 that some Christians at Corinth thought that Jesus never really died. Possibly they believed that after He had been crucified He was 'exalted' or taken up into heaven. (We

remember Elijah's being taken up: 2 Kings 2.11.) But if Jesus had not died, then God would not have raised Him from the dead. If so, then 'resurrection' does not happen. So Paul had to remind them that Jesus really died and that God really raised Him.

2. **For our sins:** This means 'because of our sins', or 'in order to deal with our sins', or 'in order that we may be forgiven'.

For some people this is all they want to know: 'Christ died and I am forgiven. Praise the Lord!' But others ask the question: '*How* can Christ's death result in our being forgiven?'

We find several answers to this question in the New Testament, not one only. One of the best-known passages is Romans 5.1–11, in which Paul used the word 'reconciliation'. (See also 2 Cor. 5.15–21.) Jesus offered Himself to God in complete obedience and gave up His life on the Cross. We human beings who need to be forgiven cannot make ourselves fit to be forgiven. There is a barrier between God and ourselves which our sin has created. But we can accept that Jesus became one with us. In this way we can be 'reconciled' to God through Jesus.

But this does not mean that a loving person (Jesus) had to die in order to persuade an angry person (God) to forgive mankind. It was God Himself who was at work in Jesus to forgive us.

15.3c. Christ died . . . in accordance with the scriptures: Paul wrote this in order to show that what had happened was part of God's purpose for the world. But Jesus was not 'fated' to die; nor did He die by chance. Nor did His death take God by surprise. According to the 'scriptures' (i.e. the Old Testament writers) God made plans to deal with the sin of mankind. His sending Jesus to share in the life and suffering of human beings was part of that plan. Paul was giving the Corinthians greater confidence in God by reminding them of this.

According to Luke 24.26 Jesus said the same. 'Was it not necessary that the Christ should suffer?' And Peter said that God delivered Jesus into the hands of the Jews 'according to the definite plan and foreknowledge of God' (Acts 2.23).

Some readers ask questions, e.g.:

1. Did these Old Testament writers know that Christ would come and that He would be killed? Is that how we should interpret such passages as Isa. 53.4–6; Ps. 118.22; and Deut. 21.22?

Some people say, 'Yes. God gave these writers this miraculous knowledge.' Others say, 'No. God certainly does miracles, but this is not one of them. "In accordance with the scriptures" means that God planned to save mankind, and this plan is what these writers understood.'

2. Did God send Jesus in order to die? It is unwise to say 'Yes', since it might seem from that answer that God is a cruel God. What writers in the New Testament say is this:

(a) Jesus came to save mankind from sin;

(b) He could not do this without being killed.

15.4. That He was buried, that He was raised on the third day in accordance with the scriptures: This is the great truth which Paul wanted to emphasize, i.e. that God truly raised Jesus to life.

1. **Was buried:** He began by saying that Jesus was buried, because this shows that He had really died. If He really died, Paul said, then God really raised Him from the dead. If God raised Him, then He will raise us.

2. **Was raised:**

(a) It was God's act. There are some verses in the New Testament in which it is said that Jesus 'rose', but far more often we read that He was raised, i.e. that God raised him. God Himself did this.

(b) It is not only a past event. What Paul actually wrote was 'has been raised', i.e. has been raised and is now alive as our Lord.

(c) This simple statement does not answer the questions which people often ask today, e.g. 'How do we know that this is true?' 'What does "raising" mean?' 'What happened to the body?' 'Why did Paul not say that the tomb was empty, as is stated in the Gospels?' But Paul's simple statement is enough. All the first Christians agreed in saying 'We believe God raised Jesus.' If they had not believed it there would have been no Christian Church.

3. **In accordance with the scriptures:** See the note on these words in v. 3b. What do the words refer to in v. 4? They may refer to the fact that Jesus was raised. We see in Acts 2.31–35 that Peter quoted Psalm 16.8–10 and 110.1 in order to teach that the resurrection of Jesus was part of God's plan.

Or the words may refer to the 'third day'. Some people point to Hosea 6.2 as a passage to which Paul was referring: 'On the third day He will raise us up.' But it does not seem likely that Hosea was thinking of the Messiah (Christ) when he said this.

15.5. He appeared to Cephas . . . :

(a) How often did Jesus appear? In 15.5–8 Paul referred to six people or groups of people to whom He appeared. But according to the Gospels there were other times and other people to whom He appeared (see, e.g., Matt. 28.1–10; Luke 24.13–31; John 20.1–14; 21.4–14).

(b) Why did Jesus appear? Chiefly in order to show His followers what they must do. 'As the Father has sent me, even so I send you . . .' (John 20.21).

(c) What sort of risen body did Jesus have? It is not clear. (1) In Luke 24.39–42 we see that the disciples could touch it. But (2) according to John 20.19 His body could become visible without passing through a doorway. And Paul used the same word for Jesus's appearing to the Twelve (v. 7), and for His appearing to Paul himself in a 'heavenly vision' (see v. 8 and Acts 26.12–19).

Many people say that they cannot believe that God raised Jesus. This may be because they have a wrong idea about His risen body, i.e. they think that it was a body like ours. But it is clear from the above that His risen body was not like our bodies.

Paul did not try to answer these questions, just as he never tried to 'prove' that Jesus rose. What he wanted to explain was that all the apostles had experienced the 'appearing' and that they were all preaching about it (see 'so we preach', v. 11). As a result, they were (a) changed people, (b) apostles who had received their orders.

15.9. I am the least of the apostles: In vv. 9–11 Paul said:

1. 'People who say that I do not deserve to be called an apostle are quite right.'

2. 'But because God was generous to me' (see note on v. 10), 'I am an apostle' 'I am not in the least inferior to these superlative apostles' (2 Cor. 11.5).

3. I and the other apostles preach the same Gospel.

Jesus appeared to Paul while he was actually persecuting the Christians (see Acts 8.1–3; 9.1–7). This is why Paul felt that he had become a Christian 'at the wrong time'. He was like a baby born at an unexpected time (see v. 8). Therefore, he was the 'least of the apostles', and 'unfit' to be called apostle.

15.10. I worked . . . though it was not I, but the grace of God: After saying that he worked harder than other Christians, Paul corrected himself. He said, 'But I only did my work because God gave me the power to do it.' A student broke his leg in two or three places and was in hospital for some weeks. After some time he was able to play football again and with great success. He did not say 'Look how clever I am', but 'Look how clever and kind the doctors and nurses were who helped my leg to mend.'

See Phil. 2.12,13: 'Work out your own salvation . . . for God is at work in you.'

STUDY SUGGESTIONS

WORDS

1. 'There are some verses . . . in which it is said that Jesus "rose", but far more often we read that He "was raised"' (p. 194).

   (i) How is this phrase in 15.4 translated in the AV and in another language version known to you?

   (ii) Which phrase is used in the following passages (RSV)?

   (a) Rom. 6.4 (b) Rom. 8.34 (c) 1 Cor. 15.14 (d) 2 Cor. 5.15

   (e) 1 Thess. 4.14

   (iii) Why did Paul write 'was raised' and not 'rose' in 15.4?

CONTENT

2. What were Paul's two chief reasons for writing 15.1–11?
3. Why did he emphasize that Christ was buried?
4. When he wrote about 'the scriptures' in 15.3,4 what was he referring to?
5. The notes on 1 Cor. 15.1–11 refer to the following wrong ideas about Christianity. Explain in each case in what way they are wrong:
   (a) Jesus is alive today. What He did on earth is not important (p. 189).
   (b) We should swallow the Gospel like medicine (p. 190).
   (c) We shall be saved if we behave well (p. 190).
   (d) Jesus had to die in order to persuade an angry God to forgive mankind (p. 193).

BIBLE

6. (i) 'In 15.5–8 Paul referred to six people or groups of people to whom Jesus appeared' (p. 194). Who were they?
   (ii) 'There were other times and other people to whom He appeared' (p. 194). Who were the others, according to each of the following passages?
   (a) Matt. 28.1–10   (b) Luke 24.13–31   (c) John 20.1–14   (d) John 21.4–15
   (iii) 'Jesus appeared chiefly in order to tell His followers what they must do' (p. 194). What did He want them to do, according to the following passages?
   (a) Matt. 28.1–7   (b) Luke 24.44–49   (c) Acts 26.16.
7. The word 'save' occurs in the following passages. Say in each case:
   (i) whether it refers to something that has happened, or is happening, or will happen.
   (ii) (if possible) what the people are being saved from:
   (a) Matt. 1.21   (b) Rom. 5.9,10   (c) 1 Cor. 3.15   (d) Eph. 2.5,8   (e) 1 Tim. 2.4   (f) Titus 3.5

DISCUSSION AND RESEARCH

8. 'These verses (1 Cor. 15.1–11) are a sort of summary of the Christian "good news"' (p. 189).
   Are there any Christian truths which are *not* included in these verses, but which you regard as being of equal importance with the truths you find here? If so, what are they?
9. 'How can Christ's death result in our being forgiven?' (p. 193). What is your own answer?
10. 'What sort of risen body did Jesus have?' (p. 194).
    (a) What answer to this question do the writers of the Gospels give?
    (b) Do you think it is an important question? Give reasons for your answer.

11. 'Did these Old Testament writers know that Christ would come and that He would be killed?' (p. 193).
(a) What is your own opinion?
(b) If they did not know, then what did Paul mean by 'in accordance with the scriptures' (15.3c)?
12. 'Paul never tried to . . . "prove" that Jesus rose. He simply said, "We all agree . . . that we have experienced His appearing"' (p. 199).
(a) Are there any events nowadays which you believe took place mainly on the grounds that many people say that they experienced them?
(b) If so, what sort of events are they?
(c) Because many people experienced that Jesus was alive after His crucifixion, does that prove that He rose?
(d) If it does not, what, if anything, does it prove?

15.12–34 New Life

God is the giver of new life

OUTLINE

15.12–19: If it were not true that God raises people from the dead, then our Christian teaching would be nonsense.
15.20–28: But God does raise the dead. He raised Christ, and He will, in the end, give life to those who belong to Christ.
15.29–32: The way in which I and other Christians live shows that God raises the dead.
15.33,34: If you think that God does not raise the dead, then it is clear that some ignorant people are leading you astray.

INTERPRETATION

In these verses Paul was continuing his reply to those Corinthians who did not believe that God could give new life to those who had died. His answer is in three parts: Consider: (1) What God has done in the *past*, (2) God's power in the *present*, (3) The *future* for which Christians hope.

1. The *past* event is that God raised Jesus after He had been killed. Paul had said this in vv. 1–11. In vv. 12–17 he referred six times to 'Christ being raised'.

The past event was the foundation on which Paul built his teaching about God's activity in the present and the future. In the same way Christians today, by reading (in the Bible) what God did in the past, get guidance concerning God's activity now and in the future.

2. In vv. 14–19 and again in vv. 29–34 Paul wrote about his own *present* experience and that of the Corinthian Christians. For example, they were experiencing the new life that God gives to sinners through His gift of forgiveness (v. 17). Paul said that this new life had come to them as a result of Jesus's being raised. If anyone said, 'But God does not raise the dead' (v. 12b), they knew that this was nonsense because of their daily experience of God.

When someone 'believes in the resurrection' he does not only believe that on the first Easter Day God's power was stronger than the powers which had injured and destroyed Jesus. He also experiences that this is true *now*. We may think of the badly injured man in Cairo who had spent years as a patient in hospital. He was often in great pain and he thought that his useful life was at an end. Then, to his surprise, he found that he could design and make food-trays for patients in bed. Because he had been a patient himself, he could make trays of exactly the right weight and size. Because he was a Christian he was able to recognize that this was God's present power giving him new life. He did this work till he died, ten years later.

3. In vv. 20–28 Paul looked ahead to the *future*, to the time for which Christians 'hope' (see v. 19), the time when God will complete His whole work of 'raising'. Although we do now experience God's power to give new life, we do not see the whole effect of His power here on earth. We ought not to be disappointed that we do not see more of it. God's great 'raising' will come at 'the end' (see note below on v. 24). So Christians are like students in a college. They work hard at each task but are also hoping for the completion of their course. Christians have hope and confidence that God in Christ will complete His work of raising.

Note on the word 'resurrection': From the above we see that Paul used the words 'resurrection' and 'being raised' to mean at least four different things. It is important to distinguish between them in order to understand this whole chapter. For Paul, 'being raised' meant new life which:

(a) God gave to Jesus Christ after He had been killed (e.g. in v. 20a): this is 'past' resurrection;

(b) God is giving to us in the present (e.g. in v. 29b);

(c) God will give to us when we die (this is what Paul referred to in v. 20b);

(d) God will give to everyone who belongs to Christ when He comes again at the end of the world (e.g. in v. 22). In this Guide the word Resurrection is printed with a capital R when it refers to the time when Christ will come again.

NOTES

15.13. If there is no resurrection: In vv. 12–19 Paul was answering people who said, 'God does not give new life to people who have died.'

'For Paul, "being raised" meant new life which . . . God will give to us when we die' (p. 198).

Some Christians think of dying and being raised as the crossing of a bridge from this life into another life — as these Londoners cross a bridge over the river Thames on their way to work each morning.

In your opinion, is this a helpful way of thinking about death and resurrection?

199

In his answer Paul did not try to prove that God raises the dead. He said, 'If you say that, then you are denying your own experience; e.g. you are denying that God has given you new life by forgiving you, "you are still in your sins" (v. 17). But this is nonsense! You *know* that God has forgiven you.'

Paul also added: 'If you say that there is no resurrection, then God did not raise Jesus (vv. 13–16). And in this case you are like runners running towards a finishing post that is not there' (v. 19).

15.17. If Christ has not been raised . . . you are still in your sins: As we have seen in the above note, Paul was not 'proving' that God raised Jesus. No one can ever do that. He was saying that, just as God had the power and the love to raise Jesus, so He has the power to raise us when we have fallen into sin. We read about God's deeds in the Bible and we experience God's deeds in ourselves.

15.19b. If for this life only we have hoped in Christ, we are of all men most to be pitied: Christians are people who 'hope'. But they do not hope only for a good life on this earth. They hope for a new and glorious life which God, through Christ, will give them.

In the New Testament the word 'hope' has almost the same meaning as 'trust' or 'have faith', but it means 'trusting in God as regards the future'. And writers often added the reason for this trusting, i.e. because God raised Jesus. See 1 Peter 1.3: 'We have been born anew to a living hope through the resurrection of Jesus Christ.' See also Col. 1.27 ('hope and glory') and 1 Peter 1.13.

In modern conversation the word 'hope' often has a different meaning. Someone who says 'I hope she will be punctual', may mean 'I want her to be punctual.' It does not mean this in the New Testament.

15.22. As in Adam all die, so also in Christ shall all be made alive:

1. *The great truths* to which these words point are:

(a) All human beings are sinful, and all need to be rescued by God and to be given new life by Him.

(b) New life is now possible for mankind because Jesus was raised. Jesus is like the first crop on a farm. The farmer knows that the rest of the harvest will follow. See 'Christ the first-fruits' vv. 20, 23. The 'rest of the harvest' is the new life which God offers us now, and which He will give to all who belong to Christ at the end of the world.

(c) Jesus was really human. See 'a man' (v. 21) and 'one man' (Rom. 5.17) and note below on 15.45. Yet He is God Himself who became man and so made new life possible for us human beings.

(d) We are so closely bound to Jesus that what He did affects us all. He and we belong to one community. Just as human beings were affected by Adam's sin, so those who are 'in Christ' are affected by His being raised.

There are some Christians who know that as individuals they need God, but who have forgotten the truth which Paul referred to here – i.e. the truth that they belong to one community, the community of all Christians. For this reason they find it difficult to see how the action of one person (Jesus) could affect everyone else.

But most people in the world do not have this difficulty. Most people live in places where if a man commits adultery, all the people, and not only his family, know that they have been affected by his action. If a student fails his final exam the whole class suffers the failure. If a student is honoured by gaining a place in an Advanced Course, the whole class is honoured. People who live like this do not find it difficult to see that we today are affected both by what our ancestors did, and by what Jesus Christ did.

2. *Making a distinction.* In the note on 7.25b we noticed that it was important to make a distinction between things that are different (p. 93). In this paragraph we should distinguish between: (1) these great truths which we have just noted, and (2) the beliefs of some Jewish teachers and 'rabbis', to which Paul seems to have referred in vv. 20–23. These beliefs were:

(a) That there was once a single male human being called Adam;

(b) That because Adam did wrong he was condemned to die instead of living for ever;

(c) That all human beings who have ever lived were in some way part of Adam's body;

(d) That, as a result, all human beings do what Adam did: they sin and they die. 'In Adam all die.' See also Rom. 5.12.

Some, but not all, Jews accepted all these beliefs. So today some, but not all, Christians accept them. A Christian needs to study not only this verse, but also what other New Testament writers and other Christians have said, in order to make up his mind about such matters.

15.24. Then comes the end:

1. What did Paul say about the 'end'? He said that:

(a) It is the time when Christ will come ('His coming', v. 23).

(b) God will give new life to those who are in Christ ('all shall all be made alive', v. 22).

(c) Christ will have completely destroyed all evil powers, including death, before the end ('after destroying every rule', v. 24).

(d) So Christ's work as God's representative Messiah will be finalized ('He must reign until . . .', v. 25).

(e) Christ will give back to His Father, God, the authority which His Father has given Him ('He delivers the kingdom to God', v. 24).

2. In what ways is this teaching most important for us? Not all that Paul wrote in 15.20–28 is equally important, but there are ways in which these words are clearly good news for us, e.g.:

(a) Events will not go on everlastingly repeating themselves. There will be an end to the sort of life that we human beings are living at present.

(b) God has a plan for His whole human family. Things are not happening by chance.

(c) In the end God will completely overcome all evil. When we fight against evil we are not wasting our time. We are taking part in a battle which God will one day win for ever.

3. How did Paul know what will happen in the end? He did not 'know' about the end. He was saying that there were three things the Corinthians did know: (a) What sort of God is in charge of the world (they knew this from reading the Old Testament); (b) That God raised Jesus; (c) That He was giving them new life. Out of this knowledge, Paul said, we can say in hope (v. 19) what God will do in the end.

Naturally, there are questions to which Paul gave no clear answer, e.g.:

(a) *When* will the 'end' come? Paul probably thought that it would come very soon after he had written this letter (see 7.29a). But Jesus once said that not even the angels or He Himself knew when it could come (see Mark 13.32).

(b) *Who* will be raised 'at the end'? Certainly those who 'belong to Christ' (v. 23). But what will happen to other people? Paul said nothing about them here. In the New Testament there are some verses from which it seems that God will save all human beings in the end, because that is His intention. See 1 Tim. 4.10 and note on p. 212, but there are other verses from which it seems that *not* all will be saved (e.g. Mark 9.43).

(c) *How long* will the coming of Christ last? There is no answer in these verses. Some readers think that His 'coming' in v. 23 is different from the 'end' in v. 24. According to some interpreters of the Book of Revelation its author believed that there will be 1,000 years between the 'Coming' and the 'End' (see Rev. 20.6).

We had better trust God to bring to an end what He has created in the way that He has planned, and be content to leave many questions about the end unanswered.

15.28. The Son himself will also be subjected to him: Paul was here comparing Christ to the general of an army. A general was often sent by his king to fight the king's enemies. When he had won the war, he came back and reported to the king to whom he was 'subject'.

Did Paul at one time think that Jesus was 'subject to' God Himself? It seems so from this verse (but see the note on 11.3b, p. 145).

15.29. Being baptized on behalf of the dead: As we have seen, some members of the Church at Corinth had said that there was no such thing as 'resurrection'. So Paul reminded them in this verse that they also had members who were 'baptized for the dead'. This showed that those members believed in resurrection.

It seems that some Christians were troubled about their relatives and friends who had died before being baptized. So these Christians were baptized again in order that their relations should be 'raised'.

Perhaps those who did this did not really believe that God is merciful. Perhaps they felt that unless they were baptized in this way, God would let their relatives be lost for ever. Perhaps this is why members of the 'Mormon' sect today practise baptism for the dead. They believe that God will refuse to save anyone except Mormons or those people for whom Mormons are baptized. So Mormons spend much time finding out who their ancestors are, and then being baptized for each of them.

15.32a. I fought with beasts at Ephesus: Paul was saying once again, 'We show by what we do that we believe in resurrection.' Probably he did not mean that he had really fought with beasts. (If he had done so, he would surely have said so in 2 Cor. 11.23–30.) His meaning here is, 'I would not risk my life preaching in public unless I believed that God would in the end give me "resurrection". But I do risk my life every day.' See 'I die every day' (v. 31) and Acts 19.29 and 30.

15.32b.'. . . Let us eat and drink, for tomorrow we die': Paul was comparing two ways in which people who know that they will one day die live their lives:

1. His own way: 'I am willing to live a dangerous life because I hope for resurrection at the end' (v. 32a).

2. The way of people who have no such hope, and who (according to Isa. 22.13) say, 'Let us eat and drink, for tomorrow we die', i.e. 'we can do what we like because we have no hope of a life after death.'

This comparison which Paul made is very important. But we should also note that:

(a) Paul did not live that sort of life *only* because he hoped for resurrection. The other reason was that he had devoted his whole life to the service of Christ, whatever the consequences.

(b) There are many people who do not believe in any life after death, and who have a different attitude from those whom Isaiah quoted. These people say, 'Since this life is the only one which we have, let us use it as well as we can, e.g. in serving other people.'

STUDY SUGGESTIONS

WORDS

1. The words 'raised' and 'resurrection' occur frequently in 15.12–34. Say, in each of the following passages,
   (a) Whether past or future resurrection is meant;
   (b) Whose resurrection is referred to.
   (i) 'raised from the dead' (v. 12)   (ii) 'has been raised' (v. 20)   (iii) 'be made alive' (v. 22).

2. What is the difference between the meaning of the word 'hope' (v. 9) as writers used it in the New Testament, and as people use it in ordinary conversation today?

CONTENT

3. (a) For what special reason did Paul write vv. 12–34?
   (b) What is the chief teaching about God to which this passage points?
4. What experience of God's 'power to raise' people did Paul refer to in v. 17?
5. The words 'a man' occur twice in 15.21. To whom do they refer in each case?
6. What five different words did Paul use in 15.24–26 to describe the evils which Christ will destroy when He comes?

BIBLE

7. (a) What single truth about Jesus do we find in Rom. 5.17; 1 Cor. 15.21; and 1 Tim. 2.5?
   (b) Why is this truth important?
8. 'I die every day' (15.31).
   (a) What does this mean?
   (b) What events did Paul refer to in 2 Cor. 11.23–27, in which he was in danger of being killed?
9. (a) Why did Paul call Christ the 'first-fruits' in 15.20?
   (b) In what way is the teaching in 15.20 like the teaching of 2 Cor. 1.22; 5.5; and Eph. 1.13, 14?
10. What 'answer' to the question 'When will the end come?' do we find in each of the following passages?
    (a) Mark 13.33   (b) 1 Cor. 7.29–31   (c) 1 Thess. 5.2   (d) 2 Thess. 2.1–4   (e) 1 Peter 4.7

DISCUSSION AND RESEARCH

11. (a) Why do you think that groups such as Jehovah's Witnesses feel that they need to know when the end will come?
    (b) Do you agree that it is better to 'leave many questions about the end unanswered' (p. 202)? Give reasons for your answer.
12. A story is given on p. 198 about a man in hospital, and the comment is that 'this was God's present power giving him new life.' If you can, tell a story concerning yourself or someone else who has had this sort of experience.
13. 'Just as human beings were affected by Adam's sin, so those who are in Christ are affected by His being raised' (p. 200).
    (a) In what verse of 1 Cor. 15 do we find these ideas?
    (b) If someone said that these ideas were absurd, how would you explain them to him? Illustrate your explanation with at least one example from everyday life.
14. (a) Of all the teaching that Paul gave about the 'end' in 15.22–28, what do you think is the most important?
    (b) Is 'the end' bad news or good news? Give reasons for your answer.

15. (a) Why were some people in Corinth baptized on behalf of their ancestors (p. 202)?

(b) What is your opinion of this practice?

16. 'Since this life is the only one which we have, let us use it as well as we can, e.g. in serving other people' (p. 3).

(a) Give examples of people, living or dead, who seem to have or to have had this attitude to life.

(b) What difference do you think it would make to their lives if they accepted Paul's teaching about life after death?

15.35–58 Life after Death

Thank God that He will give us new life after death

OUTLINE

15.35–41. God gives newness to all his creatures: When people say they don't believe in the resurrection of people who die, tell them this:

1. It is always God's way to bring new life from what is dead or seems to be dead (v. 36).

2. All creatures which have this new life are given a body which is different from their first body, and is more glorious (v. 37).

3. Just as God has made different creatures, so He has made different human beings. At the Resurrection He will give each person a new and glorious body which is suited to his own self (vv. 38–41).

15.42–50. Our future body will be different from our present body: It will never wear out (v. 42). It will be full of glory and strength. It will be controlled by God's spirit (vv. 43, 44).

God gave us the first man, Adam, and afterwards He gave us the new Adam who is Christ. In the same way, after we have finished with our physical bodies, God will give us a new and spiritual body (vv. 45–49).

I repeat, the body which God will give us at the Resurrection will be different. It will not be a body of flesh and blood (v. 50).

15.51–58. The resurrection at the coming of Christ:

1. It will be a time of great change, both for those of us who are still alive, and for those who have died (v. 51).

2. It will happen suddenly (v. 52).

3. At that time it will be clear that death is not the conqueror. Although death is a punishment for our sins, God will give a life that comes after death to those who have faith in Jesus (vv. 53–57).

If you believe this, you will discover that all the work we have done for God is worth doing (v. 58).

INTERPRETATION

1. *The main thought* in vv. 35–58 is that, through Jesus, we shall receive a new and splendid body. The Corinthians had asked Paul the question: 'What sort of body shall we have after the Resurrection?' It is a question which people ask today. A soldier who was seriously wounded and lamed for life asked, 'Shall I still be lame in heaven?' The answer was, 'No, thank God!' Paul said:

(a) You will be a changed person (see vv. 38, 45–49, 51–53).

(b) You will continue to be the same personality as you are now. Your 'self' will continue, although changed (see vv. 37, 50).

We compare what Paul said here with what people of other religions have said, in Special Note D on p. 215.

2. *Hope rather than information.* Paul did not say that in these verses he was giving information. What he did was to share with the Corinthians his hope and faith as a Christian about life after death and the 'Coming of Christ'. They had asked him a question, so he did his best to give an answer.

This becomes clear if we compare these verses (35–58) with vv. 1–11 of the same chapter. In the earlier passage Paul said, 'I am passing on to you information which all the Apostles pass on, and am describing what I have experienced.' But in vv. 35–58 it was his own hope which he expressed.

God, not Paul, knew the answers concerning the future of His people. As John wrote later, 'It does not yet appear what we shall be' (1 John 3.2). In 1 Corinthians 2.9 Paul referred to Isaiah 64.4 'No eye has seen . . . what God has prepared for those who love Him.' Why should we be surprised that God has not yet told us everything? As one Christian has said, 'Those who have heard God speak can bear His silence.'

But Paul based these hopes on beliefs about God and experiences of God which he and his readers shared. It was because of these beliefs and experiences that Paul had hopes about what kind of body Christians will one day have. These beliefs were, for example:

(a) God loves those whom he has created;

(b) God made Adam, and later on He sent Jesus;

(c) God raised up Jesus from the tomb;

(d) God still has the power to give a new sort of life to us: now at the time of our conversion, when we die, and at the great Resurrection.

3. *The word 'resurrection':* We have already seen that Paul used this word in different ways (see p. 198). In these verses he had two chief ideas in his mind:

(a) The time when Christ will come again. It was Paul's special aim to write about this.

(b) The new life which God gives to those who have faith in Jesus, now and when they die.

4. *Teaching about the present:* These verses were important for the present lives of Paul's readers. He was saying, 'Since you can safely entrust your future to God's hand, turn your attention to your present lives and your present work.' (See Note on v. 58.)

NOTES

15.36. Foolish man! What you sow does not come to life unless it dies: Someone had asked: 'If Christians live after death, with what sort of body will they live?' Paul said, 'That is a foolish question because you can answer it yourself by looking at your farm. Seeds (that seem to be dead) grow into living plants. If God can create a whole tree out of a seed, He can do the same for us.'

Some readers have said that Paul's argument is weak, because our bodies really die, but seeds do not really die when they turn brown and are buried in the soil. But what Paul was saying was that God can turn a created thing into something new. He probably knew that seeds do not really die.

15.37. What you sow is not the body which is to be: Paul again compared the body we have in this life to the different sort of body which God will give us in the future. He said it again, in v. 50: 'Flesh and blood cannot inherit the kingdom of God,' i.e. the new life will not be a repetition of this one.

It is useful to compare this with two different ways in which people think about life after death:

1. All over Asia and Africa there are people who believe that the spirit of a person can, after this life, return to earth and live again, in a new-born baby or in some other creature. This is the belief in what people usually call 'reincarnation'. Hindus and Buddhists use the word 'migrate' to describe the way in which, they believe, a person's soul occupies one body after another. The sort of body that the soul occupies depends on the deeds (*karma*) done in the present life.

Does belief of this sort contradict Paul's belief? In reply to this we should remember that Paul was talking about 'resurrection' in at least two ways in this chapter: (a) resurrection or new life when someone dies; (b) the Resurrection at the end of the world (see p. 198). Many Christians do not think that belief in 'reincarnation' contradicts Paul's statement. But they point out that in the end, at the great Resurrection, all reincarnations cease, and all the bodies suited to this life give way to a new sort of body. 'Reincarnation' is not the same as 'Resurrection'.

2. In Paul's time some Jewish Pharisees taught that at the Resurrection people's bodies would be lifted up to heaven, in the same condition in which they had been on earth. For centuries many Christians believed this. In some Western European countries, when people put a corpse into a grave, they placed the head to face Jerusalem. This was in order that, when Jesus

'Paul was saying . . . that God can turn a created thing into something new' (p. 207).

When land was cleared for a housing project in Tanzania, trees had to be cut down and 'die' before the timber could be used for building the new houses.

Think of some other ways in which created things are 'turned into something new'.

returned at the Resurrection (to Jerusalem), the body would be ready to move quickly to Jesus! Such Christians did so because they had not understood this verse or verse 50.

15.38. To each kind of seed its own body: Although a person is changed when he dies, he remains the same person. On a farm a maize seed grows into a maize plant, not into a banana tree. So when someone dies, his or her personality will not be abolished. It will not be replaced by a different personality. It is that same person who, having committed himself to Christ in this life, will have fellowship with God at the Resurrection.

For this reason everyone's personality is precious. There are some countries and some schools where the authorities try to make people as much like each other as possible. But if we follow the truth in this verse, we shall encourage each different personality to remain different from all others.

Paul was saying here, 'Just as you express your own special personality by using your present body, so God will give you a different sort of body by which to express yourself, and with which to serve Him.'

For the meaning of the word 'body' in Paul's letters see note on p. 65.

15.42. What is sown is perishable, what is raised is imperishable: In vv. 42–44 Paul showed some differences between our present 'body' and our Resurrection 'body'. He was *not* saying that our present flesh and blood body is different from our eternal souls. He did not think of body and soul as being separate. He was saying that our whole personality at the Resurrection will be superior to our whole personality now (see note on 'body' on p. 65).

Paul wrote of the difference in four ways:

1. This present body has been born into an age which will come to an end. This age and everything in it are 'perishable' (v. 42b). The Resurrection body will belong to an age when everyone will acknowledge God as Lord. That age will be 'imperishable' (v. 42b).

2. This body is 'dishonourable' (v. 43). This means that it does not yet have the glory that it will have. Paul did not, of course, mean that we should neglect our present bodies or that we should treat dead bodies with disrespect. It was simply his way of emphasizing that the future body will be 'glorious'.

3. This body has no power to give itself life ('sown in weakness' v. 43). The future body will have God's power fully working in it ('raised in power' v. 43).

4. This body is 'physical' (v. 44), i.e. filled by the spirit which is natural to all creatures of this age. The future body will be 'spiritual' (v. 44), i.e. filled with God's Spirit.

The great truth on which Paul based these thoughts is this: God recreates and changes those whom He has created, just as He raised Jesus from the dead.

209

15.45. 'The first man Adam became a living being'; the last Adam became a life-giving spirit: We have seen (p. 206) that in vv. 35–58 Paul was expressing his own hope about the future of Christian people. But we also saw that he based these thoughts on events which had already taken place. He based them also on his and his readers' experience of Jesus Christ. Here in v. 45 he referred to some of these events: 'We know that God first made Adam, and that at a later time He sent Christ ("the last Adam"). This is why I believe that we first have a physical body and that at a later time God will give us a Resurrection body. God has arranged His creation in that way. There is development. One thing is followed by a different thing.'

As Paul wrote about Adam and Christ he had two other important thoughts:

1. Adam and Christ are the heads of two great families of the human race. For Paul, Adam was the head and representative of all human beings as they were before Christ came. This is why he quoted from Gen. 2.7: 'man became a living being' (and added to it the words 'first' and 'Adam'). Then there is another family, the 'new age', consisting of all who are 'in Christ', of which Christ is the head and representative.

2. All human beings share the nature of the 'first Adam' – the nature which Paul called 'physical' in vv. 44 and 46. This 'first Adam' is the common ancestor of all humans: 'We have borne the image of the man of dust' (v. 49a). Then those who have chosen to live 'in Christ' (and have been baptized as the outward sign that they make that choice), share in Christ's nature: 'We shall also bear the image of the man of heaven', i.e. of Christ (v. 49b).

All Christians thus belong to two families:

(a) They belong to the human family, and show that they belong to it by the way in which they are concerned for the welfare of all its members, no matter what clan or tribe or race the others belong to.

(b) They belong to the Christian family, of which Christ is the head, and show that they belong to it by caring for the other members (see chapter 16).

15.51. I tell you a mystery. We shall not all sleep, but we shall all be changed:

1. **Mystery:** In chapter 4.1 the word meant 'truths which God has now shown to us' (p. 43). But here it means a 'strange thing', 'something we cannot fully understand'. What Paul wrote in vv. 51–54 was especially strange to his non-Jewish readers. They were not familiar with visions about the end of the world, such as the Jews read of in Dan. 7.27 and 12.2. But, as we have already noticed, the 'end' is a mystery to all human beings. This is why not all Christians today hold the same ideas about it, and why it is important for us to respect other Christians who hold ideas different from our own.

2. **We shall not all sleep:** 'Sleep' here means 'die'. Paul said that some

people will have already died when Christ comes at the Resurrection, but others will still be alive. Since he said 'we', he may have thought that he himself would be one of those who would still be alive (see note on 1 Cor. 7.29).

Some readers have wrongly thought that Paul wanted to give information about the End. So they are very troubled to think that he perhaps thought the End would come in his life-time. They say 'How can we take Paul seriously? If it is possible that he made a mistake here, perhaps he made mistakes in other teaching which he gave.' But Paul was not giving information in this verse (see Interpretation, p. 206). Paul probably changed his mind about this, and later thought that the Coming would not take place soon. See 2 Thess. 2.1–2.

3. **We shall all be changed:** See note on v. 42. In this verse (51) the words are 'be changed', i.e. it is God who will change us; it is He who will give us life in Christ. This was very different from the ideas which most Greeks had about life after death. According to many Greek philosophers, the soul of a wise man lived in the body as a prisoner lives in a prison. They thought that when the body dies, the soul is naturally and automatically free to walk out into a new life. The different idea which Paul repeated in v. 53 was that: 'mortal nature must put on immortality' – just as a person puts on new clothes. And it is God who gives the clothes.

Some Christians have thought that the words 'be changed' refer to the changes that must take place in a person between his death and the Resurrection when Christ will come again. They say that no one when he dies is ready to meet God, and that everyone needs to be changed and purified after death. They quote such verses as 'In my Father's house are many rooms', i.e. stages on the journey (John 14.2). This is sometimes called the doctrine of purgatory or purifying.

Others, however, point to other verses, e.g. 'Today you will be with me in Paradise' (Luke 23.43). 'My desire is to depart and be with Christ' (Phil. 1.23). Such verses, they say, do not support the doctrine of purifying after death.

15.52. The trumpet will sound: Jewish readers must have already been familiar with this language. Their prophets had used it when speaking about the Coming of God on the 'day of the Lord' (see Isa. 27.13 and Zech. 9.14).

Paul, like Jesus, expressed his thoughts in the picture-language which was familiar to him. When we read a New Testament passage we need to distinguish between: (a) the picture-language, and (b) the thoughts which lie behind that language. In this case the important thought is that Christ will come and will complete His work. (It may be that we who read this do not use a trumpet with which to greet a Very Important Person when he arrives. In our country we may, for example, beat drums or put on our best clothes or put out flags or explode fireworks. Thus for some readers the meaning of this verse would become clearer if we translated it 'the drums will beat' or 'the flags will wave', instead of 'the trumpet will sound'.)

15.55. O death, where is thy victory? O death, where is thy sting?: Paul used two quotations (from Isa. 25.8 and Hos. 13.14) to say that death will no longer conquer us. Death has 'lost its sting', i.e. it can no longer terrify or destroy us. We read the reasons in v. 57: (1) 'In Christ' we have already experienced that God forgives us; (2) 'In Christ' we have already a life that goes on beyond death.

This shows, Paul said, that the sayings of Isaiah and Hosea have 'come to pass'. What Isaiah hoped for, and what Hosea feared would never happen, is now going to take place. Death *will* be overcome.

These words have supported very many people who were afraid of death and what follows death. Perhaps we cannot be free from all fear of dying, because in spite of modern medicine the time of dying is sometimes hard to endure. But 'in Christ' we can be free from the fear of what follows death.

15.56. The sting of death is sin: Paul probably believed that God had given human beings the 'sting' or pain of death as a punishment for their sin. This is what some Jewish rabbis taught. See note on 15.21, para. 2 (p. 201).

But some people interpret it in a different way, i.e. 'men fear death (it has a "sting") because they have sinned and they do not know how to get forgiven.' This is certainly a true statement.

Paul added (and he said it more fully in Rom. 7.7–11) that 'law' causes us to sin: 'the power of sin is the law'. 'Law' shows us what sin is, and, therefore, makes us want to commit sin. If a teacher tells his class before the lesson begins 'Don't make any unnecessary noise', some of the pupils will begin to think of interesting ways of making a noise (see note p. 69).

15.57. But thanks be to God who gives us the victory through our Lord Jesus Christ:

1. Thanks to God because, although we sin, God has a gift for us: forgiveness and victory over death. Paul wrote 'God gives' not 'God will give', because he already belonged to the body of those who were 'in Christ'. It is this body to whom at the Resurrection God will give complete victory over all evil.

2. God will give us this gift 'through Jesus', i.e. to those who are trusting Jesus now in this life. People often ask, 'Will God give this gift to all human beings because He is merciful, or only to Christians, i.e. to those who are "in Christ"?' In this chapter Paul wrote as if only Christians could receive the gift, although God offers it to everyone. But see 'reconcile to Himself *all things*' (Col. 1.20) and 'God is the Saviour of *all men*, especially of those who believe' (1 Tim. 4.10).

15.58. Therefore . . . be steadfast . . . In the Lord your labour is not in vain: Your future is safely in God's hands and His enemies are already being defeated. Therefore, give all your attention to your present work and responsibilities, steadily trusting God.

Some readers of 1 Cor. 15 may have wondered why Paul spent so much time writing about the future of Christian people (about which no one knows very much). It is now clear that he wrote about our future life so that the Corinthian Christians should stop worrying about it and get on with their work. In saying this he was repeating what he said in 15.30–32: 'I can endure my present troubles because I know that my future is safely in God's hands.'

So at the end of chapter 15 we, the readers, turn to our daily work and realize that if it is done 'in the Lord' none of it is ever wasted. We are citizens, so 'in the Lord' we serve on village or town councils, and work faithfully for our wages. We are members of the Church, so 'in the Lord' we take our share in the life of the congregation. We are parents, so 'in the Lord' we give time and love to our children. In ways like these we show that we believe that life after we have died is safely in God's hands.

It is clear that doing our work 'in the Lord' does not mean saying prayers to God throughout the day. A bus-driver who prayed instead of watching the rest of the traffic would not be driving 'in the Lord'! Working in the Lord means: (a) to do His will as far as we can know it, (b) to put ourselves and our whole day inside the hands of God, probably in a time of prayer at a special time of the day, (c) then to give our whole attention to the people and things around us.

STUDY SUGGESTIONS

WORDS

1. (a) Which four words in the following list have nearly the same meaning?
   personality   completeness   selfishness   person   self
   everybody   individuality   eternity
   (b) What word (which appears ten times in 1 Cor. 15.35–50) has the meaning of those four words?

CONTENT

2. What question had the Corinthians asked Paul, to which he gave an answer in vv. 35–58?
3. Why did Paul refer to (a) grain (v. 37), (b) Adam (vv. 45–50)?
4. What did he mean by saying
   (a) This body is 'dishonourable'? (v. 43)
   (b) The resurrection body will be 'spiritual' (v. 44)?
5. What are the most important thoughts about the Resurrection at the Coming of Christ that we find in vv. 51–58?
6. For what did Paul thank God in v. 57?

BIBLE STUDY

7. Read 1 Thess. 4.13–17; 2 Cor. 5.1–10; and 1 Cor. 15.51–53.
   (a) What is the most important single idea in all these passages?
   (b) Why do you consider it is important?
8. 'Therefore be steadfast', i.e. 'give your attention to your present work and responsibilities, steadily trusting God' (p. 212). What 'present work' did Paul encourage his readers to attend to in each of the following passages?
   (a) Rom. 12.13   (b) Eph. 4.1,2   (c) Phil. 4.1,2   (d) Col. 3.23
   (e) 1 Thess. 4.11.

DISCUSSION AND RESEARCH

9. It is said (p. 206) that in 1 Cor. 15.35–58 Paul was expressing his hope and faith as a Christian about life after death . . . rather than giving information.
   If that is true, what is the value of those verses?
10. 'Some readers say: "If it is possible that Paul made a mistake here (in thinking that the End of the world would come in his life-time), perhaps he made mistakes in other teaching which he gave"' (p. 211). What is your opinion?
11. 'Some Christians say that no one, when he dies, is ready to meet God, and that everyone needs to be changed and purified after death' (p. 211).
    (a) What do you think?
    (b) Why do you think that?
    (c) Why do you think there is so little teaching about this in the New Testament?
12. A note on p. 212 refers to people who 'were afraid of death and what follows death'.
    (a) Why are many people afraid to die? What are they afraid of?
    (b) In what ways can such people be helped?
13. What are the two chief ways in which Paul's beliefs about life after death are different from the beliefs of those people in your neighbourhood who are not Christians?
14. What reply would you make to each of the following statements?
    (a) 'People believe in life after death not because there is evidence for it but only because it makes them happy to believe in it.'
    (b) 'The fact that God raised Jesus does not prove that God will give us life after death.'

Special Note D
Life after Death

This note has been added to draw attention to Paul's thoughts about life after death by comparing them with the thoughts of other people on the same subject.

1. PAUL'S THOUGHTS

We have seen that in 1 Corinthians 15 Paul was chiefly writing about the 'great Resurrection', the 'Coming' of Christ. But he probably expected that his own life on earth would continue until the 'Coming' (see 15.51). So we can say that Paul was not only referring to the 'Coming', but was answering the question 'What comes after life on this earth?' (in the NEB we find that 'Life after death' is the title at the head of 1 Corinthians 15).

The most important truth that Paul has given to us is that since God had the love and power to raise up Jesus, He will (with the same love and power) give us life after death. We know enough about God already to be able to trust Him concerning life after death.

If we look in 1 Corinthians 15 for other thoughts that Paul had we notice:

1. Life after death will be a gift from God. It is not a possession that belongs to us. 'God gives . . . Thanks be to God' (vv. 38, 57).

2. It is our whole person which will live, not only a part of us called our 'soul'. The whole person is what 'body' means in chapter 15.

3. The way we live now has something to do with what happens to us after death. Although Paul perhaps believed that God would in the end save all men, he usually said that it was those who were 'in Christ' who would be saved and given life after death (vv. 18, 57).

4. The body we shall have after death is a new kind of body. Life in the new body will not be a repetition of this life. 'What you sow is not the body which is to be' (v. 37).

5. Our self or personality will not disappear or be lost when we die, but will continue in a changed form. 'God gives to each kind of seed its own body' (v. 38).

2. OTHER VIEWS

It is useful to note under five heads those who have held views which are different from Paul's.

1. *Those who say that there is no life after death*, e.g.:
(a) The Greek philosophers called Epicureans (Acts 17.18).
(b) The Jewish Sadducees (Mark 12.18).
(c) People who say that a person consists only of particles of matter

which are separated at death. Marxists add to this that the rich invented the idea of a second life in order to make the poor forget their poverty.

2. *Those who believe in a repetition of this life*, e.g.:

(a) Those who believe in personal 'reincarnation', i.e. that the spirit of a dead person is born again and lives in another body on this earth. Hindus and Buddhists believe this, but they also think that the way a person has lived in one life makes a difference to the sort of existence he will have in his next life on earth.

(b) Those 'Spiritualists' who think that after death a person's spirit lives a life rather like this one, but in another world.

(c) Some Christians in past times who thought that the pieces of the present fleshly body would be brought together again at the Resurrection, so that the next life would be like this life. Muslims hold a similar belief.

3. *Those who believe in a half-life*, e.g.:

(a) Jews who lived before Christ and who believed that a dead person went to 'Sheol', a dark place beneath the earth, where he had no feelings and could not communicate with God (Isa. 38.18).

(b) Greeks at that time, who believed that a dead person's spirit went to 'Hades'.

4. *Those who believe that at death the self is swallowed up* in something that is far greater, as a drop of water is swallowed up in an ocean.

(a) Those Greek philosophers who were called Stoics (Acts 17.18).

(b) Buddhists, who believe that a truly good man, after living several lives on earth, can become part of 'Nirvana'. Nirvana cannot be described, but it is a higher state. In it individuals cease to be individuals and there is no pain.

5. *Those who consider the soul as separate from the fleshly body*, e.g. the followers of the Greek philosopher Plato. He taught that the real self was the 'soul' and that the soul of a 'wise man' was set free from the body at death. This idea is usually called the 'immortality' of the Soul, but this is not what Paul meant when he used the word 'immortality' in v. 54.

STUDY SUGGESTIONS

1. (a) Do you believe that there is life after death? If so, what is the chief reason for your belief?

(b) Collect the opinions of (i) other Christians, (ii) members of another religion, on 1 (a) above.

2. What is the difference between the ideas of Paul which we read in 1 Cor. 15 and the following:

(a) 'In death there is no remembrance of thee; in Sheol who can give thee praise?' (Ps. 6.5).

(b) 'I believe in the resurrection of the flesh' (a translation of the original version of the Apostles Creed)?

3. 'Paul usually said that it was those who were "in Christ" who would be given life after death' (p. 215).

(a) Do you think that God will give life after death to everyone, or only to Christians? On what New Testament teaching do you base your answer?

(b) What would you reply to someone who said, 'If God is going to save everyone in the end, why should I trouble to lead a Christian life?' Give reasons for your answers, and again refer to verses in the New Testament which have helped you to find answers.

4. If someone believes in reincarnation, can he also believe what Paul said about Resurrection? Explain your answer.

5. Some Christians think it is wrong for someone's body to be cremated. What is your opinion?

6. (a) How do members of your church interpret the words 'resurrection of the body' in the Apostles' Creed?

(b) It has been suggested that the words should be changed to 'resurrection of the person'. What is your opinion? Give your reasons.

7. A Christian in Papua New Guinea wrote this about the beliefs of his people: 'We believe that the spirits of the dead live in the graveyard. They continue to have a relationship with living people and watch over them. The spirits of good people who have died live separately from the spirits of bad people. If someone has lived a good life, then when he dies he shares the good life in the graveyard, until Jesus comes. At His coming, he will receive a good place in heaven.'

(a) In what way is this belief (i) the same as, (ii) different from, Paul's teaching in 1 Corinthians 15?

(b) If you were ministering to those people, what else would you want to say?

16.1–24 Practical Instructions

Show your fellowship with other Christians
in practical ways

OUTLINE

16.1–4: I want you to arrange a collection for the starving Christians in Jerusalem.

16.5–9: I shall come to see you, but not yet.

16.10–12: Accept Timothy in my place, and also Apollos.

16.13,14: Be watchful, firm, brave, strong, and loving.

16.15–18: Follow the instructions of Stephanas and his two friends.

16.19–24: Greetings to you! My love to you all!

INTERPRETATION

Several times in this letter Paul had taught that Christians show what they think and believe by the way in which they behave. So, having asked the Corinthian Christians to *think* very deeply about their belief in God, in chapter 15, he now gave them instructions, in chapter 16, as to what they should *do*. Alongside these instructions, he added further information and greetings.

1. The first matter is one about which the Christians in Corinth had written to him. We see this from the phrase 'Now concerning' in v. 1 (see note on p. 77). It seems that they knew that the Christians in Galatia were making a collection for the Jewish Christians in Jerusalem and that they wanted to know if they should take part. So Paul gave them instructions.

The Christian Jews in Jerusalem were in great need of food, and when Paul went there he was asked to 'remember' them (see Gal. 2.10). In Acts 11.29,30 and 24.17 we see that Paul did so. In Romans 15.25–27 he told his readers about the collection that was being made. In this chapter (1 Cor. 16.1–4) he told them how they could help. They seem to have been slow to take action. He had to remind them of the collection (2 Cor. 8.9; see especially 2 Cor. 8.10 and 9.2–5).

2. Secondly, he wanted them to be ready to help him on the next stage of his journey, after he had visited them again (see v. 6).

3. The other matters on which he wanted them to take action concern individual Christians. These were Timothy (vv. 10,11), Apollos (v. 12), and Stephanas (vv. 15–18). In each case Paul was saying, 'Treat these men with love and respect.'

NOTES

16.1. The contribution for the saints:

1. **Contribution:** The word which Paul used in this verse for 'contribution' means 'giving more than it is my duty to give', i.e. giving extra. It is not a tax which the Church authorities demand from a member, but something which he gives of his own free will.

In v. 3 the word he used was *charis* (a different word which is translated 'gift'), but it has the same meaning. It is the word which is also used to translate the 'grace' of God (v. 23).

In addition to these two words, Paul used several others in writing about giving. Christians can learn something about giving from studying them, e.g.:

In 2 Corinthians 8.20 the word means 'generosity'.

In 2 Corinthians 9.1 the word is *diakonia*, and means 'a practical piece of service' (see note on p. 33).

In 2 Corinthians 9.5c there is another word which means 'joyful and willing giving'.

In 2 Corinthians 9.12 the word is *leitourgia* (from which we get our word 'liturgy'). It means 'an act of service which I have offered to give'.

In 2 Corinthians 9.13c the word is *koinonia* and means 'an act which shows fellowship' (see note on p. 135).

2. **For the saints:** As we have seen on p. 6, 'saints' does not mean 'very good people', but 'the community of Christians'. In this verse it refers to the Christians in Jerusalem. These Christians were Jewish, and were in great need of food. We can see why they were in need from Acts 11.27–30.

The Christians in Corinth were mostly Gentiles, so in this verse Paul was telling them to perform a difficult task, i.e. to give practical help to Christians who belonged to a different race and who lived in a different country. When the Church of South India was formed, the newly unified body sent a worker to people who lived in a different part of the world from themselves, and promised to give them support in the future. The diocese of Ekiti (Nigeria) adopted the same plan at its foundation.

We may find it easier to make contributions to people whom we can see, or to those whose needs are like our own needs. What encourages Christians to give to those who are very far away or very different from themselves? We may say, 'genuine Christian love', or 'a belief that God cares equally for all people', or 'a vision of the Church as a great fellowship'.

16.2. On the first day of every week, each of you is to put something aside, and store it up, as he may prosper:

1. According to Acts 20.7 the Christians gave the name 'first day' to the day on which they worshipped together. They chose this day instead of the Sabbath ('seventh day') because it was on the first day that Jesus rose (Matt. 28.1). In Revelation 1.10 we find the name 'Lord's Day'.

But the way in which Christians use the day is far more important than the name which they give to it.

2. From these words (and also from v. 1) we see the ways in which Paul was telling the Christians to give:

(a) *With a purpose:* Before Paul told them to give, he explained the reason why they should give, i.e. because 'the saints' were in need (v. 1).

Christians need to know where their offerings will go. Church leaders can prepare a statement, and make it public, showing for instance that some of the congregation's money will go to pay for the upkeep of the church, some will be given away, and some will pay the Church leader. We see how important this is from a remark made by a Church member when a statement of this sort was issued. She said, 'I thought that all our offerings were given to the Minister.'

(b) *Regularly:* See 'on the first day of every week' (v. 2). Paul did not want the Corinthians to be so busy collecting money when he visited them that there would be no time for him to meet and talk with them. He was referring to the habit of regularly putting something aside rather than giving only because a special visitor had come to make an appeal.

Today it may not be possible to put anything aside 'every week', but it is possible to give money or work regularly. In some country areas the whole congregation owns a piece of land and members take turns in doing the farming. At the end of the year the crops are sold and the money is the 'contribution'. The advantages of this way of giving are:

(i) The offering is the offering of the community, not separate offerings by individuals.

(ii) The special day at the end of the year can be a great and joyful celebration.

(c) *Privately:* See 'each put something aside'. Paul did not tell them to bring their offering each week to the congregation, but to put it aside at home. Each member must give of his own free will. It is a matter between himself and God (Matt. 6.2–4). No one else will tell him how much he ought to give.

In most Churches today members bring their offerings to public Sunday services. But the amount of the offering should be a private matter. This was not so for the Jews who had to give a tenth, whether they wanted to or not (Lev. 27.30).

Giving is not private in some Churches today, e.g. where a committee 'assesses' the income of each member and tells him what he ought to pay. This has serious disadvantages, and it is now forbidden in some parts of the Church, e.g. in the Mar Thoma Church in South India (see 2 Cor. 9.7).

(d) *Proportionately:* See 'as he may prosper' (v. 2). See also 2 Corinthians 8.12: 'according to what a man has'. Each must decide what proportion of his money or possessions he should give. Some Christians today 'tithe' (give a tenth of what they earn). Others pay their taxes first and then give a proportion of what is left. What is important is to give in proportion to what we receive.

16.3. I will send those whom you accredit by letter: The translation in the New English Bible is better: 'I will give letters of introduction to persons approved by you, and send them. . . .'

The congregation in Corinth was responsible for appointing its own representatives to take the contribution to Jerusalem. In the same way most congregations today appoint their own treasurers. Paul knew that it was unwise for him to appoint them. They might accuse him of forcing members to make contributions or of using the money secretly. His task was to show the Christians in Jerusalem that he had given his approval to the representatives from Corinth. He planned to do this by sending letters of introduction.

16.5. I will visit you. In vv. 5–9 Paul told them as carefully as he could about the journey which he hoped to make. He did this because he did not want them to think that he was neglecting them. There were many people in the Church in Corinth who rejected Paul's authority and who would have liked to find an excuse to say, 'Paul has forgotten about us. Let us find another leader' (see note on p. 110).

His plans were:

(a) To visit Corinth, after travelling through Macedonia (v. 5);

(b) To stay in Corinth for a long time (vv. 6 and 7);

(c) To wait until Pentecost before making the visit. In Ephesus (where he was writing this letter) he was doing work which he could not finish quickly (vv. 8 and 9).

16.9. A wide door for effective work has opened to me, and there are many adversaries: Christians in many countries and in many generations have experienced what Paul described here:

(a) When an opportunity comes ('a door has opened') it is important to use it while it is there. It will not last for ever. Writers in the New Testament often call such an opportunity 'the right time'. The Greek word is *kairos*, and this is the word Paul used at the end of v. 12. According to Luke 12.56 Jesus said that his hearers did not notice 'the right time' when it came.

(b) When an opportunity for preaching the Gospel comes, there are always those who oppose the preaching. This should not surprise the Christians. Indeed, if a Christian preacher does not meet with opposition, it is likely that he is not really preaching the Gospel. In Acts 19.23–41 we read of some of the people who opposed Paul at Ephesus.

16.10. When Timothy comes, see that you put him at ease: We saw in 4.17 that Timothy was already on his way to Corinth. Erastus was with him (Acts 19.22). They were travelling over land through Macedonia, but Paul's letter was going by sea and would reach Corinth first.

Paul wrote 'Let no one despise him' (v. 11), and gave as a reason that Timothy was 'doing the work of the Lord'. Members of a congregation may sometimes not admire a Church leader for his own sake, e.g. if he is very shy or very rash or is not very well-educated. But they owe him fellowship and respect if he is doing his best to 'do the Lord's work'.

16.12. Our brother Apollos . . . will come when he has opportunity: Paul and Apollos worked together in Corinth (see notes on 1.12 and 3.5a). But some of the Christians there wanted to set up Apollos as their leader in place of Paul. That is the reason why Apollos delayed going to Corinth. He wanted to stay away in order to be loyal to Paul.

16.13,14. Be watchful, stand firm in your faith, be courageous, be strong. Let all that you do be done in love:

1. **Be watchful.** Not simply 'keep awake', but 'be ready for the end of life as it is now' (see Mark 13.35–37 and note on p. 8).

2. **Stand firm** – i.e. in the faith and trust and dependence which you have in God (see note on 15.58, p. 212). The more we depend on God who

never weakens, and the less we depend on the things which change, the 'firmer' we are.

3. **Be courageous.** Perhaps Paul was quoting from one of the Psalms, e.g. 27.14 or 31.24.

4. **In love** (see note on p. 171). In these verses 13 and 14 Paul gave a sort of summary of teaching about Christian behaviour, and (as he had done in chapters 13 and 14) he showed that the most important part of Christian behaviour was to love.

16.15. The household of Stephanas . . . devoted themselves to the service of the saints: Paul, having said 'Do everything in love', added 'Show love practically by the way in which you treat Stephanas.'

1. **Household of Stephanas:** Paul had baptized Stephanas in Corinth (1.16). But it was his whole household and not Stephanas alone whom he baptized. His family was the first whole family to be baptized in the Roman province of Achaia ('the first converts', v. 15). According to Acts 17.34, Dionysius and Damaris were the first individuals in Greece to become Christians.

This is important for Church leaders today who have to decide whom to baptize and whom not to baptize. Not all the members of a household believe in Jesus with equal strength. Paul baptized not only Stephanas who (it seems) was the first to experience the new life, but others who perhaps believed less firmly than he did.

2. **Service of the saints:** See 16.1 and note on service, p. 33. Here 'service' probably means collecting money for the starving Christians in Jerusalem. No one appointed Stephanas and his family to do this. They 'devoted themselves'. Most of the ministry which is done in the name of Jesus is of this sort. Christians see or hear of someone who is in need and set about giving 'service'.

16.16. Be subject to such men: This does not mean, 'bow down to them', but 'treat them with respect as those who are working in the name of Jesus (see v. 10); co-operate with them; follow the lead which they give.' See Galatians 5.13c.

At a later date people like Stephanas were appointed to hold some sort of official position, and were given a title, e.g. 'deacon' as in 1 Tim. 3.8. But when Paul wrote 1 Corinthians this had not yet happened.

16.17. I rejoice at the coming of Stephanas: Stephanas, with two others, had come to Paul from Corinth, bringing information about the congregation and also probably letters. Even though some of the news was bad news, Paul was glad to see them. It was far better to have bad news than to be out of touch. Also, the journey from Corinth to Ephesus was dangerous and Paul was grateful to those who made it for the sake of the fellowship among them.

Christians today often grumble at having to travel long distances to attend meetings with other Christians. Such meetings often seem to

'Christians see or hear of someone who is in need, and set about giving service' (p. 222).
In this Indian village, food is being distributed to all those in need.
What chiefly moves Christians to give service of this sort?

achieve nothing; but at least they are opportunities for Christians to share their joys and sorrows, achievements and failures (see note on 11.16).

16.19. Aquila and Prisca, together with the church in their house:

1. They were the family with whom Paul lived and worked when he first went to Corinth (Acts 18.2,3). They were refugees, having been expelled from Rome because they were Jews, who had moved to Corinth. Later, they moved to Ephesus where Paul was writing this letter. From Romans 16.3 we see that eventually they returned to Rome. They seem to have welcomed other Christians to their home wherever they went.

2. We see from this verse what a 'church' meant in those days. It did not mean a building. It meant a group of people who 'congregated', i.e. came together in a convenient place, usually in the house of one of the members. There must have been several 'house-churches' in a large place like Ephesus. Christians met for worship in this way for at least 250 years. It was not until about AD 300 that they began to build special buildings for worship.

The advantages of meeting in people's houses were, and are:

(a) Those who meet can all know each other. There is no room for a big crowd in most houses.

(b) By worshipping God in an ordinary house the worshippers are more likely to discover that God's Spirit is available to them in the ordinary events of their lives (see 10.31).

(c) The money that would be spent on building and looking after a church building can be used in caring for those who are most in need.

16.20. Greet one another with a holy kiss: Paul may simply have meant 'When you have read this letter and my teaching about love, then show love towards each other.' But it is more likely that he referred to a custom which took place at that time (and since that time) when Christians celebrated the Lord's Supper. It was, and is, a custom by which those who are about to share the bread and wine show that they are in fellowship by exchanging some outward sign of fellowship. We usually call this sign 'the Peace'. How Christians use it depends on the customs of their country. In some Churches, members turn and greet the people next to them, grasping their hands. In others, they grasp each other's shoulders, or embrace in other ways. In some Churches men greet men and women greet women; in others everyone greets everyone.

16.21. I, Paul, write this greeting with my own hand: Paul, like others in those days, usually dictated his letters to a secretary who was skilled in the difficult task of writing on papyrus, just as today many people get letter-writers in the market-place to write their letters for them. Paul employed a secretary, but in order to write his personal greetings he took the pen into his own hand (see also Col. 4.18; 2 Thess. 3.17; Gal. 6.11).

16.22a. If anyone has no love for the Lord, let him be accursed: If anyone showed by the way he treated other Christians that he was disloyal to Jesus

Christ then he should be 'cursed'. To 'curse' someone meant to declare that he was rejected by God, separated from God, and destroyed in spirit (see note on 3.17, 5.5, and 10.5, where Paul said something like this).

The following are three ways in which people have interpreted the 'curse' in this verse:

1. That Paul did not intend to curse anyone and that he only meant, 'Do not let such a person share the bread and wine with you at the Lord's Supper. He cannot honestly say that he loves Jesus and is loyal to Him if he has no love for His followers' (see NEB 'Let him be outcast').

2. That Paul referred to a real curse and that he was right to do so (see note on 10.5, p. 128). Someone who repeatedly refuses to listen to God is, in the end, unable to hear Him at all, and so is lost.

3. That Paul referred to a real curse, but that he was *wrong* to do so. Those who say this:

(a) Point out that although Jesus spoke of 'eternal punishment', human beings have no right to condemn a fellow human-being to it. If anyone condemns, it is God who does so. 'Condemn not, and you will not be condemned' (Luke 6.37).

(b) Suggest that Paul delivered this curse because he was a Jew by birth. Although he was a Christian, he could not shake off all the ways of his race. Before Jesus came the Jews had often expelled, and even condemned to death, those whom they accused of having disobeyed God (see Deut. 13.6–10; 28.15–24).

We who read this have to choose between different interpretations such as the three above.

16.22b. Our Lord, come! These words are a translation of the Aramaic word *Maranatha*. Probably this word was part of the service of the Lord's Supper in the Aramaic-speaking congregations (e.g. in Jerusalem), and the phrase was borrowed by the Greek-speaking Christians, e.g. in Corinth. (Non-Jewish Christians today are borrowing in a similar way when they say *Hallelujah*, which is Hebrew for 'Praise the Lord'.)

What did worshippers mean by it?

Either they were rejoicing that Christ was present among them, *or* (more probably) they were praying that He would soon come to bring the present world to an end and overcome all evil (evil such as 'not loving the Lord', v. 22a). It is likely that the Corinthian Christians read Paul's letter at the Lord's Supper. He had already reminded them in 11.26 that at every Lord's Supper the worshippers looked forward to Jesus's 'Coming' in this way (p. 156).

16.23,24a. The grace of the Lord Jesus be with you. My love be with you all:

1. **Grace:** Nearly all the letters of Paul which we can read today contain this word in the last verse (e.g. 2 Cor. 13,14; Gal. 6.18). He repeated the word in this way because it was the most important part of his teaching. As

we have seen (p. 7) it means, 'God has freely shown His love for us all by coming to us in the person of Jesus, and He has done this although we have not deserved it.'

In 1.4 Paul said that God had given this grace to the congregation in Corinth. Now in 16.23 he was saying, 'I pray that He will continue to accept you in this way.'

2. **Love:** We see from this that Paul was more than an apostle, theologian, teacher, leader, and writer. He was a friend who held in love those whom he led and taught – whether they were obedient or disobedient.

STUDY SUGGESTIONS

WORDS

1. Paul used several words and phrases in writing about Christian giving (p. 218).
   (i) What is the English RSV translation, and
   (ii) What is the translation in another language known to you, of the word in each of the following passages?
   (a) 1 Cor. 16.1   (b) 1 Cor. 16.3   (c) 2 Cor. 8.20   (d) 2 Cor. 9.1
   (e) 2 Cor. 9.5c   (f) 2 Cor. 9.12   (g) 2 Cor. 9.13c.

CONTENT

2. 'Several times in this letter Paul had taught that Christians show what they think and believe by the way in which they behave' (p. 218). Give one example of this from any part of 1 Corinthians.
3. (a) What do we learn in 1 Cor. 16 about the following customs of the Christians at the time when Paul wrote 1 Corinthians?
   (b) How far, in each case, does your Church today follow those customs?
     (i) The day on which the congregation met for worship;
     (ii) The place of such meeting;
     (iii) The greeting during the Lord's Supper;
     (iv) The way in which Church leaders wrote letters.
4. What was the purpose of the 'contribution' which Paul told his readers to make?
5. Why did Paul want to stay in Ephesus instead of visiting Corinth immediately?
6. In chapter 16 Paul referred to two Christian leaders and the way in which his hearers should treat them.
   (a) Who were they?
   (b) How did Paul want the members to treat them?
7. What sort of person did Paul have in mind when he wrote 'let him be accursed' (16.22a)?

BIBLE

8. (a) Why were the Christians in Jerusalem suffering?
   (b) Who gave them help?
   Some passages to consult are: Acts 11.27–30; Rom. 15.25–27; 1 Cor. 16.1; 2 Cor. 8.1–5; 2 Cor. 9.1–5.
9. Who were (a) the 'adversaries' (16.9), and (b) Paul's friends in Ephesus, according to Acts 19 (see especially vv. 9, 23–37).
10. (i) What can we discover about Aquila and Priscilla from the following passages?
    (a) 1 Cor. 16.19   (b) Acts 18.1–3,18–26   (c) Rom. 16.3,4
    (ii) In what way do you think Christians like them are needed in the present times?

DISCUSSION AND RESEARCH

11. 'Paul was telling them to give practical help to Christians who belonged to a different race' (p. 219).
    Examine the income and expenditure of one local congregation and see what proportion of the income is spent on: (a) the maintenance of buildings, (b) paying the. staff, (c) giving away to people outside the congregation.
12. It is said on p. 219 that Paul told his readers to give: (a) with a purpose, (b) regularly, (c) privately, (d) proportionately. Consider each of these four ways and say in each case how far it is possible for the members of your congregation to give in that way.
13. (a) Make a rough map showing the journey which Paul planned to make over land, beginning at Ephesus, according to 1 Cor. 16.5–9.
    (b) How long is that journey approximately?
14. 'A "Church" did not mean a building. It meant a group who congregated . . . usually in the house of one of the members' (p. 224). What are (a) the advantages, (b) the disadvantages of having a special building called a 'church' where Christians usually meet for worship?
15. 'How Christians use "the Peace" depends on the customs of their country' (p. 224).
    (a) What is your experience, if any, of having 'the Peace' in a service of Holy Communion?
    (b) Do you think that it expresses fellowship which exists already, or can create this fellowship?
16. 'Let him be accursed' (1 Cor. 16.22a). The notes on p. 225 refer to three ways in which people interpret these words:
    (a) Which interpretation do you follow?
    (b) Why do you choose that one?

Key to Study Suggestions

1.1–9

1. (a) (i)   A building.
     (ii) All Christians.
     (iii) One part of the Church.
     (iv) The Christians at Bida.
     (v) All Christians.
  (b) ii, iv, v.

3. See p. 7.

4. See p. 3, numbered para. 1, lines 5–13.

5. See p. 7, note on 1.2b.

6. (a) 9.
  (b) V. 1: Paul was His apostle.
     V. 2c: He is Lord.
     V. 7. He will come again.
     V. 9: He is God's Son, *and* We can have fellowship with Him.
  (c) See p. 5, note on 1.1b, lines 1–8.
  (d) See p. 5, note on 1.1b, lines 8–11.

7. (a) John the Baptist.
  (b) Jesus.
  (c) Christians at Rome.
  (d) Christians at Corinth.
  (e) Christians at Corinth.
  (f) Children of Christians.
  (g) Christians at Philippi.
  (h) The Old Testament.

8. (a) That God had given His grace to the Christians at Corinth, and all the gifts which they needed.
  (b) For the partnership of the Philippians with Paul.
  (c) Because of their faith and love, and because they could hope for eternal life.
  (d) Because their faith and love for each other was increasing, and because of their steadfastness and faith under persecution.

9. There will be a day of judgement when Jesus comes.

1.10–31

1. (a) 17, 19, 20, 21, 22, 24, 25, 26, 27. 30.
  (c) See p. 11, numbered paras 1 and 2.

2. Free, release, rescue, ransom, liberate, deliver, save, unloose.

3. See p. 12, numbered para. 2 and note on 1.12.

4. See p. 14, lines 13, 14.

5. See p. 14, lines 29–39.

6. (a) and (b) See p. 15, note on 1.22.

7. See p. 16, lines 2–5.

8. (1) Eloquent (v. 24).
   (2) Knew the Old Testament (v. 24).
   (3) Was interested in the Gospel (v. 25).
   (4) Fervent (v. 25).
   (5) Could teach about Jesus (v. 25).
   (6) Was willing to learn (v. 26).
   (7) Argued with the Jews (v. 28).

9. (a) (i) Peter.
   (ii) Some were very sad, and said, 'What shall we do?' and were baptized.
   (b) (i) Peter.
   (ii) He and John were arrested, and many believed.
   (c) (i) Paul.
   (ii) The congregation said 'come again', and many Jews followed Paul.
   (d) (i) Paul.
   (ii) Some mocked, others asked to hear Paul again, and others joined Paul and believed.

10. (a) (i) Poor and needy.
    (ii) The Lord as their help and deliverer.
    (b) (i) Meek and poor.
    (ii) Fresh joy and exultation.
    (c) (i) Humble and lowly.
    (d) (i) Those of low degree.
    (ii) Exaltation.
    (e) (i) Blind and lame, and lepers and deaf, dead and poor.
    (ii) Sight and strength to walk, and cleansing and hearing, and raising and good news.

11. Based on p. 11, last 17 lines.

12. (a) See p. 12, lines 8–13.

Special Note A. Corinth

1. See p. 20, numbered para. 1.

2. (a) About 50 miles.
   (b) Achaia (Acts 18.18).

3. See p. 20, Special Note A, numbered para. 1.

4. See p. 20, numbered para. 2.

5. See p. 20, last 2 lines.

6. See Acts 18.7 and 8 and 12; 1 Cor. 1.14; 16.17.

7. See p. 21, lines 11–15.

8. See p. 21.

KEY TO STUDY SUGGESTIONS

2.1—3.4

1. Unspiritual, not able to understand, men of the flesh, babes in Christ, not ready, ordinary men, merely men.
2. (a) See p. 23, lines 7, 8.
   (b) See p. 24, note on v. 26a, numbered para. 2.
3. See p. 26, lines 8–14.
4. See v. 9.
5. See p. 23, last 9 lines.
6. See p. 28, lines 22, 23.
7. (a) iii; (b) i; (c) iii; (d) i; (e) iii; (f) i; (g) ii; (h) iii; (i) i.
8. (a) i; (b) i; (c) ii; (d) iii; (e) ii; (f) iii; (g) iii; (h) ii.
9. See p. 26, note on 2.15.
10. (a) Based on p. 24, note on 2.3.

3.5–23

1. *Service:* work, task, job, duty, function.
   Position: office, grade, class, rank, post.
2. See p. 31, Interpretation lines 1–12.
3. (a) See p. 32, lines 5, 9, 12.
   (b) See p. 32, lines 5–14.
4. See p. 34, last 7 lines of note on 3.8.
5. (a) Jesus Christ.
6. (i) (a) relief; (b) ministry; (c) aid; (d) service; (e) offering.
   (ii) (a) Jesus and His disciples; (b) Jesus; (c) Gentiles; (d) The Church at Cenchreae; (e) Paul.
   (iii) (a) Preaching; (b) Sending relief; (c) Helping others to believe; (d) Reconciling; (e) Helping Paul in prison.
7. (a) and (b) See p. 39, paras 3–5.
8. See p. 37, lines 18–25.
9. (a) ii; (b) i; (c) ii; (d) ii; (e) i; (f) i; (g) i; (h) ii.
10. (a) See p. 32, note on picture-language.
    (b) (i) E.g.: *Advantage:* it is a united group; *Disadvantage:* a flock is a flock of sheep who do not have opinions of their own.
    (ii) E.g.: *Advantage:* it is a group of people of different ages and interests and yet concerned for each other; *Disadvantage:* Sometimes a congregation is too big for everyone to know each other.

4.1–21

1. Housekeeper, agent, caretaker, warden.
2. Faithful, reliable, dependable, loyal, responsible.
3. E.g. fools, weak, disrepute, hunger, thirst, ill-clad, buffeted, homeless, reviled, persecuted, slandered, refuse, off-scouring.

231

4. (a) See p. 43, lines 11, 16, 17.
   (b) See p. 44, lines 20–27.
5. See p. 45, 9–12.
6. (a) See p. 48, lines 1–9.
7. See p. 47, lines 19–24.
8. (a) 1; (b) 1; (c) ii; (d) ii; (e) ii; (f) i; (g) ii; (h) i.
9. (a) Persecuted, struck down.
   (b) Beatings, hunger.
   (c) Beatings, hunger, thirst.
10. Vv. 12 and 13.
11. (a) Son of a Jewish Christian; his father was Greek; he had a good report from Christians at Lystra and Iconium; was not circumcised till Paul circumcised him.
    (b) He stayed in Beroea with Silas after Paul had left.
    (c) He and Silas were with Paul when Paul wrote to the Thessalonians.

Special Note B. Paul

1. (a) See Acts 23.6b; Phil. 3.5; etc.
   (b) See Acts 22.3.
   (c) See Acts 22.25–28.
   (d) See Acts 9.1–5; 22.6–8; 26.12–15.
   (e) See Acts 16.9, 10; 18.9, 10; 22.18–21; 23.11; 27.33; 1 Cor. 1.4; 2 Cor. 12.3, 4; etc.
   (f) See Phil. 3.12, and Note 8, pp. 53, 54.
2. See p. 51, note 2.
3. See p. 51, note 3.
4. (a) See p. 52, note 4, lines 1, 2.

5.1–13

1. Control, educate, correct, train.
2. See p. 60, line 3 from foot.
3. See p. 55, last 3 lines, and p. 56, lines 1–4.
4. See p. 57, last line.
5. Mourn (v. 2); be removed (v. 2); deliver to Satan (v. 5); cleanse out (v. 7); not to associate (vv. 9, 11); not to eat with (v. 11); judge (v. 12); drive out (v. 13).
6. See p. 57, lines 6–9.
7. See p. 60, note on 5.6.
8. See pp. 59, 60, note on 5.5.
9. (i) (a) Tempter; (b) evil; (c) devil; (d) Satan; (e) ruler of this world; (f) evil one.
   (ii) (a) 1; (b) 1; (c) 3; (d) 3; (e) 3; (f) 3; (g) 2; (h) 2.

6.1–20

1. Sovereignty, rule, supremacy.
2. Person, personality, self.
3. (a) See p. 71, lines 6, 5 from foot.

4. See p. 66, numbered para. 1.

5. See p. 67, lines 11–17.

6. See p. 66, lines 7–3 from foot, and p. 67, note on 6.7.

7. (a) Adulterers, greedy, drunkards, joins himself to a prostitute.
   (b) The body for the Lord (v. 13); Glorify God in your body (v. 20).

8. See p. 74, note on 6.19b, 20, numbered paras 1 and 2.

9. See p. 67, lines 5–8.

10. (i) See p. 68, note on 6.11.
    (ii) (b), (c), (d), (e).

15. See pp. 69, 70, notes on 6.12a and 6.12b.

7.1–16

1. (a) and (g); (b) and (j); (c) and (f); (d) and (i); (e) and (h).

2. See p. 77, Interpretation, para. 2.

3. See p. 77, Interpretation, para. 3.

4. (a) and (b) See p. 77, last 5 lines, and p. 78, first 5 lines.

5. See p. 79, lines 10–30.

6. See p. 82, lines 8–19.

7. Vv. 3 and 5.

8. (a) Each partner has an equal right.

9. See p. 83, numbered para. 2, sections (a) and (b).

11. See p. 82, last 2 lines, and p. 83, first 6 lines.

7.17–40

2. See p. 87, last para, and p. 88, lines 2–12.

3. Circumcised people; uncircumcised people; slaves; unmarried people; married people.

4. See p. 90, numbered para. 3.

5. (a) Untrue: see p. 88, last para.
   (b) True: see p. 92, lines 11–end.
   (c) Untrue: see p. 95, lines 25–42.
   (d) True: see p. 94, last 7 lines, p. 95, lines 1–8.
   (e) Untrue: see p. 96, lines 12–17.

6. (a) Keeping God's commandments.
   (b) Faith working through love.
   (c) New creation.

7. (a) We are truly 'free' when we are no longer slaves to sin.
   (b) When we are no longer slaves to sin, we are free to be slaves of God.

8. (i) 1. Worrying and not trusting God.
      2. Being thoughtful about someone else's welfare.
   (ii) (a) 1; (b) 1; (c) 2; (d) 2; (e) 1.

9. Because v. 21 is about slaves, and Paul was writing to Philemon about his slave.

8.1—13

2. See p. 105, lines 17, 18.

3. (a) See p. 99, Interpretation, section 1, lines 1—17.
   (b) See p. 99, Interpretation, section 2.

4. See p. 99, Interpretation, section 2(b).

5. (a) See p. 99, last 6 lines.

6. (a) See p. 102, last 7 lines, p. 103, lines 1—9.

7. (i) (a) They must not be made and must not be served.
   (b) They have been created by people and have no life of their own.
   (c) They are a burden. They have no power to save those who carry them.
   (ii) (a) They have no real existence.
   (b) Have nothing to do with them.
   (c) They are dumb.

8. Rom. 14.7, 13, 15, 20—21. See pp. 106, 107, note on 8.12.

9. When we love a fellow-Christian, we are loving Christ.
   When we sin against a fellow-Christian, we are sinning against Christ.

9.1—18

1. (a) Being entitled, having the authority, being free, having the right.
   (b) 4, 5, 6, 12, 15, 18.

2. We have rights.

3. See pp. 109, 110, note on 9.1a.

4. They were a sign that he was a real apostle. See p. 110, last line, p. 111, lines 1—26.

5. (a) See p. 111, note on 9.4, lines 1—8.
   (b) Food and hospitality.

6. (a) V. 8.
   (b) See p. 110, lines 19—30.

7. (a) They all refer to Paul seeing Jesus.
   (b) They all refer to the right to be rewarded which workers have.

8. (a) The names of the brothers were James, Joses, Judas, and Simon.
   (b) At one time they did not believe in Jesus.
   (c) They, together with Jesus's mother and other women, joined in praying with the eleven disciples after Jesus had risen.
   (d) They had the right to be married.
   (e) James and Paul met in Jerusalem.

9. (a) (i) Paul; (ii) Looking after himself, and those with him.
   (b) (i) Apostles; (ii) Working with their hands.
   (c) (i) Paul and his helpers; (ii) Worked day and night.
   (d) (i) Paul and his helpers; (ii) Earning money to buy food.

9.19—27

1. (a) (i) We; (ii) servants; (iv) Christ.
   (b) (i) Those 'called'; (ii) slave; (iv) Christ.

KEY TO STUDY SUGGESTIONS

(c) (i) Paul; (ii) slave; (iv) All.

(d) (i) All believers; (ii) service; (iv) 'the Lord'.

(e) (i) Stephanas's household; (ii) service; (iv) the 'saints'.

3. See p. 118, Interpretation.

4. See vv. 19c, 20a, 20b, 21b, 22a, 22b, 23b, 25c.

5. (a) See p. 120, note on 9.20.

(b) See p. 120, note on 9.21(a).

6. (a) and (b) See p. 123, note on 9.24b, para. 1.

(c) (i) and (ii) See p. 123, note on 9.24, para. 2, p. 124, last 8 lines, p. 125, lines 1–3.

7. (a) In 9.20–23 he emphasized the things which he had in common with his hearers, but in 2.1–5 he emphasized the new and special message about Jesus which he preached.

(b) In both passages he showed that he wanted his hearers to follow Jesus.

8. (i) The truth that Christians need to make progress, that they have a goal towards which they are moving.

(ii) E.g. (a) race, run, obtain, receive; (b) press on, straining forward, goal, prize; (c) run, race.

10.1–13

2. See p. 131, note on 10.13b.

3. See p. 127, Interpretation, para. 1.

4. (a) 1 Cor. 8.

(b) See p. 102, note on 8.4b, numbered para. 3.

5. See p. 129, note on 10.9.

6. See p. 131, note on 10.13a, numbered para. 1.

7. (1) (a) The Israelites walked under a cloud by which they found the way.

(b) Exodus 13.21.

(2) (a) They crossed the Red Sea. (b) Exodus 14.21, 22.

(3) (a) They ate manna in the wilderness. (b) Exodus 16.13–17.

(4) (a) Moses obtained water from the rock. (b) Numbers 20.11.

8. (i) (a) Jesus was in the beginning. He was with God. (b) It was like being rich. (c) God kept Jesus with Him until it became the right time for Jesus to become man. (d) Everything was created in Jesus, and through Him and for Him.

(ii) Based on p. 128, note on 10.4, numbered para. 2.

9. (a) Because they were too confident of their own powers (see v. 12).

12. See p. 131, note on 10.13b.

10.14—11.1

1. Partnership, fellowship, sharing, communion, partaking.

2. See p. 134, Interpretation, para. 2.

3. (a) See p. 134, Interpretation, para. 1.

4. (a) See p. 134, last 2 lines, p. 135, lines 1–10.

(b) See p. 135, note on 10.16b.

5. (a) (i) All who believed. (ii) Everything.

235

KEY TO STUDY SUGGESTIONS

(b) (i) 'We' (i.e. we Christians). (ii) Wine and bread.
(c) See p. 136, note on 10.18.
(d) (i) Paul and the congregation at Philippi. (ii) The grace of God.
(e) (i) The writer and his readers. (ii) Fellowship with the Father and the Son.
6. (i) (a) To serve other gods or to serve the Lord. (b) To serve 'mammon' or to serve God. (c) To share in Holy Communion or to share in the worship of 'demons'.
7. (i) See pp. 138, 139, note on 11.1, para. 2.
(ii) (a) Christ: He did not please Himself. (b) Paul. (c) God: to walk in love.
(d) Christ: He took the form of a servant. (e) Paul. (f) Paul and his companions: they received the word with joy. (g) Christ: he suffered for others.
10. (a) V. 27.

11.2–16

1. (a) Helper, subject, dependent, obedient, subordinate.
2. See p. 141, Interpretation, lines 9–11, and p. 145, last 4 lines.
3. See p. 146, note on 11.11.
4. See 11.5 and 11.13.
5. (a) Simon and Andrew depended on Christ and existed to serve Him. See p. 142, note on 11.3a.
(b) Everyone exists because of Christ.
(c) Everyone was created through Christ and for Christ.
6. (a) See p. 146, note on 11.11.
(b) See p. 144, note (b) on 11.36, lines 13–19.
(c) A husband and a wife each have an equal responsibility to care for the other.
7. (i) (a) Galatia. (b) Asia. (c) Macedonia. (d) Judea.
(ii) (a) 400 miles. (b) 250 miles. (c) 200 miles. (d) 600 miles.

11.17–34

1. Assemble, church, meet together, wait for one another.
2. (a) See p. 151, numbered para. 1.
(b) See p. 6, lines 1–23.
3. (a) See p. 155, note on 11.25, numbered paras. 1 and 2.
4. (a) See p. 149, Outline lines 4, 5.
(b) See p. 149, Outline lines 5, 6, p. 154, last 6 lines, and p. 155, lines 1–3.
5. See p. 152, note on 11.23a, numbered para. 2.
6. See p. 154, note on 11.24b.
7. See p. 155, last 2 lines, p. 156, lines 1–6.
8. Loving God and loving each other go together. See p. 152, note on 11.20.
9. (a) This is my body.
(b) Covenant.
15. (b) See p. 155, note on 11.24c, numbered para. 2.
18. (a) See p. 156, note on 11.28.

12.1—31

1. (a) Something which God gives to us because of His grace. See p. 163, note on 12.4.

2. See p. 160, Interpretation, para. 1.

3. (a) See p. 161, lines 18—23.
   (b) See p. 161, lines 24—31.

4. To show that in a congregation each member is (a) necessary, and (b) different. See p. 160, lines 13—6 from foot.

5. That each member needs to consider what is best for the whole congregation.

6. (a) Prophet, apostle, teacher, healer, miracle.

7. (i) (a) Body; (b) body; (c) building; (d) house; (e) flock.

11. (a) See p. 164, note on 12.5.

13.1—13

1. (i) (a) and (f).

3. See p. 169, Interpretation, numbered para. 1.

4. Based on pp. 171—174, notes on 13.3.

5. See p. 171, note on 13.1, section 3.

6. See p. 175, note on 13.12.

7. (a) We love other people because God loves us.
   (b) A loving person does not give up quickly when loving becomes difficult.
   (c) If we really love people, we shall show it in practical ways.
   (d) A loving person loves even his enemies.

8. (a) V. 20 or v. 26 or v. 27.
   (b) Probably v. 25.
   (c) V. 21
   (d) V. 36 or v. 48 or v. 50.
   (e) V. 5.
   (f) V. 34.

11. (a) Speaking in tongues, prophesying, understanding and knowing, having faith, generosity, self-sacrifice.

14.1—40

1. (a) Build up.
   (b) See p. 179, note on 14.3.

2. (i) That someone who 'prophesies' is more easily understood (v. 16).
   (ii) Therefore he is more likely to build up the members (v. 17).

3. (a) See p. 182, note on 14.24.
   (b) If they can understand what is said.

4. (a) See p. 177, Interpretation, lines 2 and 3.
   (b) See p. 177, last 3 lines.

5. (a) and (b) See v. 34 and pp. 182, 183, note on v. 34.

6. See p. 183, lines 9—5 from foot.

7. See p. 182, lines 4—6.

8. (a) Prediction or foretelling. (b) Preaching. (c) Building up and giving consolation and encouragement.
14. (a) E.g. 5, 26, 27, 29, 31, 39.
    (b) See p. 182, note on 14.26, numbered para 1.

Special Note C. Speaking in Tongues

2. See p. 186, 'Note' at end of numbered section 3.
3. See 12.29, 30.
    (a) It is one of many gifts which God the Holy Spirit may give.
    (b) Some have this gift, some have not.
    (c) It is worthless unless it is accompanied by love.
    (d) It is not understandable.
    (e) It is less useful than 'prophesying' in building up the Church.
    (f) It is a good thing to do. But unless it is interpreted it is less important than prophesying.
    (g) He was glad that he could speak in tongues.
    (h) It is to be allowed.
4. (i) (a) A large crowd which included Gentiles. (b) About 12 disciples at Ephesus.
    (ii) (a) They first received the Holy Spirit and were baptized afterwards.
        (b) They were baptized first and received the Holy Spirit afterwards.

15.1–11

1. (iii) See p. 194, note on 15.4, numbered section 2.
2. See p. 189, last 10 lines, p. 190, lines 1–4.
3. See p. 194, lines 5–8.
4. See p. 193, note on 15.3c, lines 4, 5.
5. (a) See p. 189, last 8 lines, p. 192, note on 15.3a, numbered section 2.
    (b) See p. 190, note on 15.1, numbered para. 2(a).
    (c) See p. 192, lines 16–18.
    (d) See p. 193, lines 18–20.
6. (i) Cephas, the Twelve, 500 brethren, James, all the apostles, Paul.
    (ii) (a) Mary Magdalene and the 'other Mary'. (b) Cleopas and his friend.
        (c) Mary Magdalene, (d) Peter and the other disciples.
    (iii) (a) To tell the disciples that He had risen. (b) 1. To preach about forgiveness and repentance beginning from Jerusalem. 2. To stay in the city until they are 'clothed with power'. (c) To serve and bear witness.
7. (a) (i) Will happen. (ii) From their sins.
    (b) (i) Will happen. (ii) From the wrath of God.
    (c) (i) Will happen.
    (d) (i) Has happened.
    (e) (i) Is happening.
    (f) (i) Has happened.
10. (a) See p. 194, note on 15.5, para (a).
11. (b) See p. 193, note on 15.3c, lines 1–3.

15.12–34

1. (i) (a) Past; (b) Christ's.
   (ii) (a) Past; (b) Christ's.
   (iii) (a) Future; (b) 'All'.

2. See p. 200, note on 15.19b.

3. (a) See p. 197, Interpretation, lines 1, 2.
   (b) See p. 197, Interpretation, para. 1, line 4.

4. See p. 198, lines 3, 4.

5. The first time Adam; the second time Christ.

6. Rule, authority, power, enemies, death.

7. See p. 200, note on 15.22, section 1(c).

8. (a) See p. 203, note on 15.32a, lines 4–7.
   (b) Being stoned, being shipwrecked, in rivers, from robbers, from cold and exposure.

9. (a) See p. 200, note on 15.22, section 1(b).
   (b) In all four passages Paul taught that God has given us a promise of new life in the future.

10. (a) You do not know. (b) Soon. (c) When we are not expecting it. (d) After rebellion and the revealing of the 'man of lawlessness'. (e) It is at hand.

13. (a) V. 22.

14. (b) See pp. 201, 202, note on 15.24.

15. (a) See p. 202, last 3 lines.

16. Based on p. 203, note on 15.32b.

15.35–58

1. (a) Personality, person, self, individuality. (b) Body.

2. See p. 206, Interpretation, line 3.

3. (a) See p. 209, note on 15.38.
   (b) See p. 210, note on 15.45.

4. (a) See p. 209, note on 15.42, numbered para. 2.
   (b) See p. 209, note on 15.42, numbered para. 4.

5. See p. 205, Outline.

6. See p. 212, note on 15.57, numbered para. 1.

7. (a) God will give us new life.
   (b) We depend on the grace of God to give us this gift.

8. (a) To give Christians who are in need; be generous.
   (b) To be lowly and meek and patient and forebearing.
   (c) To stand firm in the Lord; to agree in the Lord.
   (d) To work heartily.
   (e) To live quietly, to mind their own affairs, to work with their own hands.

Special Note D: Life After Death

2. (a) See p. 216, numbered section 3.
   (b) See p. 216, numbered section 2(c).

4. See p. 215, numbered section 1, 4, and p. 216, numbered section 2(a).

16.1–24

1. (a) Contribution; (b) gift; (c) liberal gift; (d) offering; (e) willing gift; (f) service; (g) contribution.
2. E.g.: 1.10; 5.1, 2; 6.2, 7; 11.20–22; 14.1; etc.
3. (i) (a) The homes of the members (16.19).
   (ii) (a) It was the first day of the week (16.2).
   (iii) (a) A holy kiss (16.20).
   (iv) (a) They usually dictated notes to a secretary. See note on 16.21.
4. See p. 218, lines 7–18.
5. See p. 221, lines 9–11.
6. See p. 221, notes on 16.10 and 16.12, p. 222, note on 16.15, 16.
7. See p. 224, last 2 lines.
8. (a) There was a famine.
   (b) Barnabas and Paul; the Churches in Macedonia and Achaia.
9. (a) Those who did not believe Paul's preaching in the synagogue; Demetrius and his fellow silversmiths.
   (b) Tyrannus, Gaius, Aristarchus, some of the Asiarchs.
10. (i) (a) The Church met in their home.
    (b) They were Jews from Pontus, who were expelled from Italy. They were tentmakers. Paul stayed with them. They travelled with Paul to Ephesus. At Ephesus they gave Christian teaching to Apollos.
    (c) They risked their necks for Paul's life.
13. (b) About 650 miles.

Index

Bold type indicates those pages or sections where a subject is discussed in detail.

241